Introduction to the
Cyber Ranges

Chapman & Hall/CRC Cyber-Physical Systems

Series Editors:

Jyotir Moy Chatterjee
Lord Buddha Education Foundation, Kathmandu, Nepal

Vishal Jain
Sharda University, Greater Noida, India

Cyber-Physical Systems: A Comprehensive Guide
By: Nonita Sharma, L K Awasthi, Monika Mangla, K P Sharma, Rohit Kumar

Introduction to the Cyber Ranges
By: Bishwajeet Pandey and Shabeer Ahmad

For more information on this series please visit: https://www.routledge.com/Chapman-HallCRC-Cyber-Physical-Systems/book-series/CHCPS?pd=published,forthcoming&pg=1&pp=12&so=pub&view=list?pd=published,forthcoming&pg=1&pp=12&so=pub&view=list

Introduction to the Cyber Ranges

BISHWAJEET PANDEY
SHABEER AHMAD

CRC Press
Taylor & Francis Group
Boca Raton London New York

CRC Press is an imprint of the
Taylor & Francis Group, an **informa** business

A CHAPMAN & HALL BOOK

First edition published 2022
by CRC Press
6000 Broken Sound Parkway NW, Suite 300, Boca Raton, FL 33487-2742
and by CRC Press

4 Park Square, Milton Park, Abingdon, Oxon, OX14 4RN

CRC Press is an imprint of Taylor & Francis Group, LLC

ISBN: 9781032072401 (hbk)
ISBN: 9781032251424 (pbk)
ISBN: 9781003206071 (ebk)

DOI: 10.1201/9781003206071

Typeset in Palatino
by KnowledgeWorks Global Ltd.

Contents

Preface

My coauthor, Dr. Ahmad, and I share a common research interest for cybersecurity and cyber physical systems. Shabeer had worked on modeling a hybrid cyber range based on a real water supply system. I worked on designing an emulator of water supply systems during my thesis. Over the years, we both have actively, and independently, contributed to these research arenas. The idea behind this book was to communicate our knowledge and develop interest and participation for cybersecurity aspects and cyber ranges within readers.

Cyber ranges are widely used research, development, and training platforms. They have applications ranging from military to academia to commercial sectors. Our goal is to provide the reader with a simple but detailed insight on cyber ranges. This book brings together theoretical and technical knowledge along with comprehensive case studies on several existing cyber ranges. We hope that this book encourages our readers to contribute to and further explore the frontiers of cyber ranges.

Bishwajeet Pandey

About the Authors

Prof Bishwajeet Pandey has completed his PhD in CSE from Gran Sasso Science Institute, L'Aquila, Italy, under guidance of Prof Paolo Prinetto, Politecnico Di Torino (World Ranking 13 in Electrical Engineering). He is working as an Associate Professor at Jain University, Bangalore, India. He has worked as an Asst. Professor in Department of Research at Chitkara University, Junior Research Fellow (JRF) at South Asian University, and Lecturer in Indira Gandhi National Open University. He has completed his Master of Technology (IIIT Gwalior) in CSE with specialization in VLSI, Master of Computer Application, R&D Project in CDAC-Noida. He has authored and coauthored 137 papers available on his Scopus Profile: https://www.scopus.com/authid/detail.uri?authorId=57203239026. He has 1400+ Citation according to his Google Scholar Profile: https://scholar.google.co.in/citations?user=UZ_8yAMAAAAJ&hl=en. He is experienced in teaching innovation and startup, computer networking, digital logic, logic synthesis, and system Verilog. His areas of research interest are green computing, high-performance computing, cyber physical systems, artificial intelligence, machine learning, and cyber security. He is on the board of directors of many startups of his students, e.g., Gyancity Research Consultancy Pvt Ltd.

Dr. Shabeer Ahmad received his BEng degree in ICT and Electronics Engineering and MSc degree (MS) in Information & Control Engineering (summa cum laude), both from the University of L'Aquila, L'Aquila, Italy. According to the Italian newspapers, he was the first foreigner (Asian) to graduate with a gold medal from an Italian university. In 2016, he became a visiting research assistant in Shibaura Institute of Technology, Tokyo and, subsequently, he got a permanent position as a control-systems engineer in one of the best Japanese multi-national companies, Toshiba Corporation, Tokyo, Japan, before joining one of the top Italian research institutes, Gran-Sasso Science Institute (National Institute for Nuclear Physics), L'Aquila, Italy, to continue his study of Doctor of Philosophy (PhD) in the field of cybersecurity and control systems. He got the Young Scientist Award at the 4th International Conference on Green Computing and Engineering Technologies in August 2018 at Aalborg University, Denmark. His main areas of research interest are linear and nonlinear control systems, cybersecurity for the critical infrastructures, hybrid cyber ranges, and emulation of the critical infrastructures with special emphasis on water supply systems.

List of Abbreviations

Chapter 1

AI	Artificial Intelligence
APT	Advanced Persistent Threat
AWS	Amazon Web Services
CE	Cybersecurity Exercise
CPS	Cyber Physical System
CR	Cyber Range
CRaaS	Cyber Range as a Service
CSA	Cyber Situational Awareness
GSA	Government Security Agencies
ICS	Industrial Control Systems
IDs	Intrusion Detections
IoT	Internet of Things
IPS	Intrusion Prevention Systems
IT	Information Technology
NAT	Network Address Translation
SA	Situational Awareness
SCADA	Supervisory Control and Data Acquisition
SVN	Software Virtual Network
VM	Virtual Machine
VoIP	Voice over Internet Protocol
VPC	Virtual Private Cloud

Chapter 2

AMI	Amazon Machine Images
API	Application Programming Interface
AWS	Amazon Web Service
BIOS	Basic Input/Output System
CLI	Command Line Interface
CPU	Central Processing Unit
CR	Cyber Range
CSE	Cyber Security Exercise
DoS	Denial of Service
EBS	Elastic Block Store
EC2	Elastic Compute Cloud
ESX	Elastic Sky X
HTML	Hyper Text Markup Language
HTTP	Hyper Text Transfer Protocol
IaaS	Infrastructure as a Service

ISEAGE	Internet-Scale Event and Attack Generation Environment
IT	Information Technology
KVM	Kernel-based Virtual Machine
MB	Megabytes
MHz	Megahertz
MITM	Man in the Middle
OS	Operating System
PHIL	Power Hardware-in-the-Loop
PRIME	Parallel Real-Time Immersive network Modeling Environment
RBAC	Role-Based Access Control
RTDS	Real-Time Digital Simulator
SCADA	Supervisory Control and Data Acquisition
SSF	Scalable Simulation Framework
SSH	Secure Shell
VM	Virtual Machine
VMM	Virtual Machine Monitor

Chapter 3

ACS	Automation Controls System
AI	Artificial Intelligence
AIS	Automatic Identification System
APT	Advanced Persistent Threat
ARC	Autonomous Response Controller
C-FLAT	Control-Flow Attestation
CMM	Competitive Markov Model
CPS	Cyber Physical System
CR	Cyber Range
CRAMM	Central Computer and Telecommunications Agency Risk Analysis and Management Method
DoS	Denial of Service
DPI	Deep Packet Inspection
ECDIS	Electronic Chart Display and Information System
HMI	Human Machine Interface
ICS	Industrial Control System
IT	Information Technology
MITM	Man in the Middle Attack
ML	Machine Learning
OCTAVE	Operationally Critical Threat and Vulnerability Evaluation
O&G	Oil and Gas
OS	Operating System
OT	Operational Technology
PLC	Programmable Logic Controller
RTU	Remote Terminal Unit
SA	Situational Awareness
SCADA	Supervisory Control and Data Acquisition

SOC	Security Operation Center
SWAT	Secure Water Treatment
WADI	Water Distribution
WSS	Water Supply Systems

Chapter 4

ADC	Analog to Digital Converter
API	Application Programming Interface
BCS	Baltic Cyber Shield
CCU	Central Control Unit
CIP	Common Industrial Protocol
CLI	Command Line Interpreter
CPS	Cyber Physical System
CR	Cyber Range
CRaaS	Cyber Range as a Service
CSE	Cyber Security Exercise
CTTP	Cyber Threat and Training Preparation
DAC	Digital to Analog Converter
DMZ	Demilitarized Zone
DNP3	Distributed Network Protocol 3
DNS	Domain Name System
ER	Elevated Reservoir
EVA	Emulatore di Vero Acquedotto
FOI	Swedish Defence Research Agency
GUI	Graphical User Interface
HIL	Hardware-in-Loop
HMI	Human Machine Interfaces
ICS	Industrial Control System
IEC	International Electrotechnical Commission
IO	Information Operation
IT	Information Technology
IWAR	Information Warfare Analysis and Research
MAC	Media Access Control
NIST	National Institute of Standards and Technology
OFS	Overlay File System
OS	Operating System
OSI	Open Systems Interconnection Model
OT	Operational Technology
PI	Plant Information
PLC	Programmable Logic Controller
RINSE	Real-time Immersive Network Simulation Environment
RO	Reverse Osmosis
SAP	Security Assurance Platform
SCADA	Supervisory Control and Data Acquisition
SDN	Software-Defined Networking

SVN	Software Virtual Network
SWAT	Secure Water Treatment
TCP/IP	Transmission Control Protocol/Internet Protocol
UF	Ultra Filtration
USB	Universal Serial Bus
USMA	United States Military Academy
VM	Virtual Machine
VPN	Virtual Private Network
WADI	Water Distribution
WC	Wrapper Controller
WDI	Wrapper Data & Interconnection
WSS	Water Supply System

Chapter 5

BMSL	Behavioral Monitoring Specification Language
CR	Cyber Range
GPL	General Public License
IA	Information Assurance
I/O	Input/Output
IoT	Internet of Things
IT	Information Technology
MBSA	Microsoft Baseline Security Analyzer
O&G	Oil and Gas
OS	Operating Systems
RA	Router Advertisement
SAML	Security Assertion Markup Language
SEE	Secure Execution Environment
SOAP	Simple Object Access Protocol
SSL	Secure Sockets Layer
VAPT	Vulnerability Assessment and Penetration Testing
WSDL	Web Services Description Language
WSS	Water Supply System
XML	Extensible Markup Language
XSS	Cross-Site Scripting

Chapter 6

BCS	Baltic Cyber Shield
CCDCoE	Cooperative Cyber Defence Centre of Excellence
CDX	Cyber Defense Exercise
CE	Cybersecurity Exercise
CR	Cyber Range

CTF	Capture the Flag
DOA	Defense Oriented Approach
IP	Internet Protocol
IT	Information Technology
NATO	North Atlantic Treaty Organization
OOA	Offense Oriented Approach
RAM	Random Access Memory
SA	Situational Awareness
SCADA	Supervisory Control and Data Acquisition
SOC	Security Operations Centre

Chapter 7

AODV	Adhoc On-Demand Distance Vector
API	Application Programming Interface
CLI	Command Line Interface
CR	Cyber Range
DETER	Defense Technology Experimental Research
DoS	Denial of Service
DSDV	Destination Sequenced Distance Vector
DSR	Dynamic Source Routing
FIFO	First In First Out
HAN	Home Area Network
IA	Information Assurance
IO	Information Operation
JOR	Joint Information Operation Range
JSIM	Java-based Simulation
NCR	National Cyber Range
NS$_2$	Network Simulator version 2
NS$_3$	Network Simulator version 3
OLSR	Optimized Link State Routing
OS	Operating System
OTcl	Object Tool Command Language
PARSEC	PaRallel Simulation Environment for Complex systems
PLC	Programmable Logic Controller
QoR	Quality of Service
SEC	Shell Executable Command
SUT	System under Test
TCP	Transmission Control Protocol
UAS	Unmanned Aerial Systems
UDP	User Datagram Protocol
UGS	Unmanned Ground System
VINT	Virtual Inter Network Testbed
WAN	Wide Area Network
WiMAX	Worldwide Interoperability for Microwave Access

Chapter 8

API	Application Programming Interface
CLI	Command Line Interface
CR	Cyber Range
DNS	Domain Name System
ETTD	Estimated Time to Detection
ETTR	Estimated Time to Recovery
GUI	Graphical User Interface
HMI	Human Machine Interface
IaC	Infrastructure as Code
IDS	Intrusion Detection System
IP	Internet Protocol
IPAM	IP Address Management
IPS	Intrusion Prevention System
LAN	Local Area Network
MTTC	Mean Time to Compromise
MTTP	Mean Time to Privilege Escalation
NTF	Network Traffic Flow
OS	Operating System
SCCS	Source Code Control Systems
VM	Virtual Machine
VPN	Virtual Private Network

Chapter 9

AAR	After Action Report
ANTS	Automated Network Traffic Synthesizer
ATMS	Automated Testing Measurement System
BFN	Blue Force Network
CAAJED	Cyber and Air Joint Effects Demonstration
CAD	Cyber Attack and Defense
CAT	Coordinated Attack Tool
CCDCoE	Cooperative Cyber Defence Centre of Excellence
CD	Compact Disk
CE	Cybersecurity Exercise
CEMAT	Consolidated Exercise Metrics Analysis
CKIM	Cyber/Kinetic Inference Model
CNA	Computer Network Attack
CND	Computer Network Defense
CNE	Computer Network Exploitation
CNO	Computer Network Operation
COCOM	Combatant-Command
CR	Cyber Range
C2	Command and Control

DARPA	Defense Advanced Research Projects Agency
DoD	Department of Defense
DoDCSR	DoD Cybersecurity Range
DoS	Denial of Service
EW	Electronic Warfare
GUI	Graphical User Interface
IA	Information Assurance
ID	Intrusion Detection
IO	Information Operation
IOR	Information Operation Range
IP	Internet Protocol
IPS	Intrusion Prevention System
IT	Information Technology
IWAR	Information Warfare Analysis and Research
JCOR	Joint Cyber Operations Range
JFCOM	Joint Forces Command
JIOR	Joint IO Range
JRSS	Joint Regional Security Stack
JTF	Joint Task Force
LVC	Live Virtual Constructive
MAC	Media Access Control
MACR	Military Academy Cyber Range
MAP	Modern Air Power
MCR	Military Cyber Range
MUTT	Multi-User Training Tool
NATO	North Atlantic Treaty Organization
NCR	National Cyber Range
NTA	Network Traffic Agent
NTF	Network Traffic Flow
NTS	Network Traffic Scenario
PaaS	Platform as a Service
RGI	Range Global Internet
SAB	Scientific Advisory Board
SAST	Security Assessment Simulation Toolkit
SEAL	Secure Environment for Accelerated Learning
SECOT	Simulated Enterprise for Cyber Operations Training
SGI	Silicon Graphics
SIMTEX	Simulator Training and Exercises
SLAM-R	Sentinel Legion AutoBuild Myrmidon – Reconstitution
SNA	Simulated Network Architecture
SVN	Software Virtual Network
TCP	Transmission Control Protocol
TRMC	Test Resource Management Centre
UCS	Unified Computing System
USAF	United States Air Force
USMA	United States Military Academy
VM	Virtual Machine
VPN	Virtual Private Network
XML	Extensible Markup Language

Chapter 10

ABAC	Attribute-Based Access Control
ACR	Academic Cyber Range
API	Application Programming Interface
AWS	Amazon Web Services
CNO	Computer Network Operation
CONCORDIA	Cybersecurity cOmpeteNCe fOr Research anD InnovAtion
CPU	Central Processing Unit
CR	Cyber Range
CTF	Capture the Flag
DARPA	Defense Advanced Research Projects Agency
DASH	Deter Agents Simulating Humans
DDoS	Distributed Denial of Service
DETER	Defense Technology Experimental Research
DEVS	Discrete Event System Specification
DHS	Department of Homeland Security
DNS	Domain Name System
DoD	Department of Defense
DVWA	Damn Vulnerable Web Application
EUH	European Union Horizon
FIFO	First-In First-Out
GUI	Graphical User Interface
HNS	Hybrid Network Simulation
HTTP/ HTTPs	HyperText Transfer Protocol/HyperText Transfer Protocol Secure
LAMP	Linux, Apache, MySQL, PHP
LARIAT	Lincoln Adaptable Real-time Information Assurance Testbed
MAGI	Montage AGent Infrastructure
MB	Model Base
NSF	National Science Foundation
OPNET	Optimized Network Engineering Tool
RINSE	Real-time Immersive Network Simulation Environment
RISE	Research Institutes of Sweden
SCADA	Supervisory Control and Data Acquisition
SDM	Simulator Database Manager
SEER	Security Experimentation Environment
SES	System Entity Structure
SNMP	Simple Network Management Protocol
SQL	Structured Query Language
TDL	Test Description Language
UML	Unified Modeling Language
USAF	United States Air Force
VCSTC	Virtual Cyber-Security Testing Capability
VLAN	Virtual Local Area Network
VM	Virtual Machine
XML	Extensible Markup Language

Glossary

A

AAR: A comprehensive feedback report summarizing all the events.

ABAC: It is an access control paradigm granting users access rights based on attributes.

ACS: It is an integration of devices and relevant equipment within the manufacturing plant.

ADC: Converts analog signals into digital form for data processing.

AI: A computer science branch, focusing on creation of intelligent machines that process data and make appropriate decisions by themselves.

AIS: An automatic system for tracking vessels.

AMI: It provides necessary information for launching instances.

ANTS: It recreates the networks, users, and devices for carrying out its functions.

AODV: Routing protocol for designing mobile ad hoc and wireless networks.

API (Application Programming Interface): It allows communications between two applications.

APT: Sophisticated attack tactics and exploitation techniques that are stealthy, and complex.

ARC: Group of hardware and software capable of executing control functions without any external interference for long time periods.

ATMS: It is responsible for providing an operator with means to uninterruptedly determine the status of any simulation(s) and for collecting metrics to perform analysis.

AWS: Amazon's subsidiary that provides instantaneous cloud-computing platforms, and APIs to customers on a pay-as-you-go basis.

B

BCS: A multi-national cyber defense exercise.

BFN: Affected by disrupting bandwidth or meddling with the service metrics.

BIOS: A firmware used for performing hardware initialization during the boot process and for providing runtime services for OS and other programs.

BMSL: It is used for recording the behavior and storing it in a policy database.

C

CAAJED: It is a USAF-funded project, designed with the objective to concentrate on advanced cyberwarfare.

CAD: A library of DoS, channel scanning, radio jamming, and firewall models.

CAN: Unauthorized actions aimed at disrupting, denying, degrading, and destroying information from the network infrastructure.

CAT: It delivers malicious or failed network traffic activities during an exercise.

CCDCoE: One of NATO Centres of Excellence situated in Tallinn, Estonia.

CCU: It serves as a wireless cloud gateway and a prime user interface in a network infrastructure.

CD: A digital, optical disk data storage format.

CDX: A National Security Agency annual competition where different teams design, defend, implement, and manage a cyber network.

CE: Effective approach for practicing cybersecurity related concepts.

CEMAT: Used in SAST and provides capabilities for tracking and measuring security performances.

CFLAT: It allows remote attestation of the control flow path of an application without source code.

CIP: It is used for industrial automation and related applications.

CKIM: CAAJED's Cyber/Kinetic Inference Model.

CLI: Processes commands and allows user to communicate with OS and other programs.

CMM: It is used for modeling probabilities of numerous states and their transition rates.

CND: Processes and security procedures for detecting, monitoring, protecting, analyzing, and defending network infrastructure.

CNE: The ability to gather and exploit targeted data for gaining intelligence.

CORAS: It is a European research framework project designed for assessing and managing security risks.

CPS: Modern, extensive systems having both physical, communication, and computational capabilities.

CPU: Responsible for performing basic arithmetical, logical, control, and I/O operations according to the instructions written in the program.

CRAAM: It is a risk management methodology.

CSAW [see-SAW]: It is a global, student-run cybersecurity event comprising of competitions and related conferences.

CSIRT: It is Computer Security Incident Response Team

CTF: It is a cybersecurity contest where every participant must complete certain assigned tasks to access the servers for capturing the flag (an encoded string) from some secret file.

D

DA Systems: Data Acquisition systems are responsible for data collection from various types of sensors implemented in a physical environment.

DAC: It converts digital signal (input) to an analog signal (output).

DaSSF (Dartmouth Scalable Simulation Framework): It is a parallel simulator designed for simulating extensive multiple protocols communication networks.

DCS (Distributed Control Systems): These systems are types of industrial telemetry systems. They provide sophisticated control capabilities over data collecting and related devices.

DDoS (Distributed Denial-of-Service): This attack uses several systems to target and compromise a targeted resource.

DMZ: A network perimeter protecting the local network of an organization from suspicious traffic.

DNP3: A group of communications protocols used by the automation system's components.

DNS (Domain Name System): A directory service providing a mapping between host names and their numerical address on a network.

DoS: Cyber attack which makes the systems and network devices inaccessible by the users.

DPI: It is used for evaluating data packet contents when they pass across the checkpoints on network.

E

EBS: It is a scalable and user-friendly service designed for the Amazon EC2.

EC2: It is an Amazon web service which provides resizable and secure computing capacity in the cloud.

ECDIS: It is a navigational chart system for naval ships and vessels.

ER: A water-storing container located at a certain height.

ESX: It is a server visualization platform for the VMWare.

F

FIFO: A method in which the oldest entry of the queue is processed first.

G

GSA: Governmental organizations responsible for conducting intelligence activities to ensure internal safety of the nation.

GUI (Graphical User Interface): Allows user interaction with electronic devices using icons.

H

HIL: A technique for developing and testing complex instantaneous embedded systems.

HITL (Human In The Loop): It is a simulation model that requires human interaction and conforms to human-related factors.

HMI: An interface for connecting users with the systems or devices.

HTML: It is used for designing documents that will get displayed in the web browser.

HTTP: It is an application layer protocol used for intercepting and transmitting HTML documents.

HTTPs: It is an extension of HTTP and used for providing secure communications across the Internet.

I

IA: Managing data risks for protecting information systems like computer systems and network systems.

IaaS: Online service used for providing advanced APIs and other virtualized computing resources across the Internet.

IaC: It is defined as an automation approach used for deploying extensive architecture.

ICS: Commonly used term to refer various control systems and equipment for industrial processes.

IDs: Approach for detecting intrusion attempts in complex network systems.

IEC: An organization responsible for preparing and publishing international standards for all electrical, electronic, and associated technologies.

IO: Involves collecting tactical information regarding any cyber threat.

IoT (Internet of Things): A technology paradigm aimed at combining different network devices and machines under a general infrastructure.

IPS: Network security systems responsible for examining network traffic flows and detecting system vulnerabilities.

ISEAGE: A security testbed for creating a virtual Internet for designing and testing cyber defense tools.

ISR (Intelligence, Surveillance, Reconnaissance): It is responsible for coordinating data collection, its processing, and provisioning reliable information and intelligence support.

IT: Usage of computers and related devices for creating, processing, storing, retrieving, and exchanging electronic data and information.

K

KVM: It is a complete visualization module for Linux.

L

LAMP: Linux, Apache, MySQL, PHP/Perl/Python applications.

M

MAC: A sublayer of the data link layer of OSI model. It is responsible for the transmission of data.

MB: A unit of measurement of data in context with digital media storage.

MHz: A unit of measurement of frequency, equivalent to 1 million hertz.

MITM: An eavesdropping attack focused on interrupting data transfer or communication.

ML: A branch of computer science allowing software applications to accurately predict outcomes based on collected data.

MIT License: A free, permissive software license (made in 1980) originated at Massachusetts Institute of Technology.

N

NAT: A method of mapping IP address spaces into others via modification of the network address in the IP headers of the packets when in transition across traffic routing devices.

NATO: An inter-government military alliance established among 28 European and two North American countries.

NIST: A physical sciences laboratory and non-regulatory agency of the United States Department of Commerce.

O

OCA (OpenNebula Cloud API): OpenNebula has Java-based, Ruby-based, and Python-based OCAs.

OCCI (Open Cloud Computing Interface): It is a flexible API originally designed for managing IaaS (Infrastructure-as-a-Service) model.

OCTAVE: A framework used for identification and management of cybersecurity risks.

OFS: It is a union file system operation for Linux.

OS: An interface between computer hardware and software resources that provides common services.

OT: The collection of hardware and software for detecting changes via direct monitoring or controlling industrial equipment, processes, assets, and events.

OTcl: It is responsible for the arrangement and configuration of an object and its frontend.

P

PaaS: A cloud computing paradigm for delivering third-party software and hardware tools to the users across the Internet.

PHIL: An extension of HIL, supports instantaneous simulation environment for exchanging low-voltage and current signals by the SUT.

PLC (Programmable Logic Controller): A ruggedized industrial computer for controlling manufacture processes.

PNNL (Pacific Northwest National Laboratory): It is a US-based laboratory comprising of research and scientific facilities.

Q

QoR: Measurement of overall performance of a cloud computing service or computer network.

QoS: Group of technologies that guarantee a network's ability and reliability for running high-priority applications and network traffic in limiting network capacity.

R

RBAC: An approach for limiting system access to only approved users.

RTDS: An instantaneous power system simulator.

RTU (Remote Terminal Unit): An electronic device controlled via microprocessor that transmits telemetry data to the master system. It is an interface between physical world objects and the SCADA system.

S

SAB: An international scientific professionals community occupied in life science and medical sectors.

SAML: XML-based open standard used for exchange of authentication and authorization data between two entities.

SAP: Comprised of numerous tools that allows the users to comprehend security evaluations via constant monitoring and testing.

SCADA: Computer-based systems used for instantaneous data gathering and analyses of control equipment.

SCCS: A version control system used for tracking source code changes.

SDM: Used in RINSE, for transmission of the data taking place between the iSSFNet and SQL database.

SEAL: Provides management functionalities in SAST.

SEC: It is responsible for accepting the input argument and name of the Tcl script.

SEE: An inconsistency detection environment for intercepting crawler-made system calls.

SEER: A testing environment for DETER.

SES: Represents network elements and their relations in hierarchical order.

SGI: American computing manufacturer of computer hardware and software.

SITL (Software In The Loop): It is a simulator that allows the creation, testing, and use of virtual vehicles.

SLAM-R: Used in SIMTEX cyber range for providing virtual training environments or simulators.

SNA: Network simulator used for cybersecurity research.

SNMP: Networking protocol for managing and monitoring network devices in Internet Protocol.

SOAP: An XML-based protocol used for exchanging information in distributed and decentralized application environments.

SOC: A centralized unit dealing with security issues on the organizational level and technical level.

SQL: Database language for managing and performing operations on data in relational databases.

SSD (Solid-State Drive): It is a new-gen, flash-based memory and storage device.

SSF: It is responsible for providing a compact and outstanding interface used to build isolated event simulations.

SSH: A cryptography network protocol for executing network services securely.

SSL: A protocol used for setting up a secure channel between devices connected via the Internet.

SUT: It refers to the system which is to be evaluated for some operations.

SVN: Virtual network for connecting VMs and other devices irrespective of their locations.

SWAT: A water treatment testbed for cybersecurity training and research.

T

TCP/IP: Group of communications protocols for Internet and related computer networks.

TDL: It facilitates detailed security device specifications for testing purposes.

TRMC: United States test and evaluation infrastructure responsible for maintaining military cyber ranges.

TTPs (Tactics, Techniques, and Procedures): An essential cybersecurity concept defining, identifying, and analyzing attackers' (hackers') general tactics.

U

UAS: Remotely controlled aircraft.

UAV (Unmanned Aerial Vehicle): It is a remote-controlled or ground-based controlled flying aircraft commonly called a drone.

UCS: Servers having network and storage access to a single unified system.

UDP: A communications protocol used for creating low-latency, loss-tolerating connections among Internet applications.

UF: A water purification process where water gets forced via a semipermeable membrane.

UGS: A vehicle operating on the ground without human presence.

UML: A commonly used developmental and modeling language.

USB: An external interface for connecting peripheral devices to the computer.

V

VAPT: Network vulnerability testing tools.

VCSTC: An emulation-based cyber range.

VLAN: A subnetwork capable of grouping together collections of devices spread across a LAN.

VM: A virtual computer operating within a physical server.

VMM: A software supporting creation and control of VM and managing virtualized environment atop a physical machine.

VNX: It is Virtualization, Celerra [NS20, NS40, etc.] NAS Architecture platforms, CLARiiON [CX3, CX4, etc.] SAN Architecture platforms.

VoIP: A method for delivering voice communications and multimedia over IP networks.

VPC: It is an instantaneously available and configurable shared resource pool given inside a public cloud environment.

VPN: Extends private network capabilities across a public network, enabling data sharing across both networks directly.

W

WADI: An extension of SWAT testbed and used for simulating the effects of physical attacks like chemical injections and water leakage.

WAN: An extensive telecommunications network used for computer networking.

WiMAX: A group of wireless broadband communication standards based on the IEEE 802.16 standards.

WSDL: An XML notation to describe a web service.

WSS: A network of pressure pipes, water sources, and end-users.

X

XML: Defines a set of codes emphasizing readability by both humans and machines.

XSS: A security vulnerability used by attackers to compromise web applications.

1

Introduction

1.1 CSA

In everyday context, SA can be defined as being alert and having information of the happenings in one's surrounding. The notion of SA is not constricted to any domain. For example, the corporations covet to be responsive of the susceptibilities that may be present in their business models or assets with the purpose of overcoming any kinds of manipulations of its vulnerabilities. Endsley gave a more sophisticated definition of situational awareness. According to her, SA involves perceiving physical elements of an environment, comprehending their meanings and predicting how they developed.. The four focal elements of SA that make it advantageous for decision-making are:

- **Perception** encompasses the awareness of the individual's own locus concerning the setting of additional entities and environmental factors.
- **Comprehension** of the causes, impacts, and consequences of the external influences to the systems with analyzing the changes in the situations/surroundings over time.
- **Projection** or predictions of the likely developments from the existing to approaching situation.
- **Resolution** includes the recovery and repair of the damage caused to the system.

CSA is a novel and emergent methodology used to tackle sophisticated cyberattacks and exploitation of existing weaknesses in computer networks, CPSs, and companies' infrastructures. In the academic, military, and commercial arenas, CSA is regarded as the leading edge to deal with cybersecurity issues (Onwubiko 2016). It tries to apply the focal elements of SA in context of cyberspace and cybersecurity. SA proves to be an essential constituent of cybersecurity to deal with threat exchanges for everybody like individuals, businesses, and response teams (Gutzwiller *et al.* 2020). The following examples emphasize the significance of SA in cyber systems:

a. **Managing e-commercial enterprises**
   Nowadays, a lot of transactions on e-commerce websites (like eBay and Amazon) are being processed on daily basis. For smooth flow of business, it is crucial to monitor and analyze all kinds of possible cyber threats and the vulnerabilities in the cyber infrastructure and components.

b. **GSA**
   GSA monitor millions of a country's citizens' assets, national critical infrastructures, as they are accountable for protecting the citizens within the country as well as overseas. The security of the database containing every citizen's record should not be compromised.

DOI: 10.1201/9781003206071-1

CSA incorporates people (operator/team), technology, and processes required for obtaining knowledge over time of all situations in cyber systems with earlier described factors of situational awareness:

1. Network components such as IDs, firewalls, monitoring systems, and scanners collect the data, report alerts, and generate logs. Security operator/team uses this data to perceive the situation and keep track of potential cyber threats.

2. Next, the security operator/team uses technology and processes to combine, evaluate, integrate, and compare the perceived data to comprehend the current situation and update the knowledge-base as well.

3. After this step, based on the data perceived and comprehended, the security operator/team can now put forth accurate predictions of the patterns of cyberattacks. They can now answer the questions like, what kind of cyber scenarios are probable, what are the feasible methods by which the current susceptibilities can be manipulated or worsened, and what measures can be implemented?

4. Lastly, the security operator/team is able to propose and employ the required sequence of action and countermeasure controls for resolving in-built risks or cyberattacks in cybernetworks.

CSA provides overall as well as a specific vista of cyber threats and liabilities in the systems, conceding organizations the proficiency for identifying, processing, and comprehending this information in instantaneously. CR platforms and testbed tools incorporate the CSA factors and help security analysts introduce a detailed insight of the advancement of a cyberattack and the techniques to implement highly impactful countermeasure controls to impede breaches. A CSA system must comprise test environments for delivering simultaneous sensor data, languages for describing the environment at various stages of abstraction, and integration of adversarial narrative with the setup (Okolica *et al.* 2009). CSA and cybersecurity also concern reliable risk management assessments that may be based on susceptibilities found in data, network, systems, or applications affecting mission assurance (Matthews *et al.* 2016).

Following is the list of some of the uses cases of CSA systems:

- **Data source**: the CSA system can be used for generating complete and high-quality data. This ensures the authenticity of the data for other users, stakeholders, and other systems.

- **Assets organization and interconnectivity**: the system is a common platform for assets sharing and organizing. Organizing assets and their dependencies and associations makes them easily identifiable by the users. They can be shared between the physical and the logical units of the network. New components and CSA scenarios can also be developed from the knowledge and usage of preexisting assets of the network.

- **Assessing risks**: situation comprehension and projection, both can be achieved by assessing the potential impact of a network threat scenarios. This assessment can be performed using scenario simulations or by using data on previous cyberattacks. This may help the system to better adapt measures for cyber defense.

- **System monitoring**: the users can observe the performance of the various components of the system and means of a virtual environment or visualization. This may be useful for detecting and analyzing any suspicious activities.

- **Incident handling**: for appropriate response actions, it is important to comprehend the current scenario by either spotting any issues or inspections which may elucidate any possible cyber incidents. This may help the user in drawing an in-depth analysis of the situation like identifying the sources of any attacks or the later possible consequences of an attack.

1.2 Definition

CRs are intricate virtual setups that provide a prototype of complexities of cybersecurity situations (like cyberattacks, cyberwarfare) in the real-world and execute utmost quality training in cybersecurity, deliver an environment for research as well as for the study of diverse schemas, and teach practical incident management as well as response expertise. An ideal CR as shown in Figure 1.1 provides instantaneous feedback with reliable simulation, a virtual setting where different teams can participate for training, a research environment where various teams can test their strategies, and a performance-based evaluation metrics (Urias *et al.* 2018).

CRs provide dynamic simulation arenas, participant access, infrastructure, and technical scenarios for conducting CEs that are crucial for training and testing the resilience of personnel in an organization. These cybersecurity trainings and exercises are utilized by organization's personnel to improve their dexterity with respect to incident response, malware analysis, network security, forensics, etc. Using CR, the teams work together to mitigate and minimize cyber threats and cyberattacks to the organization's infrastructure. Intra-organizational CEs aim at enhancing the crisis-management, event response, and resilience of the personnel. Cross-sector CEs are useful for establishing and providing technical skills as well as for raising cybersecurity awareness and information sharing.

One of the common tasks in CR exercises is to defend essential IT infrastructure comprising SCADA/ICS against the team of coordinated attackers (Vykopal *et al.* 2017b). The personnel are divided into four main teams, each team is assigned with different tasks

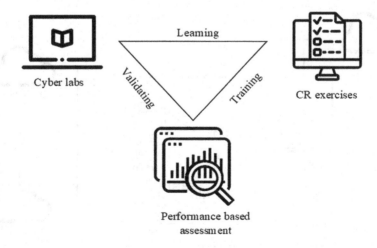

FIGURE 1.1
CR environment.

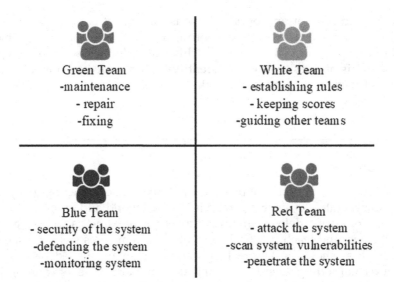

FIGURE 1.2
Roles of personnel in CR exercises.

to execute during the exercise as shown in Figure 1.2. First, the teams get to familiarize with the virtual infrastructure and rules of the exercise and after that the intensive training initiates. The red team is tasked with investigating victim's network infrastructure to find and exploit vulnerabilities in the system. And ultimately compromise all the network components and cause shutdown of the control systems. Contrary to this, the blue team is responsible for analyzing and fixing system susceptibilities and implementing strategies to flop the attacks devised by red team.

An ideal testbed environment comprises a VirtualBox Host as shown in Figure 1.3. It is a physical machine in the test-setup. It is used for hosting two VMs – Development machine and Devstack host (Hackingloops 2021). It uses a NAT adapter to enable Internet access for both the VMs. The three machines communicate with each other using host-only adapter.

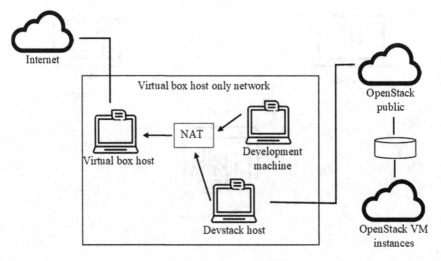

FIGURE 1.3
Testbed environment.

1.3 Need of CRs

Cyberattacks on large-scale facilities such as the Stuxnet (Denning 2012) brought into light the severity and damages caused by these incidents and the resilient requirement for personnel trainings (Benson 2021).

Stuxnet worm initially targeted the Natanz uranium facility of Iran and also spread to other countries' organizations damaging critical infrastructure and causing huge loss of assets. This incident initiated the immediate necessity for improved and novel dimension in CSA (Lallie *et al.* 2021).

The cybersecurity paradigm has shifted from seeing the user as a vulnerable link to training them to predict cyber threats and manage cyberattacks to the infrastructure reinforcing the organization's security position (Vozikis *et al.* 2020). With the rising cases of cyberattacks, organizations require sophisticated training platforms for their cybersecurity teams to gain hands-on experience in practical and immersive settings.

1.3.1 Use Cases of CRs

As shown in Figure 1.4, CRs are majorly used in academic and business sectors.

1. **In organizations**:
   a. Any commerce is dependent on virtual private network for everyday tasks of separate workforces residing in different regions of the world. These types of network architectures are exposed to cyberattacks.
   b. If a network equipment manufacturer is targeted by cyberattacks, it leads to hardware failure or exceedingly poor performance, which in turn will affect the clients and revenue.

   Organizations can use cyber-ranges for:
   a. Testing new techniques and assess the cyber capabilities of new software releases, products, and organizational restructuring

Industry
Professionals

Students

Educators

Organizations

FIGURE 1.4
Who needs CRs.

    b. Preparing their cyber teams on different organizational or technical setups and guidelines prior advancing to the organizational setting and for developing personnel skills.

2. **In separate departments:** Professionals utilize CRs for the development of both individual plus team learning and skills by practicing for diverse network-attack scenarios. These professionals can be from various arenas such as:

    a. IT

    b. law enforcement

    c. incident handlers

    d. cybersecurity

3. **In academics:**

    a. Educators use CRs as a classroom aide, to implement basic and advanced cybersecurity education courses and curricula, or to instruct and assess students virtually.

    b. Learners can use CRs for harnessing data in a virtual network setting, acquiring cyber-skills, working in teams to respond to cyberattacks, and clearing cyber-credential examinations.

1.3.2 Merits of CRs Training

- **Hands-on experiences**
  For cybersecurity/analysts/personnel teams, CRs deliver a virtual environment for collective training, improving cyber defenses skills and acquiring crucial insights into various types of investor activities in the organization. This enhances teamwork and communication within the various divisions of the enterprise as it provides the teams with an improved understanding of the responsibilities of other departments which may not be effectively possible with the conventional training models. The hands-on training helps the personnel get better equipped for the cybersecurity industry (Darwish *et al.* 2020).

- **Adapting to ever-changing and new cyber scenarios**
  The pattern of cyberattacks changes quickly, the cybersecurity personnel are required to be up to date with such changes. They should be able to keep up and respond to new attack situations. CRs empower cybersecurity teams to practice isolating and responding to cyber threats in the real-world situation with the help of a multitude of tools and runbooks. When cybersecurity teams robustly train in real-world simulations for a breach, they can most likely retain the knowledge gained and actively respond in case of an actual breach in the system.

- **Sophisticated structural security**
  CRs provide authentic and controlled training testbeds that help the team to deal with any crisis situations instantaneously. The more knowledge and experience the teams have, the better they can prepare to implement and execute tested and efficient security strategies for the organization's infrastructure.

- **Research and testing new techniques**
  Cybersecurity personnel can implement new techniques and solutions safely in a virtual environment and draw out necessary assessments before they are

implemented in the operating infrastructure or brought in for production. Simulation environment is a low-cost and low-risk method for incubating leading-edge ideas and learning from the flops. Technologies that pass all the assessments in the virtual setting could now be scaled to the organization's security strategies.

- **Improving security culture**
  CR can uncover team incoherence and help the employer in determining whether they've hired the appropriate blend of technical as well as interpersonal skills. Cyber resilience and culture are equally important. It is important that the cyber-security teams can effectively collaborate with each other as it influences how they tackle cyber-related issues under pressure.

- **Replicating cyberattacks**
  Cyberattack training is effective when dealt with real-time APTs and AI attacks. CRs effectively provide a secure environment where personnel and teams can learn and train against such real-time attacks. A replicated APT allows the cyber-security teams to validate the security of the infrastructure with respect to an advanced targeted cyberattack.

- **Evaluating potential hires**
  CR virtual environments help the employer to assess an individual's strengths and give feedback as well as assess candidates during job interviews based on how they collaborate and communicate in teams under pressure.

1.4 CRaaS

CRs can be accessed in the form of a service model that is owned and administered by CR vendors. The vendors provide cyber range service models with detailed functionalities and competences. The cyber range is developed on cloud technology and is remotely accessed by the client. For example, AWS provides several services for creating isolated cyber range (Formento *et al.* 2021):

- Amazon VPC provisions a logically remote section of AWS for launching AWS resources in a user-defined virtual network.
- AWS Transit Gateway service enables the user to connect Amazon VPCs and on-premises networks together to a distinct gateway.

CRaaS is a composition of environment and interface components provided by any cloud or data center.

1.5 On-Premise CR

These types of CRs are hosted within a physical location within an organization. These provide the training facilities like debriefing rooms and break out rooms. As compared to CR as a service, these types of CRs are quite expensive. On-premise CRs are suitable for

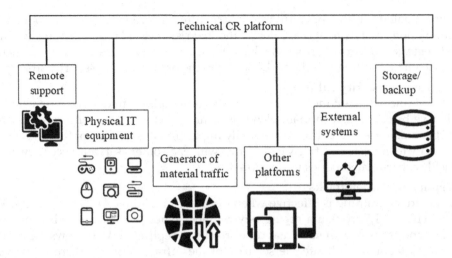

FIGURE 1.5
On-premise CR components.

fulfilling the security necessities of the organization with enhanced exercise-control and deployment of resources provided.

As shown in Figure 1.5, the platform is accessible to interfaces with external tools such as external real systems and physical IT equipment to fulfill the constraints of sophisticated environments (CyberRange 2021).

1.6 Types of CRs

CRs are of three distinct types:

- **Physical CR**
  Physical CR as shown in Figure 1.6 creates full-fledged prototype of any provided physical networks or computing infrastructures (such as the switches, routers, firewalls, servers, endpoints, etc.), for example, Cybertropolis (Deckard 2018), SCADA (Ahmed *et al*. 2016), and Swat (Mathur *et al*. 2016).

- **Virtual CR**
  Virtual CR as shown in Figure 1.7 provides a simulation of the entire computing infrastructure with the help of virtualization technologies. Every component is emulated with the help of VMs in the simulation setup. Virtual CR uses SVN technology at its core, which renders the characterization of the network structure at a suitable high-degree of reliability that the applications running on it for example video streaming, sensors collecting data, web browsing, voice communications, etc. remain unchanged atop huge emulated networks of legacy and future communication gadgets (Wihl *et al*. 2012). For example, KYPO (Vykopal *et al*. 2017a).

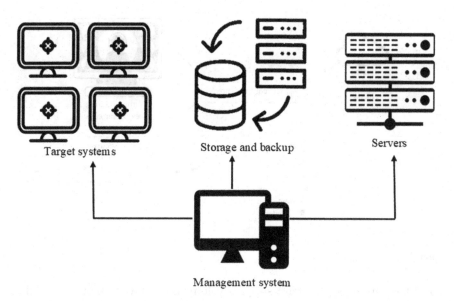

FIGURE 1.6
Some components of a physical CR.

- **Hybrid CR**
  It is a hybrid of both virtual and physical CRs. In hybrid CR environments, the virtual and physical elements as shown in Figure 1.8 are implemented and utilized as and when demanded. It is also referred to as the cyber-physical range. For example, using virtual system settings of Windows or Linux operating systems on a physical device connection for sophisticated video surveillance or some other hardware components to defend such as possibly network printers, VoIP phones or adapters, and perhaps most vitally real security tools like firewall, IPS/IDs.

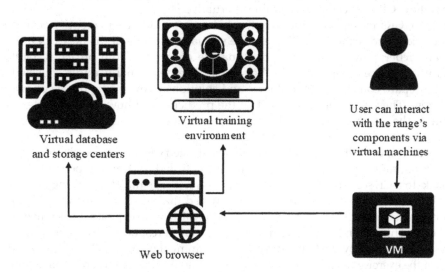

FIGURE 1.7
Some components of a virtual CR.

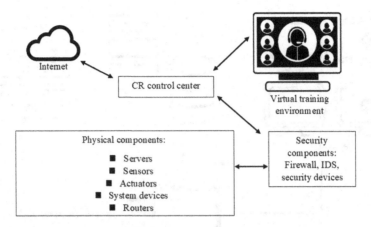

FIGURE 1.8
Some components of hybrid CR.

Hybrid CRs are used by water supply systems and power plants (Cintuglu *et al.* 2016; Holm *et al.* 2015). They are also used for monitoring security in communication protocol in smart grids (Tebekaemi *et al.* 2016). PowerCyber (Ashok *et al.* 2016) is also used for the security of smart grids.

1.7 Conclusions

CR is an effective tool for an organization for training personnel, executing cybersecurity tests, analyzing the faulty components and breaches in the system, and cultivating team work ethic. It is impractical and precarious to execute cybersecurity-tests on live IT systems; therefore, CR testbeds are a suitable alternative.

In addition, CRs incorporate the four focal elements of CSA – perception, comprehension, prediction, and resolution. CRs provide virtual prototype of the network infrastructure where cybersecurity personnel can analyze or perceive the breaches, faults, and susceptibilities of the components in the system. The personnel use this collected information to prepare counter methodologies and solutions to overcome these complications in the system. These solutions are based on the predictions of how these complexities can compromise the system. And finally, the solutions developed are tested in this virtual environment before they are sent to production.

Hence, with respect to the current scenario, sophisticated CRs are a necessity of an organization to perform multifarious technological assessments and for training personnel against a cyberattack. In a CE scenario, CR not only provides an ideal simulation setting but also team access. There are mainly four kinds of teams created during such exercises – blue team is responsible for defending attacks from the red team which try to exploit the system vulnerabilities and cause shut down of the system. The green team is responsible for fixing the breaches in the system identified by the blue team and maintaining the system. The white team decides the rules of the exercise as well as the scores of individual teams based on the task completed.

CRs are widely used in urban sectors as they facilitate and advance cybersecurity, training, education, and certifications. CRs deliver a secure environment for hands-on training, product development, security testing, and cyber skills training.

References

Ahmed, I., Roussev, V., Johnson, W., Senthivel, S., Sudhakaran, S., 2016. A Scada system testbed for cybersecurity and forensic research and pedagogy. *In: Proceedings of the 2nd Annual Industrial Control System Security Workshop*, December 2016 Los Angeles. New York: Association for Computing Machinery, 1–9.

Airbus,2021. CyberRange [online]. Available from: https://airbus-cyber-security.com/products-and-services/prevent/cyberrange/ [Accessed 27 Jan 2021].

Ashok, A., Krishnaswamy, S., Govindarasu, M., 2016. Powercyber: A remotely accessible testbed for cyber physical security of the smart grid. *In: 2016 IEEE Power Energy Society Innovative Smart Grid Technologies Conference (ISGT)*, 6–9 September 2016 Minneapolis. New York: IEEE, 1–5.

Benson, P., 2021. Computer Virus Stuxnet a 'Game Changer' [online]. DHS official tells Senate. Available from: http://edition.cnn.com/2010/TECH/web/11/17/stuxnet.virus/index.html [Accessed 20 Jan 2021].

Cintuglu, M. H., Mohammed, O. A., Akkaya, K., Uluagac, A. S., 2016. A survey on smart grid cyber-physical system testbeds. *IEEE Communications Surveys & Tutorials*, 19(1), 446–464.

Darwish, O., Stone, C. M., Karajeh, O., Alsinglawi, B., 2020. Survey of educational cyber ranges. *Web, Artificial Intelligence and Network Applications*, 1150(1), 1037–1045.

Deckard, G. M., 2018. Cybertropolis: Breaking the paradigm of cyber-ranges and testbeds. *In: IEEE International Symposium on Technologies for Homeland Security (HST)*, 23–24 October 2018 Woburn. New York: IEEE, 1–4.

Denning, D. E., 2012. Stuxnet: What has changed? *Future Internet*, 4(3), 672–687.

Formento, Jr, J., Cerini, A., 2021. What is a cyber range and how do you build one on AWS? [online]. AWS Security Blog. Available from: https://aws.amazon.com/blogs/security/what-is-cyber-range-how-do-you-build-one-aws/ [Accessed 26 Jan 2021].

Gutzwiller, R., Dykstra, J., Payne, B., 2020. Gaps and opportunities in situational awareness for cybersecurity. *Digital Threats: Research and Practice*, 1(3), 1–6.

Hackingloops, 2021. The spinning wheels behind the evolving cyber ranges [online]. Hackingloops. Available from: https://www.hackingloops.com/cyber-ranges/ [Accessed on 26 Jan 2021].

Holm, H., Karresand, M., Vidstr¨om, A., Westring, E., 2015. A survey of industrial control system testbeds. *In: Nordic Conference on Secure IT Systems*, 19–21 October 2015 Stockholm. Switzerland: Springer International Publishing, 11–26.

Lallie, H. S., Shepherd, L. A., Nurse, J. R., Erola, A., Epiphaniou, G., Maple, C., Bellekens, X., 2021. Cyber security in the age of Covid-19: A timeline and analysis of cyber-crime and cyber-attacks during the pandemic. *Computers & Security*, 105(1), 1–20.

Mathur, A. P., Tippenhauer, N. O., 2016. Swat: A water treatment testbed for research and training on ICS security. *In: International Workshop on Cyber-Physical Systems for Smart Water Networks (CySWater)*, 11–11 April 2016 Vienna. New York: IEEE, 31–36.

Matthews, E. D., Arata III, H. J., Hale, B. L., 2016. Cyber situational awareness. *JSTOR*, 1(1), 35–46.

Okolica, J., McDonald, J. T., Peterson, G. L., Mills, R. F., Haas, M. W., 2009. Developing systems for cyber situational awareness. *In: 2nd Cyberspace Research Workshop*, 15–15 June 2009 Louisiana. Louisiana: Center for Secure Cyberspace, 46–56.

Onwubiko, C., 2016. Understanding cyber situation awareness. *International Journal of Computer Science and Applications*, 1(1), 11–30.

Tebekaemi, E., Wijesekera, D., 2016. Designing an IEC 61850 based power distribution substation simulation/emulation testbed for cyber-physical security studies. *In: Proceedings of the First International Conference on Cyber-Technologies and Cyber-Systems*, 9–13 October 2016 Venice. New York: IARIA XPS, 41–49.

Urias, V. E., Stout, W. M., Van Leeuwen, B., Lin, H., 2018. Cyber range infrastructure limitations and needs of tomorrow: A position paper. *In: International Carnahan Conference on Security Technology (ICCST)*, 22–25 October 2018 Montreal. New York: IEEE, 1–5.

Vozikis, D., Darra, E., Kuusk, T., Kavallieros, D., Reintam, A., Bellekens, X., 2020. On the importance of cyber-security training for multi-vector energy distribution system operators [online]. *In: Proceedings of the 15th International Conference on Availability, Reliability and Security*, 25–28 August 2020. Available from: https://dl.acm.org/doi/abs/10.1145/3407023.3409313 [Accessed 20 Jan 2021].

Vykopal, J., Oslejsek, R., Celeda, P., Vizvary, M., Tovarnak, D., 2017a. Kypo cyber range: Design and use cases. *In: Proceedings of the 12th International Conference on Software Technologies*, 26–28 July 2017 Madrid. Madrid: SciTePress, 310–321.

Vykopal, J., Vizváry, M., Oslejsek, R., Celeda, P., Tovarnak, D., 2017b. Lessons learned from complex hands-on defence exercises in a cyber range. *In: IEEE Frontiers in Education Conference (FIE)*, 18–21 October 2017 Indianapolis. New York: IEEE, 1–8.

Wihl, L., Varshney, M., 2012. A virtual cyber range for cyber warfare analysis and training [online]. *In: Proceedings of the Interservice/Industry Training, Simulation, and Education Conference*, 2012. Available from: https://www.scalable-networks.com/sites/default/files/White-Paper–Virtual-Cyber-Range-IITSEC-2012.pdf [Accessed 20 Jan 2021].

2

Architectural Design and Tools of Cyber Ranges

2.1 Architectural Modules and Their Functions

An ideal CR aims to provide a secure, comprehensive environment where not only threats and vulnerabilities to an infrastructure are analyzed, but also testing of various security policies and products can be executed. The functionality of a CR encompasses executing threat simulations, research on potential cyber threats, training personnel for cyber incident preparedness, testing and evaluations of products, and so on. A CR may fulfill all these functionalities, or it may focus on successfully delivering only a specific utility. CRs can provide different types of specialties, for example, research, security testing, cloud-based, federal, CSE, digital forensics, and open source (Ukwandu *et al.* 2020). Depending on its purpose, the architecture of CRs and the tools used may also vary. The commonly used architecture model for designing any CR comprises the following modules as also illustrated in Figure 2.1:

- **Portal**: it supports user interface modules and front-end technologies.
- **Run-time environments**: these environments can support the execution of simulation-based tools and scenarios or emulation-based tools and scenarios. They also support traffic generation tools for replicating real-time network traffic conditions.
- **Management**: it is responsible for tasks like resource allocations, team management, and task allocations during the execution of any CSE.
- **Database**: it is used for storing different exercise modules, all the statistics of the conducted exercises, storing logs, and so on. MySQL, NoSQL are commonly used for this objective.
- **Monitoring**: it supports technologies used for monitoring of CSEs, research on cyberattacks and threats, and testing of a security product.

Tools used for portal, run-time environments, and managing of CR and their functions will be discussed in detail within this section.

2.1.1 Portal

The main function of a portal is to ensure a communication interface among the CR, its various users and test beds. There can be various types of users associated with the platform, some examples are listed as follows:

- CSE admins
- White team members

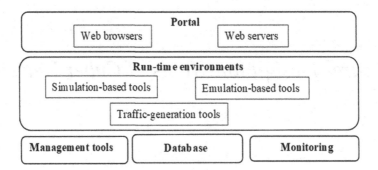

FIGURE 2.1
Architectural modules of a CR.

- Researchers
- Testbed admins
- Training personnel
- CSE trainers

Accessing virtual CRs or cloud-based CRs by the users can be achieved via browsers. Cloud-based CRs like the Virginia CR (read more in Section 10.2.5) can be accessed via the commonly used web portals. Airbus CR can also be accessed via web interfaces (read more in Section 10.1.5). NetEngine CR uses Apache as the web server (read more in Section 10.1.3).

An ideal web server navigates between the requests made by the user via internet and providing the expected responses. Figure 2.2 illustrates the working of a web server. The main task of a web server involves composing the results from various HTML files, databases, and scripting languages for generating the content user requested for. Nginx, Apache are the most commonly used web servers by CRs. Google Chrome, Mozilla Firefox, Microsoft Edge, etc. are among the list of some commonly used web browsers.

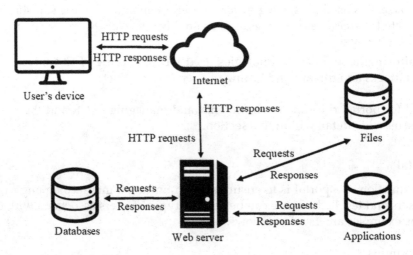

FIGURE 2.2
Working of a web server.

2.1.2 Run-Time Environments

This module comprises various types of platforms used for executing any CSE and its events. It may host either simulation- or emulation-based scenarios or both. To make the simulation/emulation more realistic, it also uses network traffic generators. These environments not only support CSE execution but also support security assessments, education and training, scenario creations, and editing. This subsection will discuss some of the tools used for simulation, emulation, and network traffic generation purposes.

2.1.2.1 Emulation-Based Tools

Some of the most commonly used tools for supporting emulations of scenarios in a CR are as follows.

2.1.2.1.1 VMWare

It is a VM emulator that was developed from research on OS conducted at the Stanford University (Nieh *et al.* 2000). It is placed as a software layer between the OS virtualizing all resources and the hardware as shown in Figure 2.3. It is responsible for the virtualization of the machine's hardware resources. VMWare creates environments where the execution of virtual hardware takes place. These environments are called the VMs. VMWare offers the following advantages:

- It allows several VMs to run simultaneously.
- The VMs are isolated from the actual hardware and additional system activities.
- Each VM can run its own OS simultaneously and on the same physical machine. The OS running on actual hardware is the Host OS and VMWare-executed OSs are the Guest OSs.

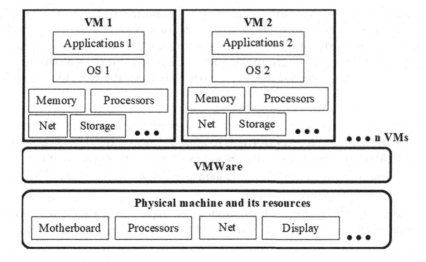

FIGURE 2.3
VMWare.

CRs like USMA IWAR, Airbus, CODE, and VCSTC make use of VMWare technology. At its core, the ESX server serves as a foundation for the delivery of distributed, virtualization-based facilities to the IT environments (Infrastructure 2006). The ESX server offers the following functionalities:

- Gets installed directly on server hardware.
- It incorporates a robust-virtualization layer between OS and hardware.
- It creates multiple, portable, and secure divisions of a physical server called VMs.
- These VMs comprise memory, processors, storage networking, and BIOS.

VMware is useful for environments that require numerous OSs, fault isolation, and kernel-level access (Nieh *et al.* 2000). The resource controls of VMWare allow users and admins to carry out precise allocation, either complete VM allocation or comparative VM importance. Without resource controls, VMs may suffer from unpredictable and unacceptable performance issues (Gulati *et al.* 2012). There are three basic resource controls implemented in VMWare:

- **Reservation**: it is expressed as MHz for CPUs and MB for the memory. It sorts a minimum definite amount of a specific resource like a lower bound employed in cases where this specific resource is heavily overcommitted. To ensure that the total of all the reservations set for the resource do not surpass its actual capacity, admission control is conducted during VM's power on.
- **Limit**: it is implemented as the upper bound on use of any specific resource, even in cases where it is less-committed. It ensures that the VM's consumption does not exceed its limit, though this may leave some resources unused. Limits are also expressed in similar units as reservations.
- **Shares**: these are expressed via abstract numerical values. It specifies the weight or relative importance of a resource.

VMWare also comprises a resource pool. It is a container and it sorts the collection of resources for allocation to a set of VMs. Admission control gets conducted at this level. Resource pool is advantageous when sharing and dividing the total capacity of resources among different user groups or VMs. The pool comprises a parent pool with sub-pools or VMs. The preferred use of resource pools is attributed to the following factors:

- It offers flexibility in resource organization. Resources reorganization, their addition and deletion all can be performed in a hierarchical order. Users can also configure the allocation settings of the resources as per their requirements.
- Different resource pools function in isolation. Changes in internal settings of one resource pool don't hinder the others.
- Users need not set resources individually for each VM. Users can control the allocation of all the resources to VMs via performing changes in enclosing pool's settings.
- Admins can manage the resources independently of actual machine that contributes the resources.

2.1.2.1.2 VM

A VM can be described as a virtual computer operating within a physical server. A VM itself runs in user mode. VMs are popularly used in the present attributing to the following benefits:

- Running several VMs on a single physical platform saves a lot of electricity and maintenance costs.
- Instead of providing a completely new environment to the developers, it is easier and time-saving to set up a VM.
- VMs can be easily moved from one hypervisor to another. They are portable and offer great backup capabilities in the case of host device failure.
- It is scalable. Users can add or remove applications or other physical resources depending on their requirements.
- As VMs run in isolation to one other and to the host OS, it can be used to isolate viruses and malware, thus protecting the host.

The performance of a VM can be evaluated based on resource interference, virtualization technology used, and interactions taking place between the VMs (Tickoo *et al.* 2010). VM emulators can be broadly categorized into hardware-bound and pure software VM emulators (Ferrie 2007). VirtualBox, VMWare, Xen, etc. are some examples of hardware-bound VM emulators. Hydra, QEMU, Bochsxiv, etc. are some examples of pure software VM emulators. Pure software VM emulators have an advantage over hardware-bound as a pure software VM's CPU need not match with the host's CPU. This allows the guest OS to move freely between the machines of varying architecture. CRs like SIMTEX, DETERLab, and Virginia CR make use of VMs in their architecture.

VMM software is the core of a VM as it is responsible for transforming the interface of a single machine into an illusion of numerous interfaces (Goldberg 1974). VMMs providing utility computing and server consolidation led to its prominence again in 2005. It's a software layer responsible for exporting a VM abstraction like the hardware running an OS. It offers the following capabilities:

- In cases where the physical machine fails, or it goes offline, or some other machine goes online, VMM remaps all the VMs accordingly.
- It also allows isolation between VMs as it mediates the interactions taking place between VM and its underlying hardware.
- It presents uniform viewing of the actual hardware. It makes the machines belonging to diverse vendors with distinct I/O subsystems look similar; allowing VMs to execute on any accessible machine.
- It is a tool for enhancing the security and robustness of the system without worrying about the space occupied by applications.

2.1.2.1.3 OpenNebula

It is a virtualization tool for managing the infrastructure (virtualized) in the private cloud (Yadav 2013). It was initially a research project by I. M. Liorente and R. S. Montero in 2005. It got publicly released in 2008. More importantly, it is an open-source platform for cloud computing as illustrated in Figure 2.4. It manages VMs for cloud and provides IaaS (Sempolinski *et al.* 2010). It has classic cluster-type architecture. It comprises the front-end

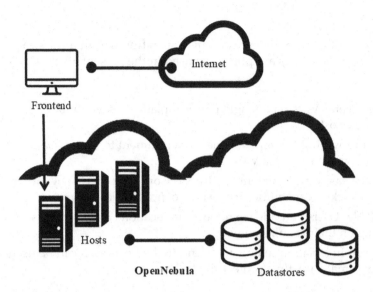

FIGURE 2.4
OpenNebula architecture.

and group of cluster nodes that run the VMs. Both components get connected to each other using a physical network. It comprises the following features:

- It has adopted AWS-compatible APIs and its services like AMI, EBS, and EC2.
- It can also deploy other types of clouds like hybrid and public.
- Majority of its components were written in languages like C++, JAVA, and Ruby.
- It also supports hypervisors like VMWare, Xen, and KVM.
- It supports Oss like CentOS, Fedora, Debian, RHEL, and Ubuntu.
- MySQL is used for its back end.

It comprises majorly nine components as listed next:

- **Front end**: it is responsible for executing all the services provided by OpenNebula. It ensures that activities like logging, authentication, resource quotas, and accounting. are carried out.
- **Host**: it is responsible for interacting with hypervisor, VMs and managing the network for VMs running in cloud. Both front end and hosts are interconnected via internet. Host also facilitates working with heterogeneous environments (like with different OSs or hypervisors).
- **Cluster**: it a pool of all the hosts. These hosts share same networks and datastores. Cluster formation leads to load balancing, high performance, and availability of the hosts (Donevski *et al.* 2013).
- **Image repository**: it comprises registered VM images within the cloud. All the VM images can be stored in various types of datastores.
- **Sunstone**: it is a web-administrative interface. It is used for managing the cloud and supporting RBAC principle.

- **OCCI, Self, EC2 services**: these allow management of the cloud with different interfaces. These are also responsible for monitoring, live migration, control, and storage access.
- **OCA**: it makes the communicating with management interface easier.

OpenNebula offers and supports the following functionalities:

- **Scalable host environments**: it allows the hybrid cloud to merge limited infrastructure with the cloud infrastructure of public cloud. It also provides cloud interfaces for VMs, network management, and storage.
- **Elastic platform**: all these services get hosted within VMs of the cloud, which can be controlled and monitored via CLI or APIs.
- It has minimum risk of breakdown as the resources (virtual) get distributed among different physical resources.
- Mapping of the virtual resources onto the physical ones increases the optimization.

2.1.2.2 Simulation-Based Tools

Some of the most commonly used tools for supporting simulations of scenarios in a CR are as follows.

2.1.2.2.1 iSSFNet

It is a network simulator supporting a network of parallel running simulations. Its kernel pattern is responsible for managing all its support functions. This network simulator assists in hosting various extensive, instantaneous, and live simulations. Its distinctive synchronization mechanism supports distributed execution. It is one of the major components of RINSE CR (read more in Section 10.1.2).

The SSF is object-oriented and is responsible for providing a compact and outstanding interface used to build isolated event simulations. It comprises five core classes – Entity, Event, InChannel, OutChannel, and Process (Cowie *et al.* 1999).

- **Entity**: it is one of the base classes. It is responsible for every simulation component as it is a container that outlines the alignment relations between the simulation's components. These interactions between components take place via event exchange across channels with lower core minimal delay (Cowie *et al.* 1999).
- **Event**: it is also one of the base classes. It is responsible for the process of significant information exchange.
- **InChannel**: it is one of the communication endpoints responsible for event exchange. Each of its instances goes to a definite Entity (Cowie *et al.* 1999).
- **OutChannel**: it is also one of the communication endpoints responsible for event exchange. It may have a core minimal delay associated with it. SSF allows both multicast InChannel and OutChannel mappings along with bus-style mappings (Cowie *et al.* 1999).
- **Process**: it is also one of the base classes. It is responsible for describing the behavior of an Entity. Each of the instances of Process is commonly associated with some definite Entity (Cowie *et al.* 1999). A Process initially waits for some Event arriving on the channel. Then it responds to that event and again moves to sleep.

The iSSFNet provides the following functionalities:

- Straightforward and simple implementation of network components and new protocols.
- High performance and high scalability on modeling of extensive infrastructures via parallel processing.
- Memory conservation is achieved by implementing SSF threads. The SSF models get converted to C++ programs.
- Processors synchronization is achieved via a mathematically proven technique. This technique ensures that all the processors get periodically synchronized for exchanging events (Cowie *et al.* 1999).
- It is substantially portable and can incorporate Linux, Windows, Solaris, etc.

2.1.2.2.2 RTDS

It is used for running instantaneous simulations of power systems or infrastructures using a parallel processing-based architecture (McLaren *et al.* 1992). RTDS costs comparatively less than the analogue simulator with comparable capabilities (McLaren *et al.* 1992). Over the decades, RTDS's applications have been encompassed in several domains:

- **Simulating cyber incidents:** On a worldwide scale, RTDS provides cybersecurity test beds as shown in Figure 2.5, for conducting simulations of cyberattacks on power infrastructures. It provides a flexible, realistic, and isolated environment for validating the security features of the power infrastructures (RTDS Technologies Inc., 2021). Some of the cybersecurity-related applications provided by RTDS include: DoS and MITM simulations, physical and cyber fault analyses, cryptography, etc.

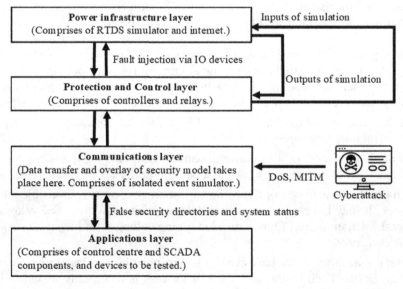

FIGURE 2.5
RTDS simulation.

- **Research and training**: As RTDS provides fastest and instantaneous outputs, several tests can be performed and validated by the users. This saves a lot of time when testing for varying incidents and conditions. It also helps in training and confidence building of novice cybersecurity personnel.

- **PHIL test beds**: these test beds are for testing the actual power hardware connected to the simulated setup. It makes use of four-quadrant amplifiers. It comprises some custom-built interfaces aiding in minimizing the PHIL delays. This is cost-effective for the users. These test beds support motor testing, characterization, and behavior studies of the power systems.

- **Test beds for protection equipment**: these test beds aid in testing and deployment of latest security algorithms and schemes under a secure, isolated, and flexible environment. As the simulations are instantaneous, such equipment can be physically linked to the simulation setup. Security algorithms can be tested instantaneously and prior to pursuing hardware availability.

RTDS provides the following functionalities:

- **Flexibility and scalability**: RTDS provides an execution of a comprehensive simulation, thus validating and configuring hardware components. It ensures that extensive and complicated simulations run accurately and are stable. It also ensures that there is minimum-to-zero performance loss. NovaCor is a custom-built and powerful hardware platform present at the core of RTDS. It is responsible for demonstrating varying power systems.

- **Instantaneous data exchange**: RTDS allows exchange of data via several communications protocols with either external software or hardware. It supports the following communication protocols: Ethernet, MODBUS, TCP/UDP sockets, PLAYBACK, DNP3, IEC 61850-9-2, etc.

- **Modeling library**: RTDS provides an extensive, flexible, diverse, and accurate modeling library for simulations. It comprises expertise and resources useful in creating customer-specific models or features.

- **RSCAD**: it is the incorporation's proprietary software developed specifically for RTDS as it does not require any third-party components. It comprises comprehensive documentations and manuals, a component and circuit builder, and operator's module. It also supports automation of C-type scripts.

- It can execute stable, multi-rate simulations. This allows the users to minimize the number of hardware components required for simulations when representing extensive networks.

2.1.2.2.3 PRIME

It is parallel simulations execution engine supporting instantaneous network simulations (Li *et al.* 2009). It has incorporated hybrid traffic and isolated event modeling techniques. These are useful in accelerating the execution of simulations, harnessing computing resources, and reducing computational demands (Liu 2010). It is able to support instantaneous simulations by focusing on timeliness and responsiveness.

- **Timeliness**: it indicates the ability of the system to perform in real time. To avoid timing faults, simulations must be able to instantaneously characterize the networks' behaviors in the case of extensive network traffic flows and network entities. The simulator can be less responsive with frequent amounts of timing faults.

- **Responsiveness**: this property indicates that the simulation should be receiving inputs and responding promptly to instantaneous events within a set deadline.

The simulator also deploys priority scheduling algorithm to support instantaneous processing of events (Li *et al.* 2009).

It also offers the following capabilities:

- **Hierarchical synchronization**: this scheme allows the simulator to improve performance on allocated memory machines. This aids in reducing communication cost between allocated and shared memory machines.
- It efficiently simulates various extensive network scenarios and types of nodes. The simulation conducts events like carrying out network packets, delays and losses, and traffic generations.
- **Accuracy**: the simulator provides comprehensive network packet transactions. Realistic traffic generation, applications, and services increase simulation fidelity.
- **Repeatability**: producing repeatable simulation conditions is imperative for evaluations and protocol developments.
- **Scalability**: operations like forwarding network packets are easier to parallelize, therefore aiding in scaling up or down of simulated network.
- It also extends DaSSF capabilities (Liu 2010). This allows the simulator to implement real applications interacting with the simulator instantaneously.

2.1.2.3 Traffic Generation Tools

Some of the most commonly used tools for supporting traffic generations in a CR are as follows.

2.1.2.3.1 SSH

It is a network protocol used for securing network services and remote logins (Ylonen *et al.* 2006) as shown in Figure 2.6. It comprises three components – SSH-TRANS,

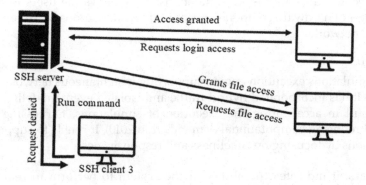

FIGURE 2.6
SSH implementation.

SSH-CONNECT, and SSH-USERAUTH (Ylonen *et al.* 2006). These components ensure client and server authentications and encryption of channels. The prime application of SSH is to ensure the establishment of a secure channel between any two hosts (Song et al. 2001). It follows client-server architecture and automatically encrypts sent data and decrypts the received data (Barrett *et al.* 2005). The protocol was developed by researcher T. Ylönen in 1995.

At present, this protocol is employed on servers worldwide. It is also used in cloud-based and on-premise Linux and Unix systems. Over the years, it has been useful in configuring, managing, operating and maintaining several servers, firewalls, and routers of critical network infrastructures. Its main functions include:

- Establishing secured users and processes accesses.
- Delivering commands remotely.
- Automated and shared transfer of files.
- Management of network components of critical systems.

The protocol makes use of hashing and symmetric algorithms for ensuring data integrity and privacy when exchanged between any two hosts. SSH keys are public keys employed for ensuring authentication. SSH keys are employed by system administrators and developers in backup systems, scripts, and management tools. They remove the requirement of re-signing in by the user every time while navigating between accounts. This feature of SSH keys makes it highly convenient to be used in major organizations. Although they can automate server access, they may cause heavy risks if remained unmanaged.

2.1.2.3.2 MODBUS

It is an extensively used communication protocol for industrial automation (Peng *et al.* 2008). It is employed in massively used industrial equipment like RTU, DCS, and PLC. It follows master-slave architecture where master diagnoses the repaired slave equipment. It ensures reliable data transfer between master and slave components within a set deadline. It is a hardware-independent protocol responsible for defining the information structure that is distinguishable by the controller and can use it.

MODBUS supports two types of communications: query/response, as shown in Figure 2.7, and broadcast. Communication between one master and one slave falls under

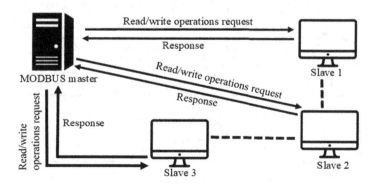

FIGURE 2.7
Broadcast MODBUS communication.

the former category. Communication between one master and many slaves is under the latter. Some of the possible attacks by exploiting MODBUS' vulnerabilities include DoS, MITM, replay, and unauthorized execution of commands attacks (Fovino et al. 2009). It primarily does not comprise protection against such attacks. Its widespread use can be attributed to its availability and user friendliness.

The data transaction taking place via MODBUS comprises register addresses, data, and function code. If there is any error in transaction, it can be sent to the master in form of error codes when requested with diagnostic data. Therefore, it also acts as a medium of transaction of data. The master and slave equipment are responsible for interpreting the data and providing accurate information. Using MODBUS for ensuring safety must be assessed for any inadvertent risks to integrity or protection of data transaction.

2.1.2.4 Management Tools

This module discusses the tool commonly used for managing resources, events, metrics, and rules during the execution any CSE. There are different teams' interactions taking place during a CSE. Therefore, it is imperative to ensure that all the CSE-related components and modules are well managed. This confirms a smooth and constructive execution of CSE.

2.1.2.4.1 ISEAGE

It is a configurable test bed, as illustrated in Figure 2.8, designed for imitating internet and for carrying out cybersecurity activities (Rursch *et al.* 2013). It allows simulating cyberattacks against the network infrastructure and therefore demonstrates realistic security-related concepts. This tool provides users the following functionalities:

- Cyber-defense-related contests for students enrolled in various academic institutes.
- It supports a validated classroom and laboratory-related activities.
- Testing and research environment for the network devices and related issues.

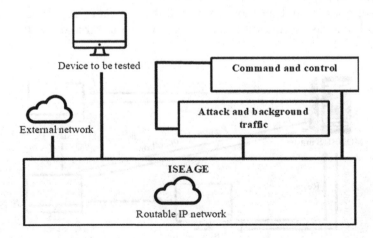

FIGURE 2.8
Test bed architecture.

It was developed with the aim to prevent predictable attacks and misconfigurations on realistic networks by novice personnel. It follows latest security paradigm enabling innovative research to resolve existing security issues in critical infrastructures. The test bed also serves organizations' product testing trials. ISEAGE architecture comprises external network, attack and background traffic, and command and control (Rursch *et al.* 2013).

References

Barrett, D. J., Silverman, R. E., Byrnes, R. G., 2005. *SSH, The Secure Shell: The Definitive Guide*. California: O'Reilly Media, Inc.

Cowie, J. H., Nicol, D. M., Ogielski, A. T., 1999. Modeling the global internet. *Computing in Science & Engineering*, 1(1), 42–50.

Donevski, A., Ristov, S., Gusev, M., 2013. Comparison of open source cloud platforms. *In: 48th International Scientific Conference on Information, Communication and Energy Systems and Technologies*, 26–29 June 2013 Ohrid. North Macedonia: Faculty of Technical Sciences – Bitola, 175–178.

Ferrie, P., 2007. Attacks on more virtual machine emulators. *Symantec Technology Exchange*, 55(1), 369–386.

Fovino, I. N., Carcano, A., Masera, M., Trombetta, A., 2009. Design and implementation of a secure MODBUS protocol. *In: International Conference on Critical Infrastructure Protection*, 23–25 March 2009 Hanover. Switzerland: Springer, 83–96.

Goldberg, R. P., 1974. Survey of virtual machine research. *Computer*, 7(6), 34–45.

Gulati, A., Holler, A., Ji, M., Shanmuganathan, G., Waldspurger, C., Zhu, X., 2012. VMware distributed resource management: Design, implementation, and lessons learned. *VMware Technical Journal*, 1(1), 45–64.

Infrastructure, V., 2006. Resource management with VMware DRS. *VMware Whitepaper*, 13(1), 1–24.

Li, Y., Liljenstam, M., Liu, J., 2009. Real-time security exercises on a realistic interdomain routing experiment platform. *In: 2009 ACM/IEEE/SCS 23rd Workshop on Principles of Advanced and Distributed Simulation*, 22–25 June 2009 Lake Placid. New York: IEEE, 54–63

Liu, J., 2010. Parallel and distributed immersive real-time simulation of large-scale networks. *Journal of Parallel and Distributed Computing*, 1(1), 221–246.

McLaren, P. G., Kuffel, R., Wierckx, R., Giesbrecht, J., Arendt, L., 1992. A real time digital simulator for testing relays. *IEEE Transactions on Power Delivery*, 7(1), 207–213.

Nieh, J., Leonard, O. C., 2000. Examining VMware. *Dr. Dobb's Journal*, 25(8), 70.

Peng, D. G., Zhang, H., Yang, L., Li, H., 2008. Design and realization of MODBUS protocol based on embedded Linux system. *In: 2008 International Conference on Embedded Software and Systems Symposia*, 29–31 July 2008 Chengdu. New York: IEEE, 275–280.

RTDS Technologies Inc., 2021. Prevent and survive cyber and cyber-physical attacks [online]. Available from: https://www.rtds.com/applications/cybersecurity/ [Accessed 20 May 2021].

Rursch, J. A., Jacobson, D., 2013. When a testbed does more than testing: The Internet-Scale Event Attack and Generation Environment (ISEAGE) – providing learning and synthesizing experiences for cyber security students. *In: 2013 IEEE Frontiers in Education Conference (FIE)*, 23–26 October 2013 Oklahoma City. New York: IEEE, 1267–1272.

Sempolinski, P., Thain, D., 2010. A comparison and critique of eucalyptus, OpenNebula and nimbus. *In: 2010 IEEE Second International Conference on Cloud Computing Technology and Science*, 30 November-3 December 2010 Indianapolis. New York: IEEE, 417–426.

Song, D. X., Wagner, D. A., Tian, X., 2001. Timing analysis of keystrokes and timing attacks on SSH. *In*: *USENIX Security Symposium*, 13–17 August 2001 Washington. California: The USENIX Association, 1–17.

Tickoo, O., Iyer, R., Illikkal, R., Newell, D., 2010. Modeling virtual machine performance: Challenges and approaches. *ACM SIGMETRICS Performance Evaluation Review*, 37(3), 55–60.

Ukwandu, E., Farah, M. A. B., Hindy, H., Brosset, D., Kavallieros, D., Atkinson, R., Bellekens, X., 2020. A review of cyber-ranges and test-beds: Current and future trends. *Sensors*, 20(24), 7148.

Yadav, S., 2013. Comparative study on open source software for cloud computing platform: Eucalyptus, OpenStack and OpenNebula. *International Journal of Engineering and Science*, 3(10), 51–54.

Ylonen, T., Lonvick, C., 2006. The secure shell (SSH) transport layer protocol. *RFC 4253*, 1(1), 1–30.

3

Motivations for Construction of Cyber Ranges

3.1 IT and OT Infrastructures

OT states the use of software/hardware alongside ACSs within an infrastructure. It is majorly used in critical infrastructures like ICSs, SCADA, power, transportation, water treatment, oil and gas plants for control and monitoring functions. The main purpose of OT systems was to integrate DA systems, HMI systems, and data collection/communication systems to achieve a central solution for resource regulation and monitoring. OT systems laid the foundation for present smart infrastructures. OT systems require project-specific proprietary protocols, and over the decades, the number of operators sustaining such systems has become limited. Therefore, OT systems are a relatively easier target for cyberattacks and threats.

There have been numerous cyberattacks on OT systems and these further keep growing more dangerous, more sophisticated and occurring frequently and causing more damage. Successful cyberattacks against these kinds of systems may not only cause financial loss but also lead to loss of life or some other harmful environmental impacts. To overcome this vulnerability, many infrastructures have adopted an integrated approach where OT can be merged with IT. This convergence is also advantageous for enhancing system productivity by incorporating the latest technologies like AI, cloud computing, sensor technology, and big data (Shahzad *et al.* 2016).

Murray *et al.* (2017) list the possible outcomes from cyberattack on OT systems:

- Delay in information communication to SCADA/ICS systems from RTU. For example, delay in communicating the turbine speed or level of sensors may lead to disastrous incidents.

- Connection gets interrupted between the critical systems when trying to employ an event via security systems.

- Manipulation in the input values that may cause chain reaction of inappropriate actions or may cause shutdown of some of the systems' sections.

- Unauthorized modification of the components' operations. For example, running the turbine at an intensifying speed which may severely damage its blades.

Differences between the IT and OT infrastructures may also be a contributing factor to security issues. Table 3.1 highlights some of the key differences between the two infrastructures:

Although both the systems are distinct, they have some similarities like both the systems give significance to team outcome and are grouped as collectivist (Murray *et al.* 2017).

DOI: 10.1201/9781003206071-3

TABLE 3.1

Differences between OT and IT

OT	IT
It focuses on controlling and monitoring physical components	It focuses on security and confidentiality of the data
The physical environment is geographically dispersed	The physical environment is contained
It gives a higher priority to production activities, often ignoring security updates/patches	IT components and systems get frequently updated
It uses proprietary protocols and OSs	It uses generic protocols and OSs

Both systems bring together diverse processes, goals, languages, and tools. Therefore, cybersecurity is critical for collaboration of OT/IT systems (Schwab *et al.* 2018). Cyberattacks cause heavy damages to products or services, thus ruining their quality. This is directly associated with loss in confidential information, customer confidence, and contracts and potential opportunities.

Schwab *et al.* (2018) survey presented some of the major concern of organizations in security breach of OT/IT systems:

- Quality impairment of services and products.
- Injury/death of organizations' personnel.
- Losing customer confidence.
- Damaging organization's reputation or brand name.
- Losing confidential or sensitive information.
- Violations of essential regulations.
- Losing potential opportunities, contracts, etc.
- Environmental damages.

Almost more than half of organizations surveyed by Schwab *et al.* (2018) express their major concerns over APTs and targeted attacks. Therefore, these organizations require cybersecurity-trained personnel, implementation of new advanced security measures, cybersecurity awareness among operators and asset owners. But they often face the challenge of hiring professionals because there are few people skilled in cybersecurity aspects. With cyberattacks and threats evolving on daily basis, there is also an increasing demand for cybersecurity professionals. The need for diverse and dedicated training courses for understanding cybersecurity approach is also recognized by organizations.

Organizations' data, for example, records of customers and products, is the main target of a cybersecurity breach. All the data gets processed, communicated, and stored in components like workstations, networks, and smart devices. These components become assets and are often targeted by threat vectors for accessing data. To protect these assets, encryption controls, software patching, etc. need to get implemented. Therefore, it is crucial that appropriate security controls are applied to these assets so that threat vectors are not able to exploit their vulnerabilities. Galinec *et al.* (2017) stress on improving cybersecurity using the approach of strategy designing and action plan framework.

3.1.1 Cybersecurity Challenges to OT/IT Systems

Given the difference in the nature and priorities of IT and OT systems, there have been other contributing factors affecting the security of these infrastructures:

- Many organizations do not perform or undertake necessary countermeasures and often ignore or fail to accurately analyze the vulnerabilities present in their infrastructures. Due to this, cyberattacks may remain undetected and successfully damage the systems.
- Cyberattacks exploit the less secured links/components of the IT systems and unnoticeably penetrate into OT environments, vice versa is also possible, thus compromising the whole network infrastructure (Palmer *et al.* 2021).
- OT/IT infrastructure is mainly adopted in ICSs. These systems have specific controller components like PLCs or RTUs. As these are the central and reliable components, they often remain unchanged for long time. With advanced cyberthreats, such components are prone to get targeted and damaged. Moreover, any interference with the components may go undetected.

Therefore, it becomes imperative to understand, prepare for such risks and their consequences. Present-day systems rely on complex organization of numerous components connected via Internet. Therefore, the frequency of targeted cyberattacks on ICSs has also increased.

OT environments are required to be actively and repeatedly probed so as to detect any underlying or dormant risks. Regularly updating components may not be practical for OT environments, but actively checking the components and their security procedures may help in preparing a useful situational analysis. It may also assist in identifying and keeping track of any local changes in the devices' metadata, for example, any change in configuration or in device logic. These analyses not only provide better insights but also eliminate the requirement of monitoring every component. Therefore, it can also reduce the maintenance expenses.

The transformation of traditional infrastructure models to present-day Internet-based complex, interconnected models influences the confidentiality and security of data. This transformation has also boosted the demand for cyber-risk management skills and professionals (Kosub 2015). For an effective OT/IT system, organizations must prioritize risk-based security vulnerabilities. This approach helps in saving time and resources. This can be achieved by carrying out the following steps:

- Setting key metrics for evaluations and threat detections.
- Identifying vulnerabilities and gaps in analysis.
- Recognizing the performance and status of assets, vulnerabilities, and any other misconfigurations.
- Predicting, prioritizing, and fixing system vulnerabilities.
- Ensuring that the mitigation methods are appropriately implemented.

Security tests and updates are inadvisable to be directly implemented on a live system. Therefore, CRs serve as ideal platform for not only carrying out testing operations but also training personnel within a secured environment.

3.1.2 Cybersecurity Implementations in OT/IT Systems

Barrett (2018) describes the following functions and their corresponding categories for implementation of cybersecurity framework:

- Identifying the assets that require protection. This may include categories like asset management, governance, and risk assessment.
- Ensuring that these vulnerable assets are secured. This may include categories like cyber-risk awareness and cybersecurity maintenance.
- Detecting cyber risks or cyberattacks against the infrastructure.
- Response to cyberattacks and risks. This may include categories like mitigation of cyber risks, and cyber-risk analyses.
- Capabilities that may assist in recovery and improvement of the systems' performances and communications.

3.1.2.1 Asset Management

The essential factor that is helpful in achieving efficient asset management involves aligning the organizational infrastructure of IT with OT and with other technological capabilities being used (Haider 2011). Asset management of IT systems requires:

- Fulfilling implementation of the decided objectives.
- Aligning resources with IT.
- Developing business strategies via informed decision assistance.

OT offer control over the tasks of an asset as well as significantly contribute to decision-making. Haider (2011) classifies asset management into three levels:

- **Strategic:** this level involves taking the requirements of investors and the market. All these requirements are then grouped together to generate optimum operative and strategic set of activities.
- **Tactical and operational levels:** these involve the planning, monitoring, and review phases. Planning is done on the basis of identifying, assessing, and controlling the involved risks. The information gathered from this phase is used for building objectives, strategies, processes, policies, for monitoring resources and assets. The review phase ensures the quality, availability, and durability of resources and assets.

3.1.2.2 Governance

OT infrastructures get specifically targeted by cyberattacks and therefore, it is essential that organizations place over a holistic and effective governance. This is necessary as OT systems also have material impacts on the infrastructure's sustainability. It also extends the decision and financial reporting for OT assets, specifically in cases where OT may directly impact IT systems. Involving OT systems in core processes of the business may help in early identification of vulnerabilities and timely execution of appropriate mitigation procedures.

In the present day, the majority of organizations depend greatly on IT systems as they provide competitive advantage over traditional infrastructures. Therefore, these systems require necessary investments and sound governance to improve on its integrity and usability. IT systems are more prone to unauthorized access, modifications, usage, and sensitive information disclosures.

Ensuring accurate financial reporting of IT systems allows the investors and board members to rely and use the provided information for decision-making. Second, it also helps them in recognizing and mitigating potential risks. It is the responsibility of decision makers to ensure the placement of necessary procedures which will assist in timely risk detections.

3.1.2.3 Risk Assessment

This approach comprises identifying, analyzing, and evaluation of existing and potential risks to the systems. Cherdantseva *et al.* (2016) provide a comprehensive study on risk assessments of various SCADA systems. There are many risk assessment methodologies for IT systems used in the industries, for example:

- **OCTAVE** (Alberts *et al.* 2003): it is a strategic, threat-based, planning, and assessment security technique. It portrays the present state of security practices implemented. It prioritizes the sectors to be improved depending on which key asset is prone to risks.
- **CRAMM** (Yazar 2002): it is the qualitative risk assessing automated tool. It provides justified security investments required for the infrastructure at managerial levels.
- **CORAS** (Aagedal *et al.* 2002): it is useful for addressing security of key components of the infrastructures, and it majorly focuses on security of IT systems. It concentrates on assessing risks involved in the integration of OT and IT systems.

3.1.2.4 Cyber-Risk Awareness

There are dynamic changes happening in cyber-related technologies, threats, and attacks. Hence, it is not only essential to focus on protecting the infrastructure but also ensuring that the organization personnel have adequate knowledge and competencies about cybersecurity skills. It is imperative that personnel are aware of possible cyber risk of their systems that might be prone to.

This ensures their readiness against any cyber risk and prompt detection of any anomaly. Organization personnel not only need to depend on threat monitoring tools but also give adequate attention to vulnerability assessments and security warning reports (Al-Mohannadi et al. 2018). They should also be able to effectively communicate and coordinate with both SOC and non-SOC groups (Al-Mohannadi et al. 2018).

3.1.2.5 Cybersecurity Maintenance

This can be achieved in critical infrastructures by Schneider *et al.* (2015):

- **Maintaining malware definitions:** it is imperative to regularly update antivirus software. This helps in scanning the system for any discrepancies and includes the latest threat definitions. The software should be appropriately configured to not wrongly classify any system file as corrupt.

- **Maintaining lists of excluded activities:** having a predefined list of all the executable and not executable applications also acts as an additional defense layer, although these lists also require to be updated when vulnerabilities of a component get discovered.

- **Maintaining security logs:** these contain event reports, resource access, login attempts, etc. These files get stored in databases of the system. They can be useful when considered together with component analysis reports. They may help in detecting unauthorized user activities, any violations against security policies, etc. Similar to antiviruses and other system files, logs need to be up-to-date for providing accurate accounts.

- **Maintaining reference clock:** these clocks are useful for detecting spoofing or jamming of servers. They run on specific firmware that gets periodically updated.

- **Maintaining security policies:** this is essential because policies evolve based on any incidents of system breach, reviews, removing or adding new components to the infrastructure, etc.

- **Maintaining security patches and fixes:** this is essential for both types of software – IT and OT related. These security patches entail frequent reviews assessing their appropriate implementations, or in cases when new breaches get discovered.

3.1.2.6 Cyber-Risk Detection

Cyber-risk or cyberattack detection systems act as a multilayer defense mechanism. This layered mechanism provides sufficient time for the cybersecurity personnel to confront any cyberattack before it causes any kind of unrecoverable damage to the infrastructure. Zhang *et al.* (2019) proposed a similar detection system that uses process, system, and network data for improving early attack detection capabilities. Mubarak *et al.* (2021) use DPI analysis for detecting any cyberattacks to OT systems. It makes the OT traffic content more transparent by analyzing preprocessed datasets for any discrepancies.

3.1.2.7 Mitigation of Cyber Risk

Lamba *et al.* (2017) mention that a system-centric approach is necessary for appropriate implementation of security mechanisms. It also states that given the complex integration of both OT systems and IT systems, depending on traditional pattern, detection methods may not be practical. There is a necessity to develop an approach that not only handles cyberthreats but also balances the detection capabilities and the maintenance of components.

Kholidy (2021) discusses the latest developed ARC for responding to threats against CPSs. It offers:

- Autonomous and scalable method for protecting the assets depending upon their significance. This may operate without any personnel interventions.

- It provides the responses quickly and timely while considering the SA at every response site using the CMM.
- It has a durable response plan for optimizing continuing benefits to counter sophisticated attacks considering requirements, characteristics of CPSs, and impact of responses on it.

3.1.2.8 Cyber-Risk Analyses

Paté-Cornell *et al.* (2018) represent a framework for risk analyses. This framework considers:

- Identifying or recognizing cyberattack groups and their objectives.
- If any personnel are involved in carrying out these attacks by leaking data or important intel.
- The systems' vulnerabilities that were or may get targeted and exploited.
- Possible consequences of any successful cyberattack like loss of intellectual property, interruption in business, loss of confidential data, and capital loss.
- Appropriate implementation of countermeasures.

3.1.3 Need of CRs for WSS

WSS are a category of CPSs as it integrates computational capabilities and physical components for monitoring and controlling water supply processes. It may compose of physical components like actuators, sensors, and controllers that communicate via the network as shown in Figure 3.1.

Earlier, WSS were physically isolated and only limited personnel had access to controller components. However, in present day, many WSS are getting integrated with new technologies to transform into smart systems. This also attracts numerous cyber-related

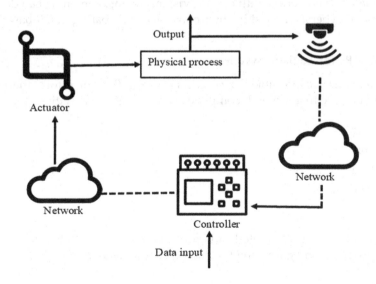

FIGURE 3.1
Layout of WSS.

vulnerabilities that get exploited by cyberattacks. There are several security aspects that can be implemented for securing this kind of systems (Tuptuk *et al.* 2021):

- **Detection models for cyberattacks:** these include physical models, ML models, statistical models, etc. Physical models are responsible for detecting discrepancies that may occur during any modification to the physical components of the system. ML model uses system data to check configuration and characteristics of the components for any anomaly. Similarly, statistical models rely on statistical analysis for detecting any cyber risks.
- **Security frameworks:** present-day critical infrastructures compose of a hierarchical, interconnected structure of components. All these components carry out data transmission via various communication networks present at every level. Therefore, applying multilayered countermeasure framework against cyberattacks help in securing all the individual infrastructure levels.

To carry out efficient construction of such models and frameworks for ensuring a secured infrastructure, a separate environment is required. CRs provide a secure, independent environment that successfully replicates the infrastructure and provide testing, training, and research services. Since it is never practical to directly implement any new technology or procedures on a live system, CRs serve as ideal substitute. There exist several CRs specifically for WSS, such as SWAT (read more in Section 4.2.2) and WADI (read more in Section 4.2.3). These CRs are useful for testing the efficiency of detection models and security frameworks.

CRs are helpful in developing datasets or using existing datasets for testing and authenticating mitigation techniques. These datasets can also be shared with the community. CRs also assist in constructing cyberattack models for exercises. These models are crucial for developing the understanding of CPS's vulnerabilities, for example, cyberattack impacts and system's resilience. These models can be used to launch adversarial attacks during the exercise. Exercises conducted in CR environment also help in building team communication and interaction with other divisions' teams. Personnel can develop attack preparedness and cybersecurity skills by frequently participating in CR-based exercises.

3.1.4 Need of CRs for Logistic Systems

Logistics systems are responsible for coordinating the flow of information of physical products from one site to another. It comprises related logistic activities like:

- Purchasing
- Production
- Forecasting
- Transportation
- Warehousing

It is an important system (illustrated in Figure 3.2) as it increases the efficacy, quality of services and products, and garnering favorable customer feedback. It always aims to fulfill two main objectives:

- Improving efficiency
- Minimizing costs

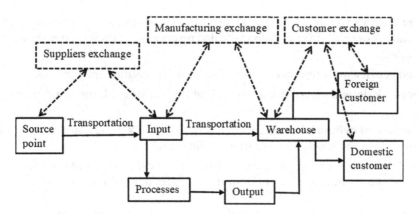

FIGURE 3.2
Layout of logistics systems.

These are essential for maximizing the company's profits and garnering positive customer support and trust. Logistic systems comprise the following elements (Wichaisri *et al.* 2013):

- **Inputs:** they can be in the form of information, materials, capital, etc. They bring in the resources to the system.
- **Outputs:** they are received in similar forms and define the values of the components.
- **Processes:** they are responsible for transforming the provided inputs into useful and beneficial outputs. The main objectives need to be considered during the operation of processes.
- **Controls:** they are used for analyzing the logistics flow of organizations from source to end points, receiving resources, converting them into valuable products, and then distributing them to the customers.
- **Feedback:** considering customer reviews, organizations need to improve on product quality and develop new products as per the customer needs.

Logistics systems have numerous interconnected devices, equipment, and software, which are also connected with the Internet. They get often categorized into Industry 4.0 paradigm. Although this also renders the enormous networks of such systems exposed, such exposure may cause misuse or unauthorized manipulations in operation flow. This may cause financial losses, damage to product quality, delay in product delivery, etc.

Sarder *et al.* (2019) provide the following attributes of cybersecurity framework as discussed in Section 3.1.2:

- **Asset management:** creating and maintaining a physical inventory. This inventory may consist of used devices, software, data flow, intercommunication setups, human resource, etc.
- **Governance:** formulating security policies, or legal requirements for protection of the systems.
- **Risk assessment:** identifying risks and system vulnerabilities, prioritizing mitigation techniques and performance analyses.

- **Cyber-risk awareness:** training IT and non-IT personnel against any potential cyberattack or risk, making managers also responsive to their own responsibilities and roles.
- **Cybersecurity maintenance:** scheduling regular maintenance checks.
- **Cyber-risk detection:** conducting vulnerability scans of all the components of the system.
- **Mitigation of cyber risk:** containing any detected risk or incident. Analyzing and documenting the newly found vulnerabilities and their mitigation plan.
- **Cyber-risk analyses:** accurately categorizing the cyber incident and then investigating if proper measures were undertaken to fix the vulnerabilities.

Therefore, CR environment can be useful for constructing a demon game (Cheung *et al.* 2019) model for addressing the issues of dependency of assets within a common network, developing new strategies for securing assets of logical systems. It may be used for similar function mentioned in Section 3.1.3.

3.1.5 Need of CRs for Maritime Systems

Unlike traditional attacks on maritime systems, present-day cyberattacks focus on stealthily exploiting the modern vessels, navigation systems, and propulsions systems for long periods of time. This often leads to disruption in business, loss of reputation, products and capital, and other legal issues. Jones *et al.* (2016) describe a cyberattack scenario where some external attack component gets undetectably smuggled into maritime vessel. The attack component may remain unnoticed until the cargo gets shipped. This component may cause interference in communications, infect port software, or loading machinery, etc. Finding and implementing countermeasures against such attacks become arduous as the vessel is physically isolated at the sea.

Maritime systems use ECDIS (Zhang *et al.* 2007) and AIS (Svanberg *et al.* 2019) as the monitoring and tracking software, although there are certain vulnerabilities discovered in both software. ECDIS lacks security patches and often admits unsecure network methods (Jones *et al.* 2016). When AIS vulnerabilities are exploited, they may cause changes in ship's course, fabricating commands, and so on (Jones *et al.* 2016), therefore making the maritime systems more prone to damage or hijack incidents.

Vessel or ship hijacking is the most common threat to maritime systems. The main target is to compromise navigation systems or propulsions systems, either by interfering, supplying false data or using ransomware and so on. The attacker can also crash the ship with another target or extensive infrastructures. This can cause heavy damages, security concerns, and legal feuds. For instance, the compromised ship may crash into an oil derrick, or damages to the ship can trigger leakage of nonbiodegradable components into the water bodies. Therefore, security of maritime systems affects personnel security, business organizations, local economy and has detrimental effects on environment and natural resources.

Another concern with lack of security in maritime systems is illegal smuggling of banned goods. The shipments travel long routes without any sophisticated monitoring. Therefore, shipments may get hacked or cargo data may get manipulated for smuggling or fraud purposes. Such possible scenarios necessitate the need to prepare suitable mitigation techniques. CRs are capable of providing situation-specific exercises w.r.t maritime systems. CRs are also useful in training personnel in mitigation and preparedness against advanced cyberattacks (Tam *et al.* 2021).

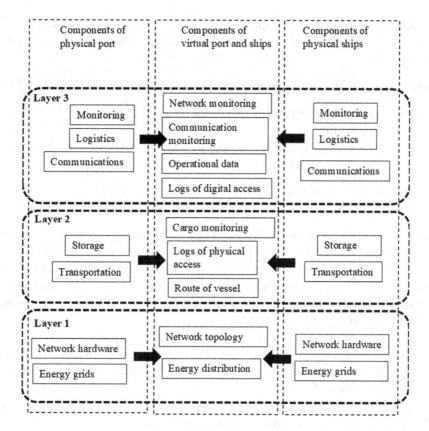

FIGURE 3.3
Layout of maritime system components.

Figure 3.3 illustrates the layered components of maritime transport systems. They bring together both OT and IT-related components (Tam *et al.* 2021). The diagram represents three layers, starting from bottom – infrastructure, transport, and digital layers. It may or may not be possible to replicate all these components present in Figure 3.3. But the main purpose of this figure is to show the components that will be required for conducting successful simulations or emulations.

3.1.6 Need of CRs for O&G Industries

Lamba (2018) highlights some of the key challenges to cybersecurity of this industry:

- Incorporating IT components into the infrastructure introduces the systems to various cyberattack vectors.
- Professional expertise is required when assessing the capabilities and configurations of the components.
- Lack of cybersecurity skills and necessary resources can hinder the prioritization of appropriate mitigation procedures and tools.
- Proper security clearance processes need to be implemented for authentic user identification and providing access to relevant data and logs.

- The modern workforces often face challenges like lack of appropriate cybersecurity-related skills and heavy workloads in this new paradigm of dynamic expertise requisites.

Stergiopoulos *et al.* (2020) classify attacks on O&G industries based on their origin types:

- **External attacks:** these comprise attacks like malware, phishing protocol attacks, hacking, and jamming.
- **Internal attacks:** these comprise attacks like MITM, USB, injection attacks, process aware, and logic attacks..

Progoulakis *et al.* (2021) conducted a survey on culture and perception of O&G industries and suggested the following measures for tackling cybersecurity-related issues:

- Using mitigation tools or methods for tackling insider threats. These types of threats can vary from unintentional actions to criminal intent to professional espionages. They ranked among the highest in the survey, in terms of recurring cyberattacks.
- Developing necessary countermeasures against unmanned platforms should they impede personnel or infrastructure security. These are capable of launching airborne, underwater, or surface attacks.
- Increasing the operational expenditure for developing appropriate cybersecurity measures as dictated by national legislations and industry standards. As it is a critical infrastructure, which contributes to the national economy, it may garner necessary funding as well.
- Collaborating with government or military personnel to raise awareness about cybersecurity and train against attack scenarios.

3.1.7 Need of CRs for Power Systems

Ten *et al.* (2007) discuss the following methodologies for conducting security assessments and modeling:

- **Attack trees:** they are logic AND, OR operators based hierarchical structures. It constitutes various kinds of intrusion events. The top node of the tree represents the main objective followed by various subgoals. The grouping of subgoals takes place using logic operators. This creates three vulnerability indices: scenario, system, and leaf. The following steps ensure systematic evaluation of these indices:
  1. Identifying the attack goals.
  2. Identifying potential vulnerabilities and constructing a corresponding attacks tree.
  3. Determining possible intrusion scenario combinations along with every cybersecurity condition present at every attack leaf.
  4. Computing the leaf vulnerabilities w.r.t implementations of password enforcements and existing technology considering the determined cybersecurity conditions.
  5. Scenario vulnerabilities can be calculated using the combinations of parallel leaf vulnerabilities.
  6. Determining system vulnerability depending on scenario vulnerabilities.

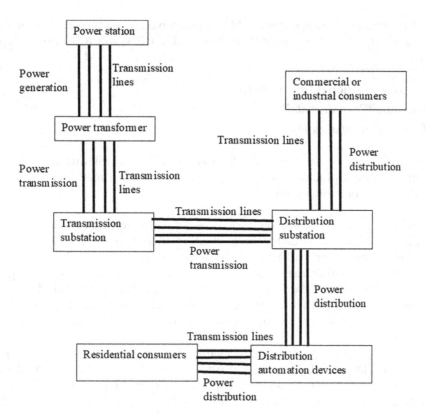

FIGURE 3.4
Layout of power system.

- **PENET:** it is a modeling framework for improving attack tress capabilities. It provides dynamic attacks, system repairing, and frequently occurring attacks. It gets implemented on OENET tool. This allows the operators to model system diagrams, perform simulations and evaluations.
- Integration of OT and IT components of the system. This is useful in understanding cascading events and evaluating overall system vulnerabilities. The integrated model facilitates threat analysis corresponding to the consequence's severity. The model can extend to incorporate analyses of economic impacts of cyberattacks on the systems, and designing appropriate mitigation procedures. Figure 3.4 illustrates the sample layout for a power system.

3.2 Cyberattacks

They have grabbed the attention of various cybersecurity-related firms, organizations, service providers, etc. The reasons behind these attacks are not only the cause of financial loss but are also capable of rapidly spreading to other components connected across the network. Information infringements, robbing smart banks or smart homes, etc. are also some of the likely cases of cyberattacks. Present-day CPSs and ICSs are susceptible to attacks like:

- False code injection (Lee *et al.* 2004).
- Code-reuse (Roemer *et al.* 2012).
- C-FLAT (Abera *et al.* 2016).

Therefore, many present-day CRs provide attack models and relevant datasets required for training and developing security paradigms against cyberthreats and related attacks.
    Cyberattacks can be categorized into:

- **Network attacks:** these exploit the exposed data for getting unauthorized entry within the network infrastructure, stealing their confidential data. Network attacks can be active and passive. In active attacks, the attacker gains unauthorized entry within the network infrastructure for reading or stealing some confidential detail or data. However, they let the data remain undamaged or unmodified. Like the active attacks, the attacker also gains unapproved entry in a passive attack. After which they alter the specific data via its deletion or encryption.
    Commonly occurring network attacks include DoS and network eavesdropping. In DoS, the targeted CPS assets get dispatched from a vast quantity of locally modified systems. Some example of DoS includes black hole (Li *et al.* 2018) and teardrop (AlEroud et al. 2013). In network eavesdropping, unsecured CPS network traffic gets captured for accessing data like passwords – this is possible by snooping, passively listening to message transmissions taking place, altering messages, etc.
- **Cryptographic attacks:** these attacks use cryptanalysis for evading security procedures. They look for vulnerabilities in key patterns, protocols, or OSs. Some of the commonly used attacks include:
    - Chosen plaintext attack
    - Brute force attacks
    - Crypto locker
    - Rubber cryptanalysis
    - Adaptive chose plaintext attack
- **Malicious software:** they assist in compromising the systems, damaging components, and cracking access control components. There exist many forms of malware, but some of them which commonly occurring include:
    - **Trojan:** it is an authentic looking malware used to fraud the users into downloading it. It then corrupts components and seal valuable data (like credentials or user activities). For example, Coreflood and Turla.
    - **Botnets:** it converts the vulnerabilities of CPS components into bots to efficiently perform an undetectable DoS attack. For example, Mootbot and Smominru botnet.
    - **Spyware:** it connects to system components stealthily for spying on the user activities or data. For example, Project Sauron and Red October.

- **Virus:** they can duplicate themselves onto other components of the infrastructure without any need of human interference. They affix at executing codes for carrying out data theft.

- **Ransomware:** it stores and then encrypts the networks info for ransom by exploiting the vulnerabilities of components of the CPS. They often target oil refineries, manufacturing facilities, healthcare, and power grids, etc. until the ransom gets paid and the data remains encrypted. For example, Lock and Siske.

- **Rootkit:** it remotely and undetectably enters the network infrastructure. They manipulate or steal the CPSs' information or damage working of components by modifying their configurations. For example, blackhole and moonlight maze.

- **Worms:** once entered a system, they start to multiply and cause servers' overloading. They exploit the OS vulnerabilities for damaging host networks. For example, Triton and Nimda.

3.2.1 Cyberattacks on Critical Infrastructures

Some of the previous cyberattacks that affected large-scale infrastructures include:

- **Stuxnet:** it was malware attack on nuclear facilities of Iran in 2010. The objective of the malware was to cause disruption in extraction of uranium and damage the machine or components involved. It consists of groups of viruses and worms specifically for targeting Windows systems. To access the OS, it would authorize default pins or keys of Siemens. It kept switching the speeds of the power centrifuges from low to high. The centrifuges were not designed to handle such rapid change in speed and therefore, they got damaged (Langner 2011).
  Since the facilities were not connected to the Internet, Iranians believed it to be non-attackable. The facilities were heavily secured by armed personnel. However, the facility was believed to be impervious to any physical attack, the operators did not deem important to:

  - Install or use any external security software like antiviruses and firewalls due to the assumptions that the facilities' locations were physically secured.

  - Download or install any regular Windows-related updates within their workstations, as none of the structures were Internet based.

  - Redundant services like MS pool were not disabled. This led to the faster transmission of malware across other workstations and components.

  - Update their system passcodes and maintain a validation list for detecting and preventing any illegal installations to the system.

- **Saudi Aramco attack:** it was a virus attack on a government-operated oil company. The attack had corrupted almost 30000+ workstations. It hindered and altered the components' configuration causing system failure. The company took 2 weeks to completely recover from the system damages and regain control (Bronk *et al.* 2013).

- Egypt Maritime Transport Sector experienced a DoS attack. It was responsible for corrupting the Egyptian government-related websites. It also corrupted websites of the Egyptian Accreditation Council, the Presidency, the Maritime

Transport Sector, the Armed Forces, the Parliament, the Large Taxpayer Center, etc. (Al-Mhiqani *et al.* 2018).

- WannaCry ransomware targeted FedEx, health departments, Renault, etc. It attacked the personal devices of telecommunication providers, tech companies, hospitals, universities, etc. within 150 countries. It spread quickly by exploiting Eternal Blue and DoublePursar. It would disable all the existing recovery options of the OS. It asked for bitcoin ransom for recovering the encrypted system data.

3.2.2 Cyberthreats to Critical Infrastructures

It can be described as the probability of a malignant effort to disorder or damage the operations of CPSs. Their usual sources include:

- Business competitors
- Hacktivists and hackers
- Disgruntled personnel
- Business spies
- Governments
- Organized crime units
- Terrorists

Different types of cyberthreats include:

- **APTs:** they are unconventional as they implement surreptitious, application-centric, and complex manipulation techniques and attack schemes. They often develop a strong foundation within the targeted systems by tracking their activities over long periods of time. They get familiarized with the system's defense mechanism to easily hamper them. Figure 3.5 describes a schema of APT.
- **Unpatched software:** it indicates identified security liabilities within system codes. Once these liabilities get recognized, operators fix them using patches that are add-ons to the existing code. They help in concealing any security loopholes.

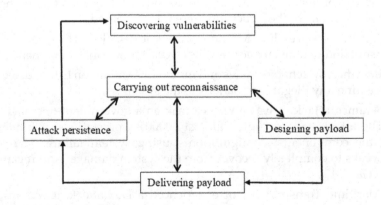

FIGURE 3.5
APT schema.

However, if this vulnerable software remains unpatched, they can be a crucial security concern. Such software are easy targets for exploitation and spreading the attack across the network.

- **Phishing:** it is a configuration of grouped manufacturing attacks for embezzling the users' data (for example, illegal access to login credentials, and credit card numbers). The hackers fool the victims into opening infected mails, links, messages, etc. by pretending to be authentic entities. After deceiving the victims into clicking malicious links, a malware starts to install in the system. The malware may cause system shutdown, information leakage, or ransomware.

References

Aagedal, J. O., Den Braber, F., Dimitrakos, T., Gran, B. A., Raptis, D., Stolen, K., 2002. Model-based risk assessment to improve enterprise security. *In*: *Proceedings. Sixth International Enterprise Distributed Object Computing*, 20–20 September 2002 Lausanne. New York: IEEE, 51–62.

Abera, T., Asokan, N., Davi, L., Ekberg, J. E., Nyman, T., Paverd, A., Sadeghi., A. R., Tsudik, G., 2016. C-FLAT: Control-flow attestation for embedded systems software. *In*: *Proceedings of the 2016 ACM SIGSAC Conference on Computer and Communications Security*, 24–28 October 2016 Vienna. New York: Association for Computing Machinery, 743–754.

Alberts, C., Dorofee, A., Stevens, J., Woody, C., 2003. Introduction to the OCTAVE Approach. *Carnegie Mellon University Pittsburgh PA Software Engineering Institute*, 1(1), 1–38.

AlEroud, A., Karabatis, G., 2013. A system for cyber attack detection using contextual semantics. *In*: *7th International Conference on Knowledge Management in Organizations: Service and Cloud Computing*, 11–13 July 2013 Salamanca. Switzerland: Springer, 431–442.

Al-Mhiqani, M. N., Ahmad, R., Yassin, W., Hassan, A., Abidin, Z. Z., Ali, N. S., Abdulkareem, K. H., 2018. Cyber-security incidents: A review cases in cyber-physical systems. *International Journal of Advanced Computer Science and Applications*, 1(1), 499–508.

Al-Mohannadi, H., Awan, I., Al Hamar, J., Al Hamar, Y., Shah, M., Musa, A., 2018. Understanding awareness of cyber security threat among IT employees. *In*: *6th International Conference on Future Internet of Things and Cloud Workshops (FiCloudW)*, 6–8 August 2018 Barcelona. New York: IEEE, 188–192.

Barrett, M. P., 2018. Framework for improving critical infrastructure cybersecurity. *National Institute of Standards and Technology, Gaithersburg, MD, USA, Technical Report*, 1(1), 1–34.

Bronk, C., Tikk-Ringas, E., 2013. The cyber attack on Saudi Aramco. *Survival*, 55(2), 81–96.

Cherdantseva, Y., Burnap, P., Blyth, A., Eden, P., Jones, K., Soulsby, H., Stoddart, K., 2016. A review of cyber security risk assessment methods for SCADA systems. *Computers and Security*, 56(1), 1–27.

Cheung, K. F., Bell, M. G., 2019. Attacker–defender model against quantal response adversaries for cyber security in logistics management: An introductory study. *European Journal of Operational Research*, 291(2), 471–481.

Galinec, D., Možnik, D., Guberina, B., 2017. Cybersecurity and cyber defence: National level strategic approach. *Automatika: časopis za automatiku, mjerenje, elektroniku, računarstvo i komunikacije*, 58(3), 273–286.

Haider, A., 2011. IT enabled engineering asset management: A governance perspective. *Journal of Organizational Knowledge Management*, 1(1), 1–12.

Jones, K. D., Tam, K., Papadaki, M., 2016. Threats and impacts in maritime cyber security. *Engineering & Technology Reference*, 1(1), 1–12.

Kholidy, H. A., 2021. Autonomous mitigation of cyber risks in the cyber–physical systems. *Future Generation Computer Systems*, 115(1), 171–187.

Kosub, T., 2015. Components and challenges of integrated cyber risk management. *Zeitschrift für die gesamte Versicher ungswissenschaft*, 104(5), 615–634.

Lamba, A., Singh, S., Balvinder, S., Dutta, N., Rela, S., 2017. Mitigating cyber security threats of industrial control systems (SCADA & DCS). *In: 3rd International Conference on Emerging Technologies in Engineering, Biomedical, Medical and Science (ETEBMS)* July 2017. New York: SSRN, 31–34.

Lamba, A., 2018. Protecting 'cybersecurity & resiliency' of nation's critical infrastructure–energy, oil & gas. *International Journal of Current Research*, 10(1), 76865–76876.

Langner, R., 2011. Stuxnet: Dissecting a cyberwarfare weapon. *IEEE Security and Privacy*, 9(3), 49–51.

Lee, R. B., Karig, D. K., McGregor, J. P., Shi, Z., 2004. Enlisting hardware architecture to thwart malicious code injection. *In: Security in Pervasive Computing*, 12–14 March 2004 Germany. Switzerland: Springer, 237–252.

Li, G., Yan, Z., Fu, Y., 2018. A study and simulation research of blackhole attack on mobile adhoc network. *In: IEEE Conference on Communications and Network Security (CNS)*, 30 May–1 June 2018 Beijing. New York: IEEE, 1–6.

Mubarak, S., Habaebi, M. H., Islam, M. R., Khan, S., 2021. ICS cyber attack detection with ensemble machine learning and DPI using cyber-kit datasets. *In: 2021 8th International Conference on Computer and Communication Engineering (ICCCE)*, 22–23June 2021 Kuala Lumpur. New York: IEEE, 349–354.

Murray, G., Johnstone, M. N., Valli, C., 2017. The convergence of IT and OT in critical infrastructure. *In: Australian Information Security Management Conference*, 5–6 December 2017 Perth. Australia: Security Research Institute, Edith Cowan University, 149–155.

Palmer, A., Rothschild, M., Ang, B., 2021. Successful cyber-risk management of operational technology and industrial control systems-technical and policy recommendations. *S. Rajaratnam School of International Studies*, 1(1), 1–17.

Paté-Cornell, M. E., Kuypers, M., Smith, M., Keller, P., 2018. Cyber risk management for critical infrastructure: A risk analysis model and three case studies. *Risk Analysis*, 38(2), 226–241.

Progoulakis, I., Nikitakos, N., Rohmeyer, P., Bunin, B., Dalaklis, D., Karamperidis, S., 2021. Perspectives on cyber security for offshore oil and gas assets. *Journal of Marine Science and Engineering*, 9(2), 112–139.

Roemer, R., Buchanan, E., Shacham, H., Savage, S., 2012. Return-oriented programming: Systems, languages, and applications. *ACM Transactions on Information and System Security (TISSEC)*, 15(1), 1–34.

Sarder, M. D., Haschak, M., 2019. Cyber security and its implication on material handling and logistics. *College-Industry Council on Material Handling Education*, 1(1), 1–18.

Schneider, J., Obermeier, S., Schlegel, R., 2015. Cyber security maintenance for SCADA systems. *In: 3rd International Symposium for ICS & SCADA Cyber Security Research 2015 (ICS-CSR 2015)*, 17–18 September 2015 Germany. Burlington: Science Open, 89–94.

Schwab, W., Poujol, M., 2018. The state of industrial cybersecurity 2018. *Trend Study Kaspersky Reports*, 1(1), 33–65.

Shahzad, A., Lee, M., Xiong, N. N., Jeong, G., Lee, Y. K., Choi, J. Y., Mahesar, A.W., Ahmad, I., 2016. A secure, intelligent, and smart-sensing approach for industrial system automation and transmission over unsecured wireless networks. *Sensors*, 16(3), 322.

Stergiopoulos, G., Gritzalis, D. A., Limnaios, E., 2020. Cyber-attacks on the oil & gas sector: A survey on incident assessment and attack patterns. *IEEE Access*, 8(1), 128440–128475.

Svanberg, M., Santén, V., Hörteborn, A., Holm, H., Finnsgård, C., 2019. AIS in maritime research. *Marine Policy*, 106(1), 103520.

Tam, K., Moara-Nkwe, K., Jones, K., 2021. The use of cyber ranges in the maritime context: Assessing maritime-cyber risks, raising awareness, and providing training. *Maritime Technology and Research*, 3(1), 16–30.

Ten, C. W., Govindarasu, M., Liu, C. C., 2007. Cybersecurity for electric power control and automation systems. *In: 2007 IEEE International Conference on Systems, Man and Cybernetics*, 7–10 October 2007 Montreal. New York: IEEE, 29–34.

Tuptuk, N., Hazell, P., Watson, J., Hailes, S., 2021. A systematic review of the state of cyber-security in water systems. *Water*, 13(1), 81.

Wichaisri, S., Sopadang, A., 2013. Sustainable logistics system: A framework and case study. *In: 2013 IEEE International Conference on Industrial Engineering and Engineering Management*, 10–13 December 2013 Bangkok. New York: IEEE, 1017–1021.

Yazar, Z., 2002. A qualitative risk analysis and management tool–CRAMM. *SANS InfoSec Reading Room White Paper*, 11(1), 12–32.

Zhang, F., Kodituwakku, H. A. D. E., Hines, J. W., Coble, J., 2019. Multilayer data-driven cyber-attack detection system for industrial control systems based on network, system, and process data. *IEEE Transactions on Industrial Informatics*, 15(7), 4362–4369.

Zhang, L. H., Zhu, Q., Liu, Y. C., Li, S. J., 2007. A method for automatic routing based on ECDIS. *Journal of Dalian Maritime University*, 33(3), 109–112.

4

Types of Cyber Ranges

4.1 Hybrid CRs

The environment of a hybrid CR as in Figure 4.1 comprises the use of virtual-based components wherever necessary in addition to the use of physical components wherever considered essential (Rev 2014). The range is the combination of real hardware and virtualization techniques. Although there may be certain limitations concerning this range, yet it provides an ideal combination of both platform scalability and inexpensive performance. The number and usage of both virtual and physical components depends upon the requirements of the scenario. Some of the firewalls, routing, functions, and desktops may either be physical or virtual. While selecting the components for building the topology, the realism of the range must not be invalidated. The design of the topology must assist in evaluation w.r.t. any event, like some realistic and extensive network attack. This type of CRs aims at providing an ideal environment for training personnel and evaluating resiliency of defense techniques of a network infrastructure. This section also discusses some of the existing hybrid CRs like EVA, DIATEAM, and CRATE.

4.1.1 EVA

The CR focuses on modeling realistic WSS. It incorporates the combination of flexibility and dynamism of virtual CRs along with a realism of a CPS (Ahmad *et al.* 2020). While designing the CR, there were three viewpoints to consider:

- Providing a simple and fast way for modifying the system's behaviors. This was necessary to ensure a smooth representation of various scenarios.
- Changing majority parts of the system's composition would result in higher maintenance cost.
- The structure is flexible to accommodate and assist all the involved teams to perform their task best.

A wrapper as shown in Figure 4.2 is placed atop every component. This ensures that without any physical modifications, the behavior of the components can be changed dynamically. It is composed of WC and WDI. WC modifies data exchange and interconnection inside the wrapper, thus controlling its behavior. It also manages WDI. WDI is responsible for defining the way the components' inputs and outputs get routed.

DOI: 10.1201/9781003206071-4

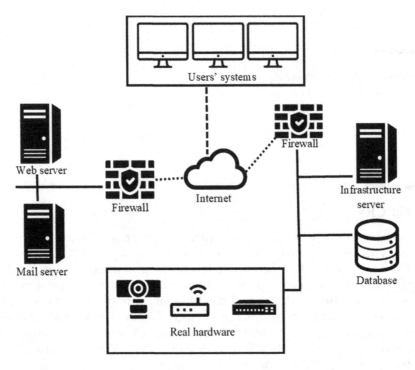

FIGURE 4.1
Hybrid CR architecture.

The use of wrapper serves the following advantages:

- It directly connects to inputs and outputs for all components, allowing arbitrarily control via selecting suitable source depending on respective scenarios like training, mock-up, or gaming.
- It provides the possibility to achieve required flexibility for operating different CR scenarios.

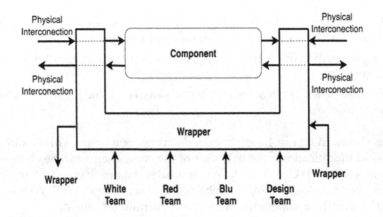

FIGURE 4.2
Wrapper.

- It can directly communicate with other wrappers via dedicated interconnection, thus avoiding any physical interconnections. This further assists in flexible implementation of the scenarios.

The wrapper assists the involved teams in conducting following scenarios:

- Mock-up operations can be conducted flexibly and on demand. The wrapper assists in adding new components to the environment without reconstructing it from scratch. It gathers information about the new components' performances prior to including them into the environment.
- The wrapper also assists in attack injections during the exercises. The red team uses the wrapper functionality to modify the inputs of the components, thus simulating an attack directly on that specific component and also appropriately modifying its outputs.
- The blue team ignores the presence of the wrapper and works on applying patches to the detected vulnerabilities. The team's interaction with the component does not get affected.
- The white team uses the wrapper to insert new vulnerabilities in the components during the designing and execution of the scenarios.
- Other than exercises, the wrapper can also be used for collecting information about the performance of any component. This is useful in early detection of any possible vulnerabilities.
- It is also helpful in emulating new components, protocols, or interconnections. Newly created components and solutions can be tested without requiring any reconstruction or modification of the environment.

The CR is capable of conducting various scenarios, training and testing environments. The working of a wrapper can be explained w.r.t. the attack scenario like injecting false data as shown in Figure 4.3. As mentioned earlier, the wrapper directly connects to inputs and outputs for all components.

This provides an arbitrary access of the components to the red team. The red team is responsible for injecting the false data. This can be done in two ways:

- The Red team controls the outputs of the component (for example, a sensor). It then sends false data to CCU, avoiding the actual output of the component.
- The Red team controls the inputs of the component (for example, an actuator). It then sends false commands to the component, avoiding the actual inputs from the CCU to the component.

4.1.2 DIATEAM CR

This hybrid CR editor is constructed by DIATEAM, which was founded in 2002 (DIATEAM, 2020). It provides both on-premise and online hand-on CR trainings. It also hosts table top exercises and serious games. The CR assists the trainees in:

- Learning, recognizing, and handling cyber threats.
- Experiencing realistic cyber crisis within a secure environment setting.

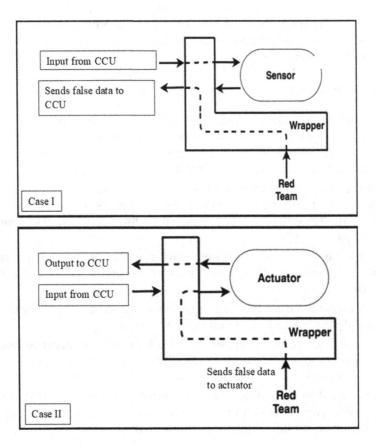

FIGURE 4.3
Using a wrapper for attack emulations.

- Process authorization and team work.
- Improving their responsive competence when facing realistic cyber crisis.

The DIATEAM CR offers the following functionalities:

- It allows its operators to further scale the environment by attaching any devices, networks, equipment, or wireless networks.
- It provides a formidable way for replication of existing information models for testing and development of skill sets like incident response and network protection.
- It provides user-friendly and tailored platforms. The hybrid CR gear comes in medium (8U), large (18U), and full stack (24U) range.
- It also aims to raise awareness among the end-users about cyber crisis using appropriate demonstrative methods for showing possible damages.

The DIATEAM CR as shown in Figure 4.4 comprises the following modules:

- **Traffic generator:** it is used by the white team for designing and constructing the exercise scenarios. The white team is responsible for ensuring that the exercise runs according to the set objectives.

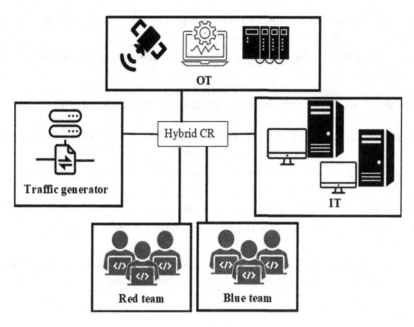

FIGURE 4.4
DIATEAM CR modules.

- **IT:** It comprises all digital tools like communications, software and hardware required for processing data.
- **OT:** it comprises software/hardware infrastructure responsible for detecting, controlling, and monitoring changes in the system.
- **Red team:** it comprises training personnel for injecting attacks during the exercise.
- **Blue team:** it comprises training personnel who detect, respond, and work on mitigating the attacks launched by the red team.
- **CR operators:** it is responsible for supervising the working of every module of the CR. They are also responsible for session development.

For conducting productive exercise and training, this CR considers the following factors:

- **Realism:** it is essential for making the exercises extensively immersive. This assists the training personnel to better adapt to the environment and improve on incident response.
- **Variety of scenarios:** the CR is capable of hosting various attack scenarios, thus testing the skill sets of the trainees.
- **Regularity:** with the everyday increase in new cyber threats and crisis, regular training is recommended. This ensures that the concerned personnel are up-to-date with recent technologies and their usage and can effectively mitigate damaging attacks.

- **Threat knowledge:** to ensure effective preparedness, having the state-of-the-art knowledge w.r.t. cybersecurity is essential.
- The personnel need to be articulate in using the defense tools when in cyber crisis situations.

The CR also provides some of the following features (DIATEAM, 2020):

- **Content catalogue:** the CR provides an extensive variety of VMs and network entities. They can be easily viewed and selected using drag-n-drop.
- **USB redirection:** it allows plug-in and redirecting of any USB to any other operational VM.
- **User-friendly GUI:** the CR provides both multiuser and multi-view features.
- **Open platform**: it provides sufficient documentation and assistance for working with the CR's APIs.
- **VMs orchestration:** the CR supports various VMs that work remotely from one another. Different actions or events can be carried out remotely.

4.1.3 CRATE

The development of this CR started in 2008, and currently it is operated and maintained by the FOI. It has served as a main platform for conducting numerous CSE and competitions at both national and international levels. It was used for hosting BCS in 2010 (Gustafsson *et al.* 2020). The CR offers the following benefits:

- Efficient deployment and configuration of approximately a thousand VMs within a moderate environment.
- It comprises traffic generators that emulate the behavior of the users and tools. This is used for generating logs and supervising the environment.
- All the emulated environments run parallelly without interfering the working of each other.
- Its core API offers various services like authentication and resource reservations.

Figure 4.5 displays some of the main components of the CR as discussed next:

- **Control plane:** it is used for managing the CR. It is isolated from the event plane and represents one of the security zones. The events executing in event plane do not affect control plane.
- **Event plane:** in this plane, all the training and test sessions get implemented. It is also one of the security zones.
- **Virtualization servers:** the CR uses approximately 500 servers for operations that run the CRATEOS (Gustafsson and Almroth 2020). CRATEOS is Linux based and operates in read-only setting. VMs and configurations get stored using OFS.
- Core API and VMs communicate via Node Agent (Gustafsson and Almroth 2020).
- **Emulated environments:** they are stored in configuration database as definitions when not operational. Simulated internet gets constructed using these environments. They comprise database, DNS, and search engines.

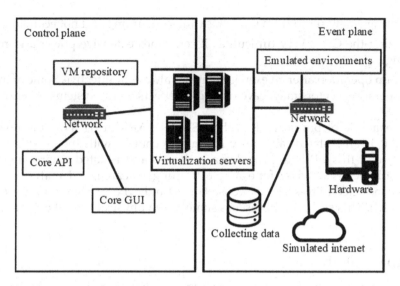

FIGURE 4.5
CRATE components.

4.2 Physical CRs

The environment of physical CR as shown in Figure 4.6 comprises the replication of the entire physical infrastructure. All the components like firewalls, servers, and routers are duplicated for training purposes. This type of CRs although provides the advantage of a realistic environment but is followed by the following disadvantages:

- Replicating and setting up of the live and complex CR environment is financially exorbitant.

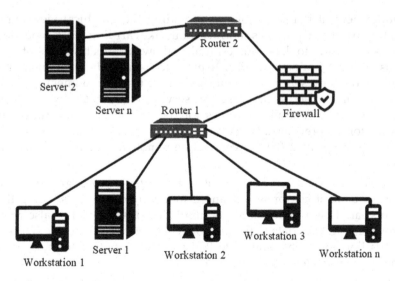

FIGURE 4.6
Layout of a physical CR.

- Recreating a new setup from scratch is time-consuming and not economical.
- Managing the CR is very difficult as it consumes extensive power and requires cooling.
- Clean-up operation after an exercise may not always be effective. Some of the complex operation vectors may leave unwanted effects on the systems or networks.

A popular example of physical CR is the USMA IWAR during its initial development stages. IWAR is an isolated laboratory having no contact with the outside world. The main purpose of this CR is to provide an authentic and isolated environment for conducting simultaneous activities for example, training, research, and analyses. Most of the researches conducted in this CR are focused on IO and cyberwarfare concepts (read more in Section 9.4.1). This section will discuss some of the physical CRs like SCADA testbeds and SWAT.

4.2.1 SCADA Testbeds

Critical infrastructures incur cyberattacks or threats that not only damage the infrastructure components but also cause loss of capital. These losses can be caused by insiders with malign intentions having the intel and access to data and controls, and hackers who use prepackaged tools to disrupt the working of the systems, sophisticated group targeting the vulnerabilities of the infrastructure (Davis *et al.* 2006). Therefore, the requirement emerges to mitigate attacks on the critical infrastructures and analyze threats. It is important to analyze their impacts and determine the possible losses. This is followed by the vulnerability identification. Using all this information, risk analysis can be performed. Risk analysis tells which vulnerability requires most protection against itself. Accordingly, the suitable defense techniques can be developed, tested, and implemented.

These were some of the motivations for developing a testbed that can also conduct CSEs. The SCADA testbed initially aimed at assessing the vulnerabilities initiated via public networks used for communication purposes. It initially comprised the following components:

- **Network client:** it is responsible for providing the graphical viewpoint of the infrastructure. It also provides control actions like carrying out independent modifications according to data sources. It also allows conducting tests of the power systems, communication networks, display, etc. None of the components affect the working of other present components within the test environment.

  It is also capable of accessing numerous servers, while following a sophisticated and configurable scheduling process for data retrieval. Fixed timed intervals can be set for data retrieval. It also supports various OSs like Linux, MacOS, and Windows (Davis *et al.* 2006). For conducting remote tests, it allows executing Java applet within the browser.
- **PowerWorld server:** it acts as a substitute for realistic power grid structures. It is advantageous as it comprises advanced modeling capabilities. Using these, the operators can design highly accurate simulation of systems. It is also responsible for providing SCADA data to the network client. For example, line status, generator status, line flow, phase angle, etc. It also accepts inputs in form of control commands by the users (clients).
- **Client server Protocol:** it is request/response type protocol assisting in carrying out communications between the client and the server. It uses TCP/IP protocol.

The client initiates the communication by either sending or receiving any type and amount of data within a session.

- **Network emulator:** it serves the purpose for emulating attacks, defenses, extensive networks, and network-related transactions. The network emulator used is RINSE. It is used as it is capable of representing realistic nodes along with virtual nodes within the simulation. It can also generate actual packets that can perform transactions even in the real world. (Read more in Section 10.1.2.)

- **Protocol converter:** it was designed for converting a customized protocol of PowerWorld into a realistic SCADA protocol. It allows an interface between actual hardware and network client. It also helps in mapping between the PowerWorld server and sophisticated physical devices. One such example is Modbus. It is the most generally utilized SCADA protocol.

- **Simulators integration:** both the PowerWorld and RINSE are integrated using proxy and VPN servers, along with VPN clients. The network client communicates with the PowerWorld using the proxy server on some specific port. The destination of the packets gets translated to PowerWorld server's virtual IP address during the simulation. The packets get delivered via VPN to RINSE nodes where they get injected into the simulation. During the simulation, using these packets, RINSE generates realistic packets having virtual IP addresses. Then they are transferred to the proxy server via VPN and also translate them and send them to the actual PowerWorld server. Using the similar procedure, the PowerWorld can also communicate with the network client.

There exists another type of SCADA testbed that successfully incorporates HIL techniques. Its main focus was on providing instantaneous simulations, handling operations of power systems and remote monitoring. This goal was extended on the SPS lab SCADA testbed developed at University of South Florida (Aghamolki *et al.* 2015). It also focuses on configuring and developing a communication interface that can be used by the packages and devices. It makes use of DNP3 and Modbus protocol for sending commands (Aghamolki *et al.* 2015).

- **DNP3 protocol:** this protocol is based on standards of IEC. It was specifically designed for optimizing data transmission of SCADA applications. It is used for sending the control commands from one system to others.

- **Modbus protocol:** it is an application layer protocol used for messaging or sending commands. In OSI model, it is positioned at the seventh layer and is responsible for providing client server type communication among the connected devices. These devices may be present on dissimilar networks or buses. It uses function codes to provide the request/reply services. It supports sending commands for both Modbus Poll and PI servers.

- **PI server:** all commands are defined as data points or specific tags. Changing the output tags results in sending the commands to Modbus. It supports multi- and single-register writings. It provides the advantage of archiving data and automatically coding operations.

- **Modbus Poll servers:** it also supports simultaneous multi- and single-register writings. Both the servers are similar in carrying out sending instantaneous commands.

4.2.2 SWAT

It is water treatment testbed designed for cybersecurity research. It served as a significant advantage for researchers, assisting them in designing of secure and stable CPSs. Its main purposes include (Mathur *et al.* 2016):

- Developing an understanding of the effects of a cyberattack against water treatment systems.
- Evaluating the efficacy of algorithms used for detecting any cyberattacks the system is experiencing.
- Evaluating the efficacy of the system's defense mechanisms in cyberattack conditions.
- Understanding the dependency of one ICS on the other and that collapse of one has cascading effects on the dependent ICS.

It has a six-stage process architecture as shown in Figure 4.7 and labeled P1, P2, P3, P4, P5, and P6.

- **P1 process:** this process involves storing raw water. It is a central buffer for supplying the water to the treatment system.
- **P2 process:** this is the pretreatment phase for evaluating the quality and properties of water-like pH level and conductivity.
- **P3 process:** this is the UF phase where a huge amount of colloidal materials and feedstuff water solids get removed. These contaminants get separated by eroding the surface of the membrane. There are two sensors for measuring differential

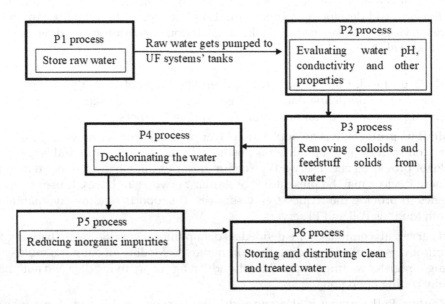

FIGURE 4.7
SWAT processes.

pressure, which are located at both ends of UF system. This process ensures the removal of small unwanted residuals present in the water.

- **P4 process:** this process involves destroying the remaining chlorines in the water.
- **P5 process:** this process uses RO system for decreasing the amount of inorganic impurities present in the water. The dechlorinated and filtrated water gets pumped past the semipermeable membranes at high pressure.
- **P6 process:** after undergoing all these process, the cleaned and treated water is stored and set for distribution purposes.

SWAT testbed comprises CLI interpreter called SWAT Assault. It has a collection of the attack modules that are responsible for launching injection and spoofing-like attacks on actuator and sensors used in the testbed (Urbina *et al.* 2016). All these modules independently load, configure, and run. PLCs act as control devices. They receive the readings from the sensors and produce control commands for actuators. It is placed in a ring topology comprising a primary and a secondary PLC. The primary PLC is responsible for the control of physical processes, communications, and receiving/relaying data. The secondary PLC follows the primary's memory state. The system will switch the control automatically to the secondary, when primary fails. A more recent study (Athalye *et al.* 2020) presents a comparison between SWAT and WADI testbeds by experimentally studying performances of detection methods.

PLCs, actuators, and sensors present in the testbed communicate using the Ethernet/IP (for network level 0) and CIP stack (for network level 1). Tools like Scapy, Wireshark, and Ettercap are used for performing network traffic decoding and monitoring. Ettercap is an attack suite used for launching wireless attacks. Scapy is used for manipulating the senor reading and actuator commands. Wireshark assists in understanding the type of communication taking place among the devices present in ring topology.

The testbed architecture is composed of four zones:

- **Zone A:** it comprises seven sets of PLCs autonomously controlling the actuators and sensors for all the six different processes.
- **Zone B:** it is also called the control system that comprises engineering workstation and operator console. Both these zones are accessed and protected using the firewall. Other zones can access them via the testbed's firewall.
- **Zone C:** it is also called the DMZ zone as it comprises smart devices and remote operator console.
- **Zone D:** it is the plant network that comprises workstation and server accessible via laptop systems.

4.2.3 WADI

This testbed was developed as an extension to SWAT. It has been operational since 2016 and serves as a significant asset in understanding the extensive range of possible cyberattacks and physical attacks against water treatment and distribution plants. It also simulates the physical attacks like injection of malicious chemicals and leakage issues. Since distribution systems compose of several pipelines covering large and open areas, they are prone to such physical attacks.

Both SWAT and WADI represent interconnected systems; thus they are crucial in understanding the interdependency of CPSs. Palleti *et al.* (2021) describe three conditions when two systems are interconnected:

- These systems may have either one or many inputs provided by another system.
- These systems together share either one or many components like sharing water tank for storage purposes. Consumption activities of one system affect the availability of resource in another system.
- Either of the components of the two systems is used for the movement of resources.

Currently, WADI testbed assists in the carrying out the following objectives (Ahmed *et al.* 2017):

- Conducting security evaluations for WADI networks.
- Carrying out experiments for assessing the detection mechanisms pertaining to possible physical attacks and cyberattacks.
- Understanding the interdependency between connected systems and what effects a system under attack have on its other connected systems.

WADI is composed of three processes as shown in Figure 4.8:

- **P1 process:** this is responsible for water supply and serves as a primary grid. It has two water tanks each having a capacity of 2500 L. The water comes from three sources – utility water, water treated from SWAT, and water from P3 process. This process also has quality sensors for monitoring water quality before it gets stored. These sensors monitor pH, conductivity, pressure, turbidity, overall chlorine residual, etc.

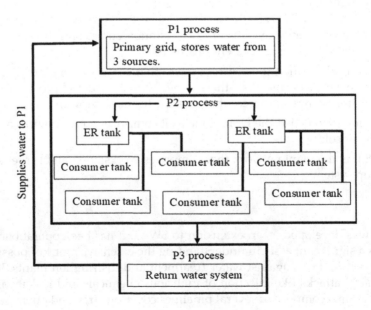

FIGURE 4.8
WADI processes.

- **P2 process:** this is a secondary process composing of two ERs and six consumer tanks. The water from P1 tanks moves to ERs depending on the set value for the tank levels. The water then moves to consumer tanks that have a predetermined demand assigned. Two stations for monitoring water quality are installed at upstream end and downstream end of the ERs.

- **P3 process:** this is also called the return water system. After the consumer tanks are filled, the water gets drained into P3 process.

The testbed network architecture is composed of three layers:

- **Layer 0:** this layer is composed of sensors and actuators.

- **Layer 1:** this layer comprises PLCs that control the layer 0 components. The components are arranged in star topology.

- **Layer 2:** it comprises devices like workstations, smart devices, and HMI for supervisory control.

- **Layer 3:** it is the DMZ layer that is also responsible for operation management. It comprises a Historian.

The PLCs and above layer components present in the testbed communicate using the Ethernet/IP and CIP stack (for network level 1). Communication between layer 0 and layer 1 components is possible for using electrical signals. The data provided by the sensors gets accessed by SCADA workstations and recorded by Historian. This recorded data is used for successive evaluations. Contamination dosing and leak detection are two of the main simulations carried out by WADI testbed. In contamination dosing, the dosing system gets prepared using a dosing pump and a tank. Analyzers for monitoring water quality (in terms of turbidity, conductivity, pH, etc.) are placed at reservoir's outlet followed by the dosing points. In leak detection, a transparent dual-containment piping unit and modulating valves are used for simulation. The valve releases into outer pipe presenting a leakage condition. The pressure transmitters detect the leakage due to difference in the pressure.

4.3 Virtual CRs

A virtual CR as shown in Figure 4.9 is entirely composed of emulated components (both software and hardware) using VMs. It uses SVN technology that is responsible for making it plausible to characterize the networking infrastructure at suitable extent of dependability. The applications getting executed on it like web browsing, video/web conferencing, and video streaming are unchangeably implemented above enormous emulated networks for communication appliances. Given this feature, virtual CRs offer the following advantages:

- As compared to physical CRs, the cost of operations and capital is significantly reduced.

- They can easily be set up or torn down on demand. This process is less time consuming.

- The CR can easily be reverted back after an exercise by disposing of attack elements.

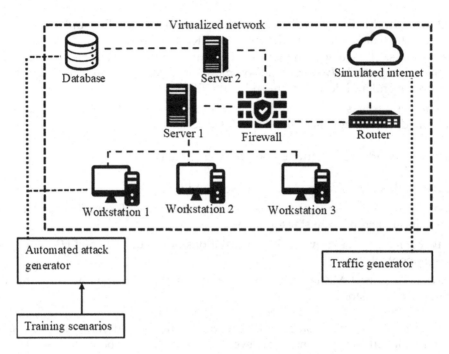

FIGURE 4.9
Virtual CR layout.

- Its resources can be scaled up and down effortlessly.
- It is always up-to-date as new updates, patches, and exploits are always available.
- The hardware becomes simpler and that's because everything is virtualized to run on relatively common off-the-shelf hardware and less expert human resources, or fewer expert human resources, are typically needed than for a fully physical notation.

However, in virtual CRs, it is always not possible to model certain scenarios exactly like a real-world situation. Realism is difficult to achieve in virtual CR environments. Realistic scenarios are critical for train-as-you-fight paradigm. Virtual CR environments face limitations when trying to precisely replicate the behavior of any physical component. For example, modeling components like firewalls and webcams in a virtual CR may be challenging and they require to be accurate and realistic. The prominent example of this type of range is Virginia CR (read more in Section 10.2.5). This section will discuss CYRA and GISOO.

4.3.1 CYRA

It provides an assurance platform allowing users (Smyrlis *et al.* 2021):

- To educate and train against numerous cyberattacks via generic or organization-specific training program.
- Conduct evaluations on how efficiently the gained expertise gets applied for enhancing security of the system.
- Create and customize training procedures.

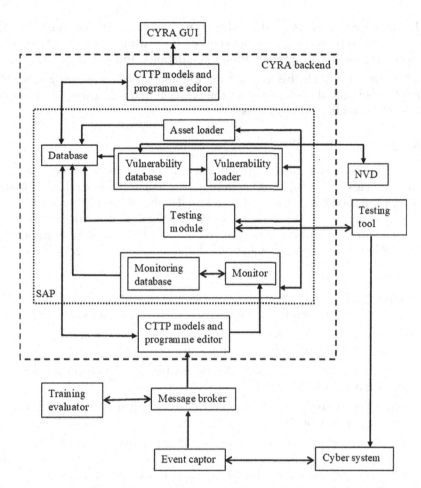

FIGURE 4.10
CYRA architecture layouts.

The CR's architecture, as shown in Figure 4.10, is composed of three major components (Smyrlis *et al.* 2021):

- **Sphynx SAP:** it comprises numerous tools that allow the users to comprehend security evaluations via constant monitoring and testing. It includes components like asset loader, vulnerability loader, monitoring, testing modules, and event captor. An asset loader is responsible for receiving system assets, security properties, security controls, and threats violating these properties. Vulnerability loader composes of known vulnerabilities.
  It updates the SAP according to the organizations assets. Monitoring module is a runtime engine containing monitor manager, event collector, and monitor. It is responsible for forwarding runtime events and obtaining monitoring outcomes. The testing module executes various penetration assessments using various open-source tools. It is responsible for discovering vulnerabilities, reporting new assets in the system. Event captor tool collects data and trigger events. It is responsible for formulating rules, monitoring and evaluating modules.

- **CTTP model editor:** it is used for the creation of training programs and CTTP models. It is a web service accessible via the CR's platforms. The training program is responsible for executing emulations, simulations, and gaming activities.
- **CTTP adaptation tool:** this is used for the adaptation of existing models and training programs. It also assists in the creation and designing of new tools to address the potential cyber threats.

4.3.2 GISOO

It is a virtual testbed used for executing authentic simulations for all components in a wireless CPS. It integrates both COOJA (Osterlind *et al.* 2006) and Simulink (The MathWorks, Inc 2021). COOJA is used for the emulation of actual embedded code beneath the authentic models for wireless and timing communications. It is flexible and scalable comprising various standard extensions and plug-ins. This integration helps GISOO to implement various wireless CPSs architectures. GISOO testbed offers the following capabilities (Aminian *et al.* 2013):

- It combines MAC and application layer together to replicate packet loss and timing rates removing the requirement for constructing abstract simulation setups.
- Embedded code for wireless communications can be emulated and directly executed on target platform without adding any changes to it.
- Computation, actuation, and control can be directly implemented in Simulink, thus proving complete flexibility.
- Comprehensive analysis of relations between communication, control, and computation components can be carried out.
- It supports wireless platforms like Contiki OS and TinyOS via COOJA.

The architecture of GISOO as shown in Figure 4.11 can be broadly categorized into COOJA and Simulink. Simulink is responsible for simulating the dynamics of physical systems and performing controller designs. Control engineers use Simulink for designing and studying control systems. COOJA is used for the simulation of wireless components within a wireless actuators and sensors network. It also facilitates cross-platform simulations within single framework at OS, application, and machine code levels. GISOO plug-in is responsible for data exchange between Simulink and COOJA. The plugins are implemented within COOJA. The plugin retrieves the data from Simulink and delivers it to wireless nodes present in COOJA and vice versa (Aminian *et al.* 2013).

This data transmission takes place using relay and sensor nodes. The synchronization between the two is maintained by time clocks. These clocks follow stop and run procedure. When any event is taking place in COOJA, it gets transmitted to Simulink. During this phase, Simulink's time clock is stopped until the event gets completes. After which, the Simulink's time clock is run until the requested time to complete the event. Once, the event gets executed the Simulink's clock is again stopped.

COOJA provides access to several debugging features like logging, breakpoints, and watches for development of wireless code. Moreover, it provides access to wireless data transmission taking place from all nodes and their statistics like power consumptions. The CR uses IEEE802.15.4 standard for wireless network and it is accessible for communication layers specifications (Aminian *et al.* 2013).

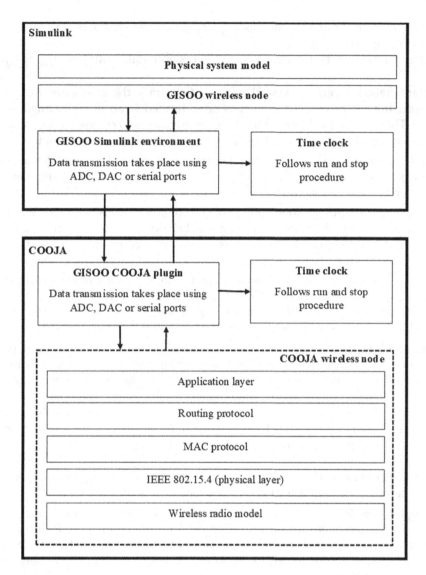

FIGURE 4.11
GISOO architecture.

4.4 CRaaS

As also mentioned in Chapter 1, CRaaS is a form of a service model that is owned and administered by CR vendors. The major advantage of CRaaS is that it provides fast and economical way for the users to execute their respective tasks. There exist numerous kinds of services available on cloud like malware simulators, hypervisors, traffic generators, and SDN. All these tools and services are provided by various cloud vendors that complicate management and automation goals set for the delivery of CRaaS (Reynolds 2019).

This prevents the CR infrastructure from ensuring optimization that is essential to meet users' needs. Without absolute control over the CR infrastructure, organizations would not be able to update or enhance the capacity or performance of the overall infrastructure, thus not fulfilling its users' demands.

Reynolds (2019) also lists the risks involved in not automating and managing CRs:

- **Instantaneous inventory visibility:** most CRs track the assets due to financial reasons, but the resource inventory is often limited to an ill-maintained spreadsheet. Therefore, it becomes difficult for the engineers to ensure the existence of a resource, whether the required resources are presently available or not.

- Without a proper documentation, it becomes complex to keep updates about the changes made by several engineers in the CR's infrastructure. This may cause costly errors and connectivity issues.

- Both private and public clouds offer isolated solutions. Tools and modules present in one type of cloud environment may not be sufficient for sharing across other dissimilar environment for numerous end users. For example, some resources may only be limited to private cloud, thus avoiding resource integration.

- Having numerous customized environments and tools without any common controlling interface leads to their limited usage within several groups. It would not only require extensive capital but also expertise in managing these components, thus limiting the management of certain resources to certain teams of personnel.

- This also leads to very less resource utilization. Creating and designing of new resources requires a lot of capital and research. If users are not able to avail these resources, as and when required, they may lead to a huge loss and wastage.

The concept of CRaaS tackles such issues to provide a CR environment that is sophisticated, accurate, productive and has high utilization. CRaaS incorporates methodologies of automation framework that offers the following advantages:

- **Cost effectiveness:** there is significant reduction in wastage and expenditure when complete device utilization is achieved.

- Using the object-oriented methods for creation, modification, and maintenance of components' templates makes an automated live documentation. Result analysis is also automated, which provides robust reports of execution. Users have a complete control over all the produced datasets allowing an ownership of outputs and metrics of the framework.

- It ensures faster allocation and deployment of resources and rapid report generation.

CRaaS provides an object-oriented and entirely integrated framework that helps the user to achieve automating development for any type of CR. This framework includes:

- An integrated, instantaneous resource inventory.
- Topology designs considering the available resources.
- Common calendar assigning topologies and resources reservations.
- A library of reusable templates and objects. They can be constructed using a range of sources.
- Resources' diagnostics
- The users or participating organizations own their test logs and datasets.

References

Aghamolki, H. G., Miao, Z., Fan, L., 2015. A hardware-in-the-loop SCADA testbed. *In*: *North American Power Symposium (NAPS)*, 4–6 October 2015 Charlotte. New York: IEEE, 1–6.

Ahmad, S., Maunero, N., Prinetto, P., 2020. EVA: A hybrid cyber range. *ELETTRONICO*, 2597(1), 12–23.

Ahmed, C. M., Palleti, V. R., Mathur, A. P., 2017. WADI: a water distribution testbed for research in the design of secure cyber physical systems. *In*: *Proceedings of the 3rd International Workshop on Cyber-Physical Systems for Smart Water Networks*, 21 April 2017 Pennsylvania. New York: Association for Computing Machinery, 25–28.

Aminian, B., Araújo, J., Johansson, M., Johansson, K. H., 2013. GISOO: A virtual testbed for wireless cyber-physical systems. *In*: *IECON 2013-39th Annual Conference of the IEEE Industrial Electronics Society*, 10–13 November 2013 Vienna. New York: IEEE, 5588–5593.

Athalye, S., Ahmed, C. M., Zhou, J., 2020. A tale of two testbeds: A comparative study of attack detection techniques in CPS. *In*: *International Conference on Critical Information Infrastructures Security*, 2–3 September 2020 Bristol. Switzerland: Springer, 17–30.

Davis, C. M., Tate, J. E., Okhravi, H., Grier, C., Overbye, T. J., Nicol, D., 2006. SCADA cyber security testbed development. *In*: *38th North American Power Symposium*, 17–19 September 2006 Carbondale. New York: IEEE, 483–488.

DIATEAM, 2020. DIATEAM, cybersecurity engineering company [online]. Available from: https://www.diateam.net/about-diateam-cyber-range-editor/ [Accessed 23 May 2021].

Gustafsson, T., Almroth, J., 2020. Cyber range automation overview with a case study of CRATE. *In*: *Nordic Conference on Secure IT Systems*, 23–24 November 2020. Switzerland: Springer, 192–209.

Mathur, A. P., Tippenhauer, N. O., 2016. SWaT: A water treatment testbed for research and training on ICS security. *In*: *International Workshop on Cyber-Physical Systems for Smart Water Networks (CySWater)*, 11–11 April 2016 Vienna. New York: IEEE, 31–36.

Osterlind, F., Dunkels, A., Eriksson, J., Finne, N., Voigt, T., 2006. Crosslevel sensor network simulation with Cooja. *In*: *31st IEEE Conference on Local Computer Networks*, 14–16 November 2006 Tampa. New York: IEEE, 641–648.

Palleti, V. R., Adepu, S., Mishra, V. K., Mathur, A., 2021. Cascading effects of cyber-attacks on interconnected critical infrastructure. *Cybersecurity*, 4(1), 1–19.

Rev. A., 2014. Cyber range: Improving network defense and security readiness real-world attack scenarios for cyber security training [online]. Ixia. Available from: https://support.ixiacom.com/sites/default/files/resources/whitepaper/915-6729-01-cyber-range.pdf [Accessed 23 May 2021].

Reynolds, C. T., 2019. Cyber range as a Service® CRaaS [online]. Available from: https://rdp21.org/wp-content/uploads/2020/11/Cyber-Range-as-a-Service-CRaaS-2019.pdf [Accessed 25 May 2021].

Smyrlis, M., Somarakis, I., Spanoudakis, G., Hatzivasilis, G., Ioannidis, S., 2021. CYRA: A model-driven Cyber range assurance platform. *Applied Sciences*, 11(11), 5165.

The MathWorks, Inc, 2021. Simulation and model-based design [online]. Available from: https://se.mathworks.com/products/simulink.html [Accessed 25 May 2021].

Urbina, D., Giraldo, J., Tippenhauer, N. O., Cardenas, A., 2016. Attacking fieldbus communications in ICS: Applications to the SWaT testbed. *In*: *Proceedings of the Singapore Cyber-Security Conference (SG-CRC)* 14–15 January 2016. Amsterdam: IOS Press, 75–89.

5

Roles of Cyber Ranges: Testing, Training, and Research

5.1 CRs for Testing

Modern CRs provide scalable and isolated environments aimed at (Chouliaras *et al.* 2021):

- Constructing competitive and realistic scenarios.
- Combining simulating and emulating features to become more adaptable and efficient.
- Producing and maintaining datasets that are useful for conducting various types of testing agendas.

Therefore, CRs serve as ideal platform for carrying out penetration testing, security testing, and software testing of the network infrastructures.

5.1.1 Penetration Testing

This process is often associated with and followed by the assessment of system vulnerabilities. It is considered more effective when tracking and finding security lapses from the beginning of the product life cycle (Arkin *et al.* 2005). It is responsible for intently exploiting the system's liabilities under authorized jurisdiction for examining the extent of damage or uncovering some new vulnerabilities as shown in Figure 5.1. It is one of the nine steps in VAPT life cycle:

- Scope
- Reconnaissance
- Detecting system vulnerabilities
- Analyses and planning of information
- Penetration testing
- Privilege intensification
- Analysis of results
- Reporting
- Cleanup

Table 5.1 lists some of the most commonly used VAPT tools, licenses, and OS specification. In terms of defense, VAPT tools are crucial when assessing and removing system vulnerabilities. Attackers also perform vulnerability assessments to gather Intel about

DOI: 10.1201/9781003206071-5

TABLE 5.1

Details of VAPT Tools

VAPT Tool	Licenses	OS
Metasploit (Holik *et al.* 2014)	Proprietary	Cross-platform
Nessus (Thacker *et al.* 2006)	Proprietary	Cross-platform
Nexpose (Goel *et al.* 2015)	Proprietary	Windows, Linux
MBSA (Goel *et al.* 2016)	Freeware	Windows
Canvas (Goel *et al.* 2016)	Proprietary	Cross-platform
Paros proxy (Ferreira *et al.* 2011)	GPL	Cross-platform
OpenVAS (Kumar *et al.* 2018)	GPL	Cross-platform

unrepaired liabilities. Timely restoration or replacement of visible liabilities can avoid adverse attacks like DoS and RA flooding (Goel *et al.* 2015).

McDermott (2001) describes either of two approaches followed by penetration testing:

- **Flaw hypothesis**: it is commonly used for the latest product testing at its last stage of development. Penetration testing uses flaw hypothesis for generating theoretical flaws which undergo analyses, filtration, and arranged priority-wise. Later, the confirmed flaws are thoroughly analyzed for any past incidents and for creating appropriate fixes.

- **Attack tree**: this approach is useful in the case of insufficient information available of the system which is supposed to undergo testing. It is logic AND, OR operators-based hierarchical structure constituting various kinds of intrusion events in the leaf. The top node of the tree represents the main objective followed by various subgoals as shown in Figure 5.2. The grouping of subgoals takes place using logic operators.

Penetration testing entails conducting IT security tests, physical security tests, and evaluations for cybersecurity awareness among employees (Dimkov *et al.* 2010). Some of the majorly used penetration testing techniques include:

- **Black box testing**: this technique is performed from external to internal networks. The tester is unaware about the network's architecture.

- **Gray box testing**: this technique can be performed either from external or internal networks. The tester has some partial knowledge of the systems' configurations.

- **White box testing**: this technique is performed from internal networks. The tester has completed and deeper understanding of the working and configurations of systems' architectures. This is necessary for providing comprehensive results.

5.1.2 Software Testing

It is crucial for validating and verifying if the software has been developed according to the set guidelines and fulfills the determined specifications. Software testing helps in preventing any errors affecting its performance. During software testing, the following objectives need to be considered:

- Verifying if the product operates as expected and validating if it carries out the tasks in the arranged and efficient manner.

- Testing should be conducted on priority bases within the schedule and budgets limitations.

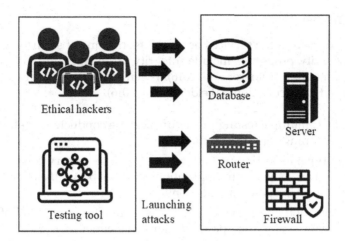

FIGURE 5.1
Penetration testing on network components.

- The requirements, user expectations, and technical limitations must be balanced during the testing phase.
- Recording and maintaining results of test process must be documented.
- Advance planning about the objectives to be tested and expected outcomes must be determined beforehand.

Sawant *et al.* (2012) define four strategies for software testing:

- **Unit testing**: it involves testing small units of code blocks. It is often referred to as the white box test. It is beneficial for improving resource reliability. It is a cost-effective technique. It is ideal for testing parts of a product or code without awaiting the availability for other parts. Debugging becomes more precise in this technique and lengthy debug cycles can be avoided.
- **Integration testing**: this is useful for systematic construction of program structure while simultaneously undergoing software testing. This associates debugging with interfacing. Integration testing can be done using either a top-down or bottom-up approach. Top-down approach integrates the modules starting with the module for main control and progressing downwards.
  In bottom-up approach, the constructing and testing activities begin at the base modules. This approach removes the requirement of subordinate stubs. All the lower level components get combined in form of clusters. These clusters have definite subfunctions. For providing test cases and coordinating them with I/O, a driver is used. Once the cluster gets tested, the drivers get removed. The clusters keep getting combined together while moving upwards.
- **Acceptance testing**: it verifies product standards and if it meets the necessary, customer-specified requirements. The testing is conducted by external party that is not concerned with the system coding but with the overall performance. It is also referred to as black box type of testing. It is conducted after the completion of product life cycle but before the product gets handed over to end users. It ensures that the designed product fulfills customer demands and it is operationally efficient (Jamil *et al.* 2016).

5.1.3 Security Testing

It is responsible for testing the services or products in terms of security requirements or criteria. These security properties include integrity, confidentiality, authorization, availability, and non-repetition (Felderer *et al.* 2016). When conducting security testing, the following factors need to be considered (Felderer *et al.* 2016):

- **Attack surface**: multiple testing procedures can be conducted together efficiently recover a wider range of vulnerabilities.
- **Application type**: as testing procedures are product- or service-specific, using a testing method on some mobile applications may not be as efficient when used for multilayer request/response applications.
- Resource utilization and performance is distinctive for every kind of product as they entail diverse computing power and manual endeavors.
- Costs of security testing licenses, support, and regular maintenance need to be integrated and fit in with the overall budget.
- Result quality must be maintained or enhanced using either false-positive rates, fix recommendations, etc.
- As security testing only supports limited tools and technologies like (interfaces, programming languages, systems, etc.), appropriate testing facilities must be availed.

The two major types of security testing techniques include threat model and web security testing.

5.1.3.1 Threat Model Testing

It is a systematic process concerning with identification, analyses, documentation, and mitigation of security threats to the system. This type of testing uses threat tress and allows the operators in comprehending threat profiles against the system from the perspective of an attacker. Marback *et al.* (2013) provide the following steps for threat model testing:

- Asset identification
- Threat determination
- Prioritizing most damage causing threats
- Threat mitigation procedures

5.1.3.2 Web Security Testing

Modern industries use various web services within their network infrastructure. It is one of the most important and vulnerable components of the infrastructure. The web services are often exposed; therefore, it becomes easier for the attackers to exploit using injection attacks or encryption attacks, etc. Web security testing ensures (Vieira *et al.* 2009):

- Operators have better understanding of the service's behavior.
- Awareness about previously attempted or executed cyberattacks.
- Comparison of the results with valid requests.

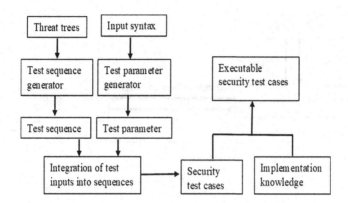

FIGURE 5.2
Threat model generation processes.

One of the most common cyberattack on web services is XSS. It injects malicious JavaScript written code in the target's WSDL. Attackers use this for stealing data, compromising servers and integrity of the system. The web services assume that the code provided by the servers is legitimate, therefore allowing access to confidential details (Salas *et al.* 2014).

The most common application attack is SQL injections. It injects malicious SQL queries for extracting and executing commands by evading authentication. These are carried out via web and focus on returning the output of the statement. Even error messages by the database are sufficient for assisting the attacker (Boyd *et al.* 2004). The attacker may force an exception for revealing more details about the database tables (Boyd *et al.* 2004).

Security testing focuses on enforcing integrity and confidentially and end-to-end communication security. It also allows security tokens like Kerberos (Neuman *et al.* 1994), SAML (Groß 2003), and X.509 (Welch *et al.* 2004). These are security specifications for verifying the authorization and authentication of the users and their access to relevant services. Figure 5.3 represents a stack of security specifications for shielding web services from external attacks.

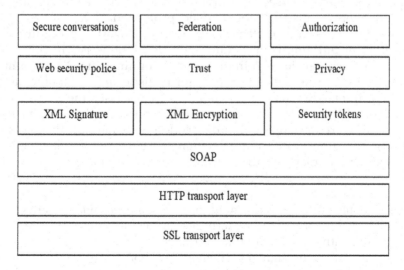

FIGURE 5.3
Stack of security specifications.

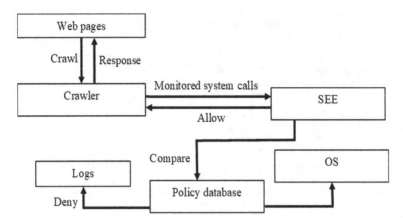

FIGURE 5.4
Working of SEE.

Huang *et al.* (2005) describe SEE as shown in Figure 5.4, an inconsistency detection environment for intercepting crawler-made system calls. If a call has malicious parameters, it gets rejected. It studies and records the behavior of crawl targets. BMSL is used for recording the behavior and storing it in a policy database. It not only acts as a self-protecting mechanism but also as a method for detecting insertion of malicious code in web-based applications.

5.2 CRs for Training

Training personnel for cybersecurity preparedness is crucial for organizations to secure their network infrastructures. Trained professionals can effectively address cyber threats or attacks and implement necessary mitigation procedures. Training is also essential for building teams' communication that assists in timely detection and reporting of discrepancies within the system. Trainings in CR environment allow the personnel to safely practice and prepare for realistic and instantaneous scenarios and combat conditions. Regular and planned trainings assist the personnel in keeping their skills and knowledge up to date. This is an essential attribute because new threats and attacks are developing rapidly. Modern CRs have all the necessary tools for conducting and supporting training exercises. They can also be scaled according to the number of participants. Unlike military, where emphasis is given on creating research and training-specific CRs, commercial sectors can rent or buy CR platforms for training purposes.

CRs serve as a substitute for performing planned exercises without affecting the live operations and systems. Some of the modern CRs can also accommodate external exercise-specific equipment within the environment provided by the participating organizations. Infrastructure simulations or emulations demonstrate both necessary and vulnerable features of the IT infrastructure to the participants. The platform is ideal for solving all the "what-if" scenarios and questions. This in return is helpful in designing improvements or confirming the adequacy of the training objectives.

Some of the most common training objectives include:

- Determining the efficiency of cybersecurity knowledge of the personnel.
- Assessing the teams' incident preparedness and effectiveness of reporting, analyzing, and remedying system vulnerabilities.
- Assessing the awareness of participants to successfully detect any suspicious activities and take necessary measures.
- The participants can become more familiar and comfortable with the network infrastructure and its components.
- Enhancing coordination and communications between the team members and amongst other operations teams.
- Understanding team roles and executing the assigned tasks.

As trainings are conducted in simulated/emulated environments, it also helps in revealing any security gaps within the infrastructure. After successful testing of any security service

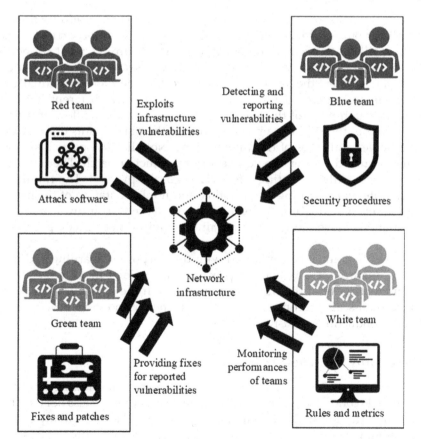

FIGURE 5.5
Common training scenario.

or patch, they can initially be used in training scenarios for providing dual validation. Most importantly, trainings help the organization to improve and strengthen their infrastructure and teams against advanced cyberattacks, thus evading any extreme security loss.

5.2.1 How to Use CRs for Trainings

Before commencing training operations, it is necessary to set training objectives, resources required, and consider level of participants. The complexity of trainings must be mapped according to the average qualifications of the participants. The objectives of training must be established and agreed upon prior to its execution and during the planning process. Using the same set of objectives or resources for distinct, application-specific training is not effective and realistic. Well-defined training objectives dictate the nature of activities that would be carried out by participants.

Therefore, adequate planning is crucial for conducting successful trainings. It becomes easier to timely organize and accommodate all the training requirements prior to the session. This is also useful to predict any potential issues that may occur during trainings. The larger the scale of training, longer the time is required for planning. The training objective must reflect realistic situations and consider the lessons learned from previous trainings.

The training scenarios must be realistic and specific. It is not useful to flood the participants with various, sophisticated cyberattacks or threats all occurring at once. Such a situation is unlikely to occur in the real world. The trainings must support realism and focus on understanding specific and related cybersecurity aspects at a time. The scenarios must not deflect the participants from working on their individually assigned tasks. Participants are divided into teams, each assigned a different list of tasks to accomplish. Although none of the teams must interfere with the flow of training. It is the responsibility of the White team to ensure that the participants do not direct away from the objectives and rules of training sessions. Not all those participants would be involved in design and testing of a new security product or patch. Therefore, the trainings must not focus only on testing effectiveness of the product. The trainings should rather concentrate on examining applicability and implementation of the new product, security patch, etc. Conducting realistic and well-planned trainings promotes active participation and achieve more form it. Training environment is composed of several participants.

Lastly, the trainings must be conducted with the purpose of learning and not just for the sake of organizing extensive and complex training sessions. In such cases, chances are that the original purpose of the training may get lost. If the objectives can be efficiently achieved in a small-scale training scenario, then it a better and more economically viable approach than conducting extensive sessions.

5.2.2 Cybersecurity Awareness Trainings

Awareness of cybersecurity is essential in present day for communicating security requirements and suitable conduct (Bada *et al.* 2019). Cybersecurity awareness not only highlights the areas of concerns, but it also encourages appropriate responses. Many organizations and industries now focus only ensuring cybersecurity awareness among their employee. Many industries have shifted to IT-based infrastructure or incorporated relevant IT aspects in existing systems. Therefore, it is essential for both technical and nontechnical employee to be aware about cybersecurity and its aspects. It assists in informed and timely detection and reporting of any anomalies in the system.

Apart from having knowledge of cybersecurity aspects, it is also necessary to emphasize on appropriate reaction. A person, having knowledge of cybersecurity aspects, may not necessarily be aware or motivated to respond accordingly. Therefore, trainings can assist in incorporating constructive cybersecurity behaviors and response habits. Zwilling *et al.* (2020) describe three levels of cybersecurity awareness:

- **Low awareness**: it can be described as when the personnel may neglect security alerts.
- **Medium awareness**: it can be described as improper handling of technical operations.
- **High awareness**: it can be described as having enough knowledge of cybersecurity aspects and competence to prevent them.

CyberCIEGE (Cone *et al.* 2007) is a cybersecurity awareness game. It not only supports training objectives but also makes team engagement interesting in form of security adventure games. It is presently used by organizations to educate and train their workforces in IA and cybersecurity. It provides training on the following awareness topics:

- Understanding definitions, descriptions, interactions, and importance of IA and cybersecurity aspects.
- Understanding information value and securing information with the highest priority.
- Introducing both necessary and flexible access controls.
- Preventing password sharing or revealing with external sources.
- Determining how to utilize resources for procuring technical settings useful for preventing the further propagation of malicious software.

5.2.3 Incident Response Trainings

A successful cyber incident response is one where mitigation procedures are timely implemented and the progression of cyberattack is under control. With the increase in the use of advanced technological assets within infrastructures, the frequency of cyberattacks proportionally increases. Therefore, there is a need for cyber incident response trainings. Such trainings help the personnel in studying the potential cyberattacks, system vulnerabilities, security gaps, etc. They are ideal to prepare for any live incidents. The personnel may be able to timely communicate and effectively respond to any attack. These trainings ensure that the personnel actively consider and report any security alerts or system discrepancies. It also involves learning from past incidents and failures. Once the cyberattack is detected, it must be contained before it can cause severe damages. It can later be used for analyses and research purposes. It can later be studied and understood. Security procedures can be developed to mitigate similar attacks in the future. Figure 5.6 shows the processes involve in incident response trainings. This is like carrying out and actual mitigation response against any cyberattack. Taking participant feedback after the training helps the training administrators to understand participant's expectations and effectiveness of the training conducted.

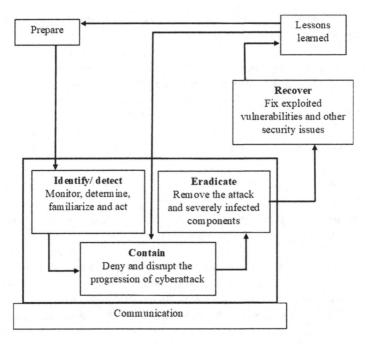

FIGURE 5.6
Processes in incident response training.

5.3 CRs for Research

CRs serve as ideal platform for conducting cybersecurity-related research. There are several academic and military institutes, which not only develop their own CRs, but also use it for research and analytical purposes. Some of the academic CRs are discussed in Chapter 10. Chapter 3 discussed the need for CRs in the critical industries like WSS, O&G, power, maritime, and logistics. However, cybersecurity- and internet-based technology is not only limited to these industries. Several other industries are also shifting to incorporate IT aspects within their infrastructure. Therefore, this provides new research areas for expanding the applications of cybersecurity aspects. For example,

- **Maintenance of IoT-assisted highways**: with the incorporation of IoT in highway maintenance, several physical devices, computing systems, and datasets have also emerged. Each of this eventually reveals potential areas or vulnerabilities for cyberattacks (Trotter *et al.* 2018). Moreover, such components are prone to intrusion attacks. The most common security concern is the basic safety of IoT-related components. In the case of highways, these components are easier to compromise because they are present in open environments. They also require regular inspections and repair.

It also requires employing specific standards and appropriate governance for addressing and managing cybersecurity-related issues. Therefore, research is required in formulating cybersecurity-specific standards. This sector also requires more research in understanding complexities of data sharing with other domains.

Research is also required in determining the errors with the roles that human resource contributes to, for example, providing authentications, detecting intrusion attempts, reporting incidents, managing operations, etc. Moreover, it is also necessary to assess and understand the risks accompanying these possible errors (Boyce *et al.* 2011). Determining risks also provides the probability of the occurrence of these errors in different scenarios. Their consequences and mitigation strategies can be studied and used for developing error-tolerant systems.

Research on cybersecurity policies is also required for understanding the use of IT in social as well as political contexts (Cavelty 2018). Cybersecurity is viewed differently from both perspectives. From social context, it is a practice of resolving affected components. From political context, it is a means of advancing political agendas. The former notion neglects the other significance of cybersecurity and the other constitutes very less knowledge about the application and working of cybersecurity aspects. Cavelty (2018) emphasizes that research is required for addressing and combining both these notions for providing improved benefits to each.

References

Arkin, B., Stender, S., McGraw, G., 2005. Software penetration testing. *IEEE Security and Privacy*, 3(1), 84–87.

Bada, M., Sasse, A. M., Nurse, J. R., 2019. Cyber security awareness campaigns: Why do they fail to change behaviour. *arXiv preprint arXiv:1901.02672*, 1–11.

Boyce, M. W., Duma, K. M., Hettinger, L. J., Malone, T. B., Wilson, D. P., Lockett-Reynolds, J., 2011. Human performance in cybersecurity: A research agenda. *Proceedings of the Human Factors and Ergonomics Society Annual Meeting*, 55(1), 1115–1119.

Boyd, S. W., Keromytis, A. D., 2004. SQLrand: Preventing SQL injection attacks. In: *International Conference on Applied Cryptography and Network Security*, 8–11 June 2004 Yellow Mountains. Switzerland: Springer, 292–302.

Cavelty, M. D., 2018. Cybersecurity research meets science and technology studies. *Politics and Governance*, 6(2), 22–30.

Chouliaras, N., Kittes, G., Kantzavelou, I., Maglaras, L., Pantziou, G., Ferrag, M. A., 2021. Cyber ranges and testbeds for education, training, and research. *Applied Sciences*, 11(4), 1809.

Cone, B. D., Irvine, C. E., Thompson, M. F., Nguyen, T. D., 2007. A video game for cyber security training and awareness. *Computers and Security*, 26(1), 63–72.

Dimkov, T., Van Cleeff, A., Pieters, W., Hartel, P., 2010. Two methodologies for physical penetration testing using social engineering. In: *Proceedings of the 26th Annual Computer Security Applications Conference*, 6–10 December 2010 Austin. New York: Association for Computing Machinery, 399–408.

Felderer, M., Büchler, M., Johns, M., Brucker, A. D., Breu, R., Pretschner, A., 2016. Security testing: A survey. *Advances in Computers*, 101(1), 1–51.

Ferreira, A. M., Kleppe, H., 2011. Effectiveness of automated application penetration testing tools.

Goel, J. N., Mehtre, B. M., 2015. Vulnerability assessment & penetration testing as a cyber defence technology. *Procedia Computer Science*, 57(1), 710–715.

Goel, J. N., Asghar, M. H., Kumar, V., Pandey, S. K., 2016. Ensemble based approach to increase vulnerability assessment and penetration testing accuracy. In: *2016 International Conference on Innovation and Challenges in Cyber Security (ICICCS-INBUSH)*, 3–5 February 2016 Greater Noida. New York: IEEE, 330–335.

Groß, T., 2003. Security analysis of the SAML single sign-on browser/artifact profile. In: *19th Annual Computer Security Applications Conference*, 8–12 December 2003 Las Vegas. New York: IEEE, 298–307.

Holik, F., Horalek, J., Marik, O., Neradova, S., Zitta, S., 2014. Effective penetration testing with Metasploit framework and methodologies. *In: 2014 IEEE 15th International Symposium on Computational Intelligence and Informatics (CINTI)*, 19–21 November 2014 Budapest. New York: IEEE, 237–242.

Huang, Y. W., Tsai, C. H., Lin, T. P., Huang, S. K., Lee, D. T., Kuo, S. Y., 2005. A testing framework for web application security assessment. *Computer Networks*, 48(5), 739–761.

Jamil, M. A., Arif, M., Abubakar, N. S. A., Ahmad, A., 2016. Software testing techniques: A literature review. *In: 2016 6th International Conference on Information and Communication Technology for the Muslim World (ICT4M)*, 22–24 November 2016 Jakarta. New York: IEEE, 177–182.

Kumar, R., Tlhagadikgora, K., 2018. Internal network penetration testing using free/open source tools: Network and system administration approach. *In: International Conference on Advanced Informatics for Computing Research*, 14–15 July 2018 Shimla. Switzerland: Springer, 257–269.

Marback, A., Do, H., He, K., Kondamarri, S., Xu, D., 2013. A threat model-based approach to security testing. *Software: Practice and Experience*, 43(2), 241–258.

McDermott, J. P., 2001. Attack net penetration testing. *In: Proceedings of the 2000 Workshop on New Security Paradigms*, 18–21 September 2001 Ballycotton. New York: Association for Computing Machinery, 15–21.

Neuman, B. C., Ts'o, T., 1994. Kerberos: An authentication service for computer networks. *IEEE Communications Magazine*, 32(9), 33–38.

Salas, M. I. P., Martins, E., 2014. Security testing methodology for vulnerabilities detection of XSS in web services and WS-security. *Electronic Notes in Theoretical Computer Science*, 302(1), 133–154.

Sawant, A. A., Bari, P. H., Chawan, P. M., 2012. Software testing techniques and strategies. *International Journal of Engineering Research and Applications (IJERA)*, 2(3), 980–986.

Thacker, B. H., Riha, D. S., Fitch, S. H., Huyse, L. J., Pleming, J. B., 2006. Probabilistic engineering analysis using the NESSUS software. *Structural Safety*, 28(1–2), 83–107.

Trotter, L., Harding, M., Mikusz, M., Davies, N., 2018. IoT-enabled highway maintenance: Understanding emerging cybersecurity threats. *IEEE Pervasive Computing*, 17(3), 23–34.

Vieira, M., Antunes, N., Madeira, H., 2009. Using web security scanners to detect vulnerabilities in web services. *In: 2009 IEEE/IFIP International Conference on Dependable Systems & Networks*, 29 June-2 July 2009 Lisbon. New York: IEEE, 566–571.

Welch, V., Foster, I., Kesselman, C., Mulmo, O., Pearlman, L., Tuecke, S., Gawor, J., Meder, S., Siebenlist, F., 2004. X. 509 proxy certificates for dynamic delegation. *3rd Annual PKI R&D Workshop*, 14(1), 1–17.

Zwilling, M., Klien, G., Lesjak, D., Wiechetek, Ł., Cetin, F., Basim, H. N., 2020. Cyber security awareness, knowledge and behavior: A comparative study. *Journal of Computer Information Systems*, 1(1), 1–16.

6

Cybersecurity Exercises and Teams Definition

6.1 Need of CEs

CEs are required in field ranging from military to commercial to academics. With the advancing cyber technologies and cyber threats, the frequency of cyberattacks has also risen exponentially in the past decades. Cyberattacks can have damaging effects on cyber-infrastructure and can compromise national security, the economy, livelihood, and safety of citizens (Clark *et al.* 2016).

Preparing for such scenarios in advance is advantageous for the personnel and saves time. For example, it is not always possible to report a cyberattack to higher officials and then wait for their timely decisions. Instead having a team of personnel who have the required expertise and experience to deal with such scenarios would be more feasible. They could later provide a damage report regarding the same. CRs provide a platform for conducting CEs for personnel trainings. CEs are critical for inculcating cyber emergency management capabilities, for example, communication between the teams, decision-making, analyzing and reporting, etc., in personnel.

These exercises are helpful in testing the abilities of government employee in operating in a cyber environment and providing insights into e-government operations and vulnerabilities (Conklin *et al.* 2006). The communities participate in these exercises as they are specifically designed for testing their personnel on a frequent basis. The aim is to assess their abilities to act in response to any cyberattacks along with representing real-life scenarios or conjectural security problems presented in realistic manner (simulations) (Sommestad *et al.* 2012).

CEs are more complex in comparison to tutorials and games (Čeleda *et al.* 2015). The CDX (Schepens *et al.* 2002) is a competition where different teams design, defend, implement, and manage a cyber network. The teams focus to conduct forensic analysis and make required security configurations to the network.

CEs are beneficial for exploring and conducting the following:

- **Security competitions**
  Various cybersecurity competitions include CSAW (NYU 2021; Figure 6.1), iCTF (Shellphish 2021), and cybersecurity challenge (Anonymous 2021). These competitions can vary due to the factors such as level of participants, simulation environment used, and incentives provided. The competitions can use two approaches: defense-oriented approach and offense-oriented approach.

  The simulation environment aims to provide real-life attack scenarios where the participants would be required to learn about the vulnerabilities of the network and fix it and generate a report. Different teams are assigned with different tasks

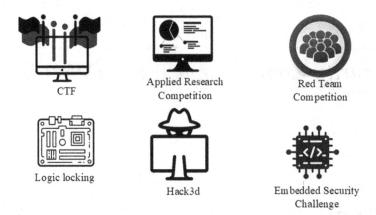

FIGURE 6.1
Security competitions organized by CSAW.

that they are required to accomplish within a given time and by the following established guidelines by the organizers. A performance report is generated for each participant as well as for the overall team.

- **Incident detection and analysis**

    These are the two of the six major steps required for an executing effective incident response as shown in Figure 6.2. Timely detection and analysis of any incident (cyberattack) facilitate in its categorization and accurate implementations of solutions and prevention of any adverse long-term impacts. In military or commercial sectors, these exercises are useful in simulating the network topology of the organization for personnel trainings against cyberattacks, finding system vulnerabilities, running security tests, and delivering a comprehensive report for the same.

    A CR can log these events and the states when an exercise is being conducted. These logs are beneficial when combined with other investigatory data to recreate

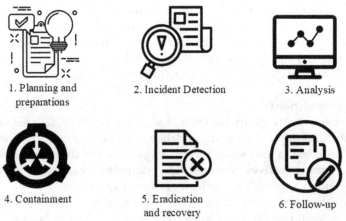

FIGURE 6.2
Steps of incident response.

a group of events occurring during the exercise. Such facility is required and significant for incident management (Mitropoulos *et al.* 2006; Werlinger *et al.* 2010) as well as forensic investigations (Meyers *et al.* 2004). Simulations of cybersecurity incidents can be useful in providing cyber threat assessments and intelligence, prevention of loss of data and IP. It also ensures response teams' readiness and a better clarity of protocols, individual roles, and establishing communication paths.

- **Improving personnel skillsets**
  To evade and respond to a cyberattack, it is important to have a team of personnel who are trained against such possible scenarios. CEs are useful for participants who have differing levels of education/training about cybersecurity, or participants with minimum grasp of concepts like internal security and spear-phishing, or participants who are more dependent on the tools and lack the knowledge to comprehend the data provided. It also helps in establishing team coordination and training personnel for prompt response to any cyberattack.

- **Identification**
  Identification can include identifying specific roles to fill w.r.t. cybersecurity, faults in the network infrastructure, reviewing faulty aspects of policies or procedures based on the identification in previous exercises. Identification can be categorized into:

  - **Technical vulnerabilities identification**: It is important to timely identify any technical flaws in the network components and architecture to prevent its exploitation by attackers. CEs also test robustness of components in a network architecture along with effectiveness of protocols that are established for incident response. These exercises are helpful in uncovering any unknown faults within the systems that may cause unpredictable technical hitches and thus preventing losses of valuable assets. CTF and military war gaming are a few examples of CEs conducted specifically for identifying vulnerabilities in cyber-oriented mechanism. Such exercises can be conducted within an organization or on large-scale basis like conducting competition or as a collective exercise between different organizations and government.

  - **Identification of policies and procedural issues**: Identification of gaps in policies or procedures developed for responses to cyberattacks is critical in ensuring cybersecurity. These gaps or areas of improvement can hider responses and/or accidentally assist in an attack. CRs provide a controlled environment where malicious attacks can be replicated without the risk of any actual damage to the infrastructure or system components. CEs highlight such faults and also provide useful insight in rectifying and enhancing the policies and procedures. Thus, reducing the impacts caused by an actual cyberattack on the network infrastructure.

- **Testing**
  It is never practical to perform any technical tests on a live cybersecurity infrastructure. CEs conducted on a CR platform can be used for testing the functioning of any new features, procedures, and components. Using simulations to test software and/or hardware prior to its deployment is commonly practiced in military and the IT industry. CEs provide a learning prospect via testing new products/features/procedures in real time without any hassle of real-world consequences.

6.2 Life Cycle of a CE

CEs can broadly be divided into three phases (Wilhelmson *et al.* 2011) as shown in Figure 6.3. Essentially, all the phases affect each other because the exercises are repeatedly held and overlapping takes place between these phases.

a. **Planning phase**

   The first stage determines the effectiveness and usefulness of the later stages. In every case, the exercise must be scoped to fit and prepare a specific subset of an organization. Depending upon the required learning outcomes and w.r.t. the requirements of the corporation, numerous exercise parameters can be extracted from the established goals and then formulated into an exercise narrative. These goals help in defining operational environment factors like functionalities, risks, threat actors, and vulnerabilities to be included in the simulation designed for exercise. Each activity's details along with the roles of each participant in the exercise need to be planned before the implementation phase is initiated.

   There are many ways for constructing exercise scenario, which is often based upon factors like threat model, availability of personnel, and specific skills that

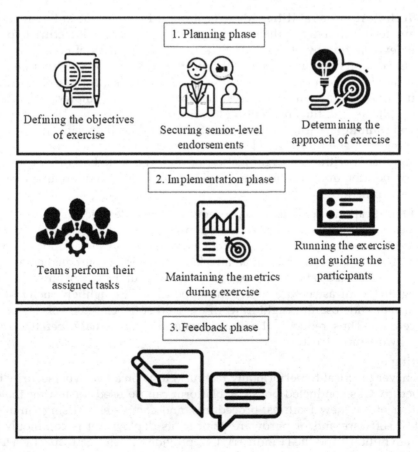

FIGURE 6.3
Phases in life cycle of CE.

would be selected after careful deliberation. The linkage between exercise's scenario and preferred learning outcomes must be specified at a level where all elements and events within the exercise are tied to some certain learning goal, thus allowing to create a technical environment incorporating the discussed goals. Without detailed planning, the technical environment created may not be able to support the learning objectives and fail in enhancing skilled performance.

It is difficult to plan an extensive CE because of various constraints, like planning time, money, and experts' readiness. The process also comprises interviewing personnel, for example, where the organizers of the exercise do not have expertise in a particular field like military or aviation and need extra support from the corporation that contracted their team.

b. **Implementation phase**

This phase differs from others in time span and it focuses on managing the exercise for achieving most of the premeditated objectives. This brings forth the necessity for keeping SA during exercise entire time. Moreover, as SA is a fundamental segment of expertise, it's often included in list of skills requiring training. Maintaining SA is among one of the challenges in directing these exercises.

SA lets the white team members to monitor participants' outcomes regarding all operation lines. During this time, the verification of participants' incident handling is also crucial. If the participants' response to the incidents do not fulfill the learning goals, the white team would adjust all the incidents to accomplish the established learning objectives. One of the most common ways of doing this is to launch new planned incidents that will bring the needed information for the participants and practically guide them toward the set learning goals.

c. **Feedback phase**

It is an essential phase of the exercise especially from individuals' learning perspectives. Accordingly, adequate time interval must be allotted for this phase. In this phase, every major operation policies and events need to be analyzed and discussed.

The participants can hence ask questions in concern with the events conducted during the CE. For most cases, it is crucial to discuss the details of course of specific incidents where the participants provide an explanation on how they responded to the given scenario and anything else they noticed concerning the exercise. This leads to the required reflection for participants toward an understanding and expectantly toward the achievements of established learning objectives.

6.3 Steps in Designing of a CE

Designing any CE entails precise planning by several personnel involved in different phases. There are seven steps essential for developing a CE as shown in Figure 6.4.

1. **Defining the necessary exercise objectives**

It is crucial for ensuring the focus of the exercise's approach. Suppose, a CE is conducted with the objective of risk analysis; it would focus on identification of the most vulnerable and critical parts of the infrastructure. The risks to be analyzed

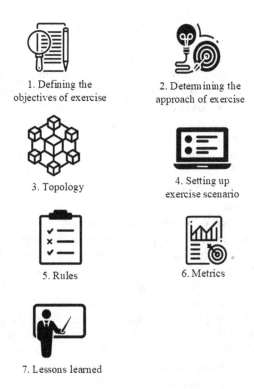

1. Defining the objectives of exercise

2. Determining the approach of exercise

3. Topology

4. Setting up exercise scenario

5. Rules

6. Metrics

7. Lessons learned

FIGURE 6.4
Design steps of a CE.

should be predetermined and based on how much harm they may do and also the chances of them occurring.

It is necessary to ensure that the participating teams have a clear understanding of the exercise's objectives and follow a well-predefined response plan. Conducting CEs for training against the infrastructure's greater threats and attacks is likely to increase endorsement opportunities. More importantly, the CEs conducted must have an established name, making it easier to differentiate and creating reference points.

To ensure all the resource needs are met, the organization's management requires rationale for running a CE. Support from the management may also increase recommendations and participations in the exercise. To secure a good funding for the resources used in the exercises, the following factors need to be addressed: focus area of the exercise and its necessity, financial and human resources required, risks or any alternatives involved, spreading awareness and communication strategies, and lastly providing regular updates on the progress of the exercises.

2. **Determining the approach of exercise**

Conducting a CE is resource intensive, and to ensure that all the objectives are fulfilled, it is necessary to select an approach that may achieve this. Demonstrating a coherent approach of the CE may also be helpful in securing endorsements. Broadly, there exist two different approaches:

a. **Tabletop exercises**: these are the dialogue-based sessions, all the team members gather for discussing their respective roles and response plans w.r.t. the cyber incident.

b. **Live-play exercises**: these are the real-time CEs, where all teams perform their respective tasks in the cyber incident simulation.

The approach selected must strengthen the exercise objectives. It is important for ensuring a thorough course of exercise for enhancing coordination among participants and teams. The following factors must be considered when deciding on an approach: exercise objectives, availability of resources, time availability for creating as well as running the exercise, which teams need to participate during the exercises.

3. **Topology of the CE conducted**
Determining the topology of the CE is useful in displaying what physical devices are live. Creating a topology map helps in displaying the interconnections of the devices and aids in their easy monitoring and ensuring proper functioning of the exercise arena. Physical devices like routers, servers, and desktops get characterized by features such as their name, IP address, logical and physical roles, and RAM.

4. **Setting up exercise scenario**
The setup of the exercise is built upon deciding the objectives and the topology. Forming bespoke teams of personnel considering their academic qualifications and IT experiences is beneficial for developing and delivering the CE to an extensive range of expertise.

Considering all the defined objectives, the participants should be provided with information about the CE like any backdrop story having real-world incidents references. Exercise injects (written or verbal) can provide relevant information, updates, guidelines for assessing participants. These may be helpful to make the CE more engaging.

While setting up a CE scenario, the following points must be taken into considerations: ensuring that the CE is as near to realistic as it can be, all the participants' activities must be monitored, identification of new lessons inferred from the exercise results and participants' performances. The timings of the CE must not clash with the organization's personnel key activity periods. This may hinder participation's as well as the organization's essential operations.

5. **Rules**
For smooth flow of the CE, it is necessary to create and circulate rules of the exercise prior. This may help the participants to adequately prepare for the CE. The rules must be defined such that they convey all the necessary contextual information, timings as well as what is expected from the participants. The rules must provide the participants a clarity of the exercise objectives and eliminate any possible confusions that may hinder the flow of the exercise.

6. **Exercise metrics**
These are useful for identifying any zones of response that may require additional development, participants' recommendations and the lessons learned during the execution of the CE. Metrics must be defined for each stage of the exercise to evaluate the performances of the teams and participants individually.

The metrics must be accurate and comprehensive for providing a holistic clarification of expected responses. Poorly defined metrics can lead to unreliable and confusing information or false lessons. While defining metrics, the following points must be considered: time taken by participants to complete the given tasks, quality of decision-making, the success rate of any taken actions, and, lastly, participants adherence to approved response plans.

7. **Lessons learned**

   Finally, these exercises must have some method of reviewing all lessons learned both by participants and organizers. Observing and recording the participants' activities and responses is useful in determining what factors worked or failed to achieve the desired objectives. Participants' feedback on conducting the exercise and its design could be crucial for further improving exercise arenas. The participants can fill a postexercise form to provide their feedbacks. This may be useful in collecting any lessons identified by participants, their recommendations, and summary of their reviews.

6.4 Different Kinds of Approaches

As mentioned in the previous section, the objectives play a major role in determining the approach of a CE. Live-play exercises can be classified into three major approaches: DOA, OOA, and mixed approach. Mostly, such exercises focus on training security administrators that require DOA. For breach testers, the approach preferred is OOA. For any wide-ranging security trainings, a mix of both approaches can be implemented, as explained below:

1. **DOA**

   In this approach, the CE aims at studying and practicing defense techniques to be implemented during any cyber incidents. These methods are more related to system administration and forensics tasks. The defender teams have to fulfill these sets of actions:

   a. **Formulating security policies**: based on previous system vulnerabilities, new security policies must be created to update the infrastructure against advanced cyber incidents.

   b. **Employing security procedures**: for example, new encryption techniques can be put to use for transmitting data via secure channels, fixing security bugs, and faulty physical components.

   c. **Security monitoring of the system and its components**: it is crucial to determine the efficacy of the formulated security policies and that they meet the said requirements. For example, to monitor unwanted network traffic, intrusion detection systems can be employed.

   d. **Security state testing after execution of procedures**: the security policies must be tested for identifying any conceivable loopholes and limitations that may cause loss of essential data.

   e. **Improving complete security of infrastructure**: all the abovementioned sets of actions are important considerations in improving security procedures to keep up with complex cyber threats and attacks.

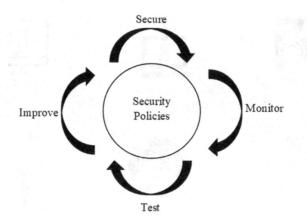

FIGURE 6.5
Security wheel.

The aforementioned set of actions comprises the "Security Wheel" as also shown in Figure 6.5. It should be implemented for securing the defended assets, monitoring system activities for early detection of any attacks and respond to them by regularly enhancing the system configurations. DOA offers the following ways for organizing the CE:

- The participants get a list of requirements as well as services that they are supposed to deliver, which they develop using their own computer systems.
- The participants have to configure and protect the provided default installations and services of specific components in a network system.
- The participants have to protect the given installed as well as configured systems from the attacker teams in the exercise environment.

An example of DOA is blue team exercise. The purpose of the exercise is to train the personnel in ensuring security of preconfigured components and gaining necessary knowledge and skills for cyber defense. These skills may include security configuration, forensic investigations of malware, or other cyber incidents.

2. **OOA**

It is also beneficial for participants to learn of the vulnerabilities or procedural issues existing in the infrastructure that can be exploited by hackers. OOA helps the participants develop a better understanding of implementing required defense measures against cyberattacks.

An example of OOA is red team exercise, which focuses on supporting the improvement of security tools and procedures against the complex cyber incidents. It simulates the protection of the infrastructure from the real-world cyber incidents. It also simulates the attack steps presented in Figure 6.6.

Other examples include conducting CE for penetration testing on targeted components and systems, detecting and assessing vulnerabilities in the system, identifying security violations, etc.

It is necessary to learn and analyze the patterns of the previous attack methodologies for developing efficient mitigation procedures or tools. OOA places the participants in an attacker's position. In this approach, the participants require

FIGURE 6.6
Tasks of Red team.

fulfilling the mentioned tasks. In an OOA, the participants must discover and exploit the vulnerabilities of a target system.

3. **Mixed approach**

   A CE can use a mix of both the abovementioned approaches to make it more comprehensive, for example, the CTF. In such exercises, the participants are split into two teams – attacker and defender teams – as illustrated in Figure 6.7. The attacker teams' aim is to collapse the working of the system by discovering and exploiting the system susceptibilities. The defender teams must fix these susceptibilities and design new security procedures for mitigating any attacks from the attacker team. Mixed approach combines all the elements of both the approaches in an exercise environment.

Table 6.1 summaries all the features and examples of previously discussed approaches.

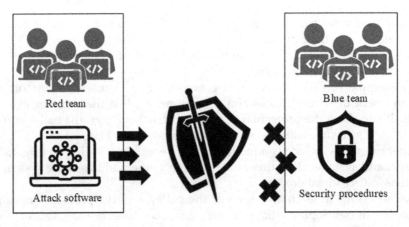

FIGURE 6.7
Mixed approach.

TABLE 6.1

Features and Examples of Different Types of Approaches Used in Designing a CE

Approach	Features	Examples
OOA	• Training personnel in security of pre-configured components. • Improving counterattack skills for neutralizing effects of cyber incidents.	• Red team exercise • Cyber Coalition
DOA	• Focuses on identification of system vulnerabilities, faulty components, and bugs. • Implementing and testing security policies and procedures.	• Blue team exercise • BCS
Mixed approach	• Real-time cyberattack and defense training. • Combination of elements from both approaches in an exercise arena.	• CTF • Locked Shields

6.5 Common Features of a CE

1. **Learning culture**

   Conducting CE ensures a learning culture within an organization. It helps in establishing the organization's resilience toward cyber incidents and practice security response plans. A CE provides a safe environment for learning and practicing with experienced personnel.

   It also helps in including the organization's values in the exercise objectives. Learning the skills to overcome the constraints, threats, and challenges only improves the organization's effectiveness in response to any cyber incidents.

2. **Scalability**

   An ideal CE can accommodate all the necessary physical resources and virtual resources for participants. It can also accommodate a huge number of participants when hosting national or international competitions.

   The CE can get updated with new complex and realistic cyber scenarios and security procedures. To fulfill all the set objectives and follow a selected approach, the design requirements of the CE can be accordingly scaled.

3. **Realistic**

   The CE provides a realistic training environment for testing security policies and new software patches, fixing system bugs, etc. It is not always feasible to replicate the entire operational network infrastructure.

   However, CEs can be used to design specific realistic infrastructure segments. The realistic environment also simulates real-world cyber threats and attacks in real time. The participants can improve on timely responding to these cyber incidents and effectively following an established response plan.

6.6 Types of CEs

There are broadly two types of CEs: full simulation and table top.

1. **Full simulation CEs**

   These are the resource-intensive exercises providing technical representation of any cyber incident. They replicate the operational network infrastructure using either physical resources or virtual resources or both. The participants are provided with realistic simulations of predefined scenarios and necessary resources to complete their respective objectives. These exercises have participants divided into different teams with different objectives to fulfill and improving on in-team communications. Hosting a full simulation exercise requires a comprehensive planning to define objectives, rules, metrics, and participants' roles. These exercises need to be planned well in advance to be able to accommodate necessary resources for its smooth execution. The exercises must also provide an immersive and interactive experience to the participants.

2. **Table-top CEs**

   These include a discussion based on a hypothetical scenario without any technological aid. These can be described as a round-table discussion on potential cyber incidents and conceivable solutions. These are aimed at discussing security policies without being under any pressure of any possible attack. They don't focus on personnel preparedness against any cyber incident scenario. They focus on building abstract solutions and developing policies. Unlike full simulations, table-top exercises are hosted in an informal setting. The exercises require fewer resources and are flexible to accommodate any number of participants.

Table 6.2 compares previously discussed types of CEs.

TABLE 6.2

Comparison Between Types of CEs

	Table-Top CEs	Full Simulation CEs
Description	It is a paper pen–driven discussion where the organizers provide scripted injects.	It is a real-time, realistic simulation of cyberattack on network infrastructure for personnel training.
Objectives	• Determining response plan of cybersecurity personnel to an incident. • Validating security procedures. • Observing and describing the processes for detecting vulnerabilities and defining a set of tools to be used for recovery.	• Training the organization personnel. • Identifying system vulnerabilities that are likely to be exploited and fixing them. • Testing security software patches and security policies. • Learning about new cyber incident scenarios and training to follow an established response plan.
Advantages	• Helpful in initiating communications among individual participants and various teams. • Sharing security Intel among other experts, partners, and organizations. • Testing skills of personnel for response capabilities against any cyberattack. • Raising awareness about cybersecurity within the organization communities.	• Provides real-time and realistic simulations. • Acts as a software and tool testing platform. New security tools, software, fixes can be safely tested in the simulations without having any consequences in a live network infrastructure. • It is useful for training and assessing the performance of personnel.
Complexity and number of resources required	These types of exercises can be planned and executed within a span of a few days. The resources require comparatively less resources which majorly depend on the number of participants involved.	These exercises require a comprehensive and detailed planning like defining objectives, rules, metrics, participants' roles, etc. The exercise requires extensive physical and virtual resources to fulfill all the objectives and ensure a proper flow of events.

6.6.1 Examples of CEs

Many examples of CEs are mentioned across the chapter, some of which are discussed and described in this section too.

1. **CTF**

   It is a cybersecurity contest where every participant must complete certain assigned tasks to access the servers for capturing the flag (an encoded string) from some secret file. Participants require to use their hacking skills to capture these flags and put them in the CTF server. The points get allotted depending on the complexity of each task. The team or the individual participant with maximum scores wins the competition.

   CTF comprises three different style events:

   - **Jeopardy style:** this requires solving a series of tasks using cybersecurity skills to capture the bits of encoded string. A new stage unlocks only after successfully completing previous stage. This style includes cryptography, pawning, steganography, forensics, and web-related challenges.

   - **Attack-defense style:** this requires two groups who compete against one another. The objective is to break into the security of another group to obtain the flag, and in the meantime, to also ensure the security of one own's systems from the opponent. Prior to the beginning of the competition, sometime is allotted to both groups for identifying the susceptibilities in their systems and fixing those. This style requires smooth coordination between team members for scoring maximum points.

   - **Mixed style:** it is a blend of both the above-discussed styles. The competition may have an attack-defense setup with jeopardy-style challenges or vice versa.

2. **Red team competition**

   It is used as a cybersecurity technique for assessing the security capabilities of an organization's infrastructure. Red team competitions also use simulated attack scenario.

   The participants and teams are assigned tasks such as identification, exploitation, and reporting the infrastructure's vulnerabilities.

   The main objective is to deliberately penetrate the defenses of an entity's infrastructure with their knowledge and identify faulty components, security loopholes, bugs, and other weaknesses. Red team competition is not same as the red team-blue team competition. This competition helps in providing the necessary experience to participants for detecting and quarantining any cyberattack. New security policies and tools can be developed based on the system vulnerability report obtained from the competition.

3. **Cybersecurity workshops and discussions**

   These are an example of table-top CEs. They are helpful in security policy analysis and identification of bottlenecks in communications. These require relatively less resources. These are advantageous for military personnel because these CEs are not time-consuming and do not require extensive preparations. They can be conducted in a matter of hours rather than days for some simulations. The workshops can utilize any scenario for planning and working through without employing any technical resources like in the case of full simulations.

4. **Locked shields**

   This exercise was developed for encouraging trainings, experimentation, and collaboration among NATO, CCDCOE, and other partner nations' members. It is an international, real-time, red team versus blue team competition involving military, business, and critical infrastructure simulations.

   The competition focuses on strategic decision-making to practice and improve in-team coordination and communications. It also focuses on realistic complex infrastructure scenarios by simulating real-world like massive cyberattack incident. The teams must ensure specialized systems' protection, provide reliable situation reports, detect and respond to the attacks using coordinated teamwork.

5. **BCS**

   It was an international cyber defense exercise conducted in 2010. The BCS involved six blue teams, comprising public, private, and academic sectors personnel. Their main was to protect virtual system networks against attacks from red team. The simulation scenario described a SCADA system needed to be protected by the cybersecurity teams (blue teams) against the hacker groups (red teams). The exercise rules were developed and managed by the white team. The green team was tasked with setting up of the technical infrastructure and other facilities like logging, recording, communications, etc. The shortcomings of the exercise included setting too many objectives, insufficient resources, and unforeseen real complexities of accommodating many participants.

6.7 Teams Definition

A typical CE involves different types of participants, usually grouped into teams according to the specific roles they play in a CE. Depending on numerous varied cyber exercises, not all the teams may be involved. The following are the four main teams commonly found in every CE:

- **Red team**: generally, this team aims at finding the vulnerabilities in the network, and exploiting those faults to collapse the system. This team uses real-time security tools to simulate real-world security incidents and cyberattacks. Their role comprises attackers gaining unauthorized access to the system to cripple its defenses. The team members can use both external attacks and insider threats like disgruntled employees during the exercise for compromising the entire system.

- **Blue team**: it is responsible for responses as well as security of the network infrastructure of an organization. Its task is the detection of any cyberattacks and providing suitable responses to mitigate the breaches and attacks led by red team. Based upon type and purpose of a CE, this team can have SOC teams or include staff from IT or operations. Eventually, its aim is to detect security attacks early and defend the infrastructure in real time.

- **White team**: it is responsible for supervising the execution of the CE while ensuring that all teams respect the rules and assist the active teams with any support issues. It also certifies that the exercise results are exact according to the prior set scoring rules as well as the tasks performed by different teams. This team can have authors of the exercise, administrators of platform as well as professionals who have overseen executions of more CEs.

- **Green team**: Its responsibilities during the execution of a CE include improving communication between all the present teams, maintaining, and mending faults identified and reported by blue team. In context of CEs, it signifies authentic users of an organization, thus presenting legitimate as well as realistic network traffic, and application logs, etc. This team is often modeled via traffic-replay, web-browser simulators, and much more advanced tools and techniques.

6.8 Conclusions

CRs are crucial for providing the suitable environment for conducting CEs. CEs are essential for the implementation of cyber SA concepts along with training personnel. It is not advisable to perform test of new procedures or fixes on a live cyber system; and so, they are executed during CEs. This not only helps in analyzing the working of new fixes and their adaptability in the infrastructure but also prevents any real-consequence disasters. The life cycle of CE can be divided into three phases – planning, implementation, and feedback. As the exercises are held often, these phases tend to overlap with each other. A few of the important features of CEs include establishing a learning culture, scalability, providing realistic scenarios. CTF, red team competitions, workshops, and discussions, etc. are some examples of CEs. Although CEs are vital for any organizations' or governments' cyber network and architecture, it still faces numerous challenges like cost of implementation, updating the exercise which often conflicts with the set of existing objectives. The most important component of a CE is its teams. Participants are generally divided into four teams, and this may vary depending on the objectives of the exercise. The four teams – red, blue, white and green, each require fulfilling their allotted tasks during the exercise. Red team is responsible for finding the vulnerabilities in the cyberinfrastructure and exploits them. Blue team needs to block the attacks from red team and find and fix the vulnerabilities with the help of green team. The white team is responsible for regulating the rules and flow of the exercise. For a successful learning experience, it's important for the teams to train together and improve on their cybersecurity skills.

References

Anonymous, 2021. Cyber security challenge [online].Available from: https://www.cybersecuritychallenge.org.uk/ [Accessed 03 Feb 2021].

Čeleda, P., Čegan, J., Vykopal, J., Tovarňák, D., 2015. Kypo – A platform for cyber defence exercises. *In*: M&S Support to Operational Tasks Including War Gaming, Logistics, Cyber Defence, 5–9 October 2015 Munich. Germany: NATO Science and Technology Organization, 1–12.

Clark, R. M., Hakim, S., 2016. Protecting critical infrastructure at the state and local level. *In:* R. M. Clark, S. Hakim, eds., *Cyber-Physical Security*. Switzerland: Springer, 1–17.

Conklin, A., White, G. B., 2006. E-government and cyber security: The role of cyber security exercises. *In*: 39th Annual Hawaii International Conference on System Sciences, 4–7 January 2006 Kauai. New York: IEEE, 1–8.

Meyers, M., Rogers, M., 2004. Computer forensics: The need for standardization and certification. *International Journal of Digital Evidence*, 3(2), 1–11.

Mitropoulos, S., Patsos, D., Douligeris, C., 2006. On incident handling and response: A state-of-the-art approach. *Computers & Security*, 25(5), 351–370.

NYU Tandon School of Engineering, 2021. CSAW – CyberSecurity competition [online]. Available from: https://www.csaw.io/ [Accessed 03 Feb 2021].

Schepens, W., Ragsdale, D., Surdu, J. R., Schafer, J., 2002. The cyber defense exercise: An evaluation of the effectiveness of information assurance education. *The Journal of Information Security*, 1(2), 1–14.

Shellphish Team, 2021. The UCSB iCTF [online]. Available from: https://ictf.cs.ucsb.edu/ [Accessed 03 Feb 2021].

Sommestad, T., Hallberg, J., 2012. Cyber security exercises and competitions as a platform for cyber security experiments. *In*: A. Jøsang, B. Carlsson, eds., Nordic Conference on Secure IT Systems, 31 October–2 November 2012 Sweden. Switzerland: Springer, 47–60.

Werlinger, R., Muldner, K., Hawkey, K., Beznosov, K., 2010. Preparation, detection, and analysis: The diagnostic work of IT security incident response. *Information Management & Computer Security*, 18(1), 26–42.

Wilhelmson, N., Svensson, T., 2011. *Handbook for Planning, Running and Evaluating Information Technology and Cyber Security Exercises*. Sweden: Försvarshögskolan (FHS).

7

Simulation and Emulation Environments

7.1 Emulation Environment

It represents the network infrastructure using a group of substitute systems and some components of SUT (Göktürk 2007). Figure 7.1 represents the layout of emulation environment. Thus, the realism provided by the replication of SUT varies depending on the components of the setup. Many CRs are developed to support emulation environments, for example, NCR (read more in Section 9.3.1), JIOR (read more in Section 9.3.2), Emulab (read more in Section 10.2.3), and DETER (read more in Section 10.2.4). Some of the factors guiding the designing of an emulation environment are:

- **Cost of experimentation**: constructing emulation environment is economical in comparison to simulation environments. However, emphasis must be given on calculating the overall cost and cost of alterations that may be necessary for incorporating new test conditions and relevant equipment.
- **Instantaneous execution**: emulation environments can lapse the time according to the training or experiment activities. Time can also be emulated and controlled to move slowly or fast. Therefore, making it possible to execute tasks using actual applications instantaneously.
- **Regulating environment conditions**: the operators have complete control over the set environment conditions and working of components. However, actual SUT components used in the environment cannot be altered or intervened. Only emulated components can be regulated by the operators according to training objectives.
- **Result generation**: as emulated environments comprise actual SUT components, which improves the realism features, they may provide insightful end results. However, if the environment uses several simplistic emulated components, the end-results may not be suitable for use in analyses. These results may or may not be completely accurate.
- **User friendliness**: the emulation environment uses either preexisting models or modules for constructing scenarios. Emulation environments are composed of library of training, testing and research modules, APIs, preexiting events, etc.; therefore, providing mobile and operational resource capabilities.

7.1.1 Need for Emulation Environment

Emulation environments are majorly used as testbeds for conducting trainings and research. However, to be more specific emulations are majorly for assessing end-to-end

DOI: 10.1201/9781003206071-7

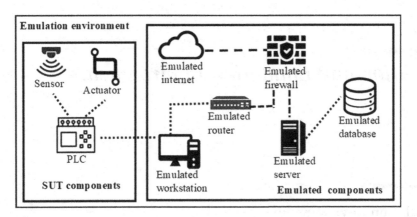

FIGURE 7.1
Layout of emulation environment.

systems' or protocols' performances (Lochin *et al.* 2012). It can also be used for preservation purposes. (Van der Hoeven *et al.* 2007) constructed an emulator for preserving digital
objects. It emphasizes providing a secured and sustained availability for the objects to
be preserved. Since the emulation environments are concerned with recreating the actual
systems, it will be ideal for emulating the original conditions and components used for
creation of digital objects.

It is also useful in handling obsolete hardware and obsolete software (Van der Hoeven
2012). Subsequent conversion of digital files from one format to another may lead to loss
of information. However, this may be prevented if the file gets recreated in the emulation
environment based on original system. Figure 7.2 illustrates a similar process. It can also

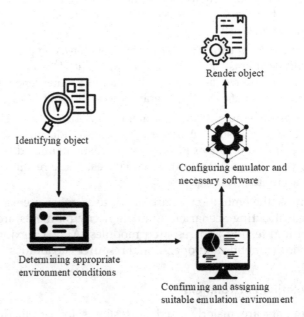

FIGURE 7.2
Steps to render objects in emulation environment.

be used and coordinated with any complex network simulator (Weingärtner *et al.* 2008). It provides an extensive environment for research in cybersecurity-related aspects like DoS, information and wireless security, and botnets (Mirkovic *et al.* 2010).

7.1.2 Types of Emulation Models

Emulation environments comprise constructing various scenarios. Majority of these scenarios can be classified into static, event-driven, and trace-based models (Lochin *et al.* 2012). As shown in Figure 7.3, these are a part of the network model of the emulation system.

- **Static model**: in this model, all the parameters are constant during the execution of any session (experiment, training, etc.) in the environment. Therefore, it is necessary to configure the parameters' settings prior to the session. It focuses on representing rational cases of artificial QoS (Lochin *et al.* 2012). It is used for testing all the prospects of a product, protocol, or service. For example, Dummynet (Rizzo 1997).

- **Event-driven model**: it is useful for schematic representation of general behaviors of a product, service, or protocol (Lochin *et al.* 2012). The SUT gets validated and compared with other SUTs under the set event conditions. These events can be clock ticks, packet numbers, etc., for example, Netshaper (Herrscher *et al.* 2002) and KauNet (Garcia *et al.* 2007).

- **Trace-based model**: it provides more realistic scenarios as the network behavior gets replicated and represented same as the original. As it is nondeterministic, it is not capable of complete replication of network behavior (Lochin *et al.* 2012). For conducting evaluations, it implements existing traces which represent intricate mobility.

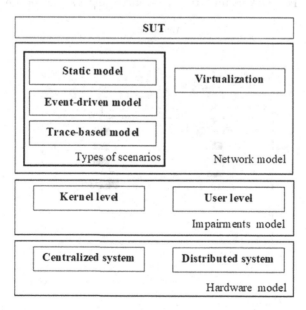

FIGURE 7.3
Emulation system architecture.

7.1.3 Emulators

This subsection discusses some of the most prominently used emulators: Dummynet, NetEm, and NIST Net.

7.1.3.1 Dummynet

This model was initially developed by FreeBSD. It is inserted within an operative protocol stack as shown in figure 7.4 for running experiments on separate system. It intercepts communications taking place among protocol layer; replicating an actual network with fixed-size queues, limited bandwidth, and delays in communication. The emulator provides absolute control over the running parameters, user-friendliness, and facilitates the usage of actual traffic generators (Rizzo 1997). It can support execution of several experiments on single system. Carbone *et al.* (2010) provide suggestions for further extending the capabilities of the emulator. It can execute several scheduling algorithms. It is employed on OSs like Linux, Windows, and MacOS. It uses pipes for implementing queues (rq, pq), link, scheduler, bandwidth, etc. The emulator also allows creation of multiple pipes, transfer of traffic to other pipes, etc. (Vanhonacker 2003).

7.1.3.2 NetEm

It provides emulation functionality on Linux OS for the testing protocols using emulated WAN (Hemminger 2005). It is capable of emulating loss, delay, and shuffling effects. It comprises a kernel module and CLI (Hemminger 2005). The kernel is responsible for queuing discipline control, and CLI is responsible for its configuration. It comprises private and nested FIFO queues (Hemminger 2005). These queues are used for prioritizing network traffic and controlling network congestions. Although it also supports numerous different queuing disciplines, it hosts network degradation at "link" level.

The emulator implements packet loss by dropping some packets randomly prior to sending them to a queue. For packet emulations, it clones the packets randomly prior to sending

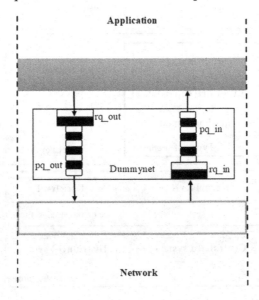

FIGURE 7.4
Dummynet operation.

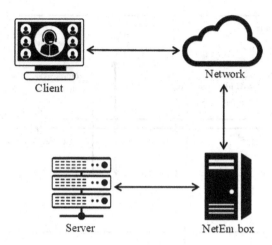

FIGURE 7.5
NetEm setup.

them to a waiting queue. The jitter emulated is comparitively lower than the provided input (Jurgelionis *et al.* 2011). Jitter can be described as variation parameters expressed by standard deviation, average value, and correlation (Jurgelionis *et al.* 2011). NetEm box (Ahmad *et al.* 2020) is a modified form of the emulator. It consists of a finite buffer. When the buffer gets full because of repetitive high delays, packet loss occurs. Therefore, it establishes a correlation between delays and packet loss similar to the actual setup. Figure 7.5 represents the NetEm setup in a network infrastructure.

7.1.3.3 NIST Net

Its first release was in 1998 and its last version in 2005. It was developed as a common-purpose tool for emulation of IP networks' performances under various network conditions. It allows complete user control over the environment applications and protocols. It is capable of emulating loss conditions caused by congestion, asymmetric bandwidth, etc. It provided the following features (Fanney *et al.* 2014):

- It inexpensively emulates intricate scenarios of network performances like bandwidth limitation, packet shuffling and replication, congestion, etc.
- Its GUI supports monitoring and selecting exclusive traffic streams going via router. It can also modify the characteristics of IP packets.
- It also supports extensions via packet handlers like data collection, packets' time stamping, etc.

The architecture of NIST Net as shown in Figure 7.6 comprises live Linux kernel. It comprises (Carson *et al.* 2003):

- **Kernel module**: it is responsible for connecting the Linux network with the instantaneous clock code. It also exports APIs.
- **User interfaces**: they are responsible for configuring and controlling emulated kernel operations by using APIs.

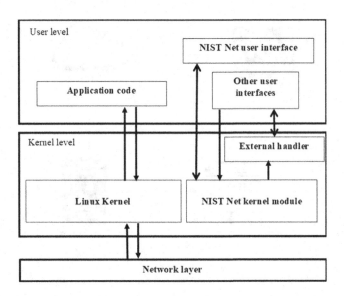

FIGURE 7.6
Architecture of NIST Net.

7.2 Simulation Environment

Ingalls (2011) describes simulation environment as a copy or a model of an actual SUT. It is crucial for network research as many research communities not only use and study it but have also developed target-specific simulations. Simulation environment provides the following advantages (Guruprasad *et al.* 2005):

- The executed scenarios can be reused and operated for experimentation purposes.
- Its components are comparatively easier to configure unlike the emulation environment.
- The environment is written in high-level languages like JAVA, C++, etc.
- It provides high realism by replicating all the components of the network infra-structure as shown in Figure 7.7.
- It is an ideal platform for analyzing system vulnerabilities at several abstraction levels.

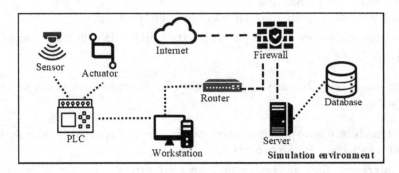

FIGURE 7.7
Layout of simulation environment.

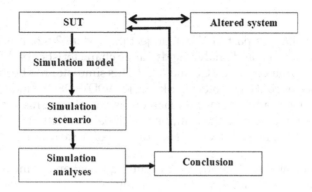

FIGURE 7.8
Basic processes of simulation.

Figure 7.8 shows some of the basic process involved for conducting simulation. The behavior and characteristics of an actual SUT can be simulated using a simulation model. The simulation model supports execution of different scenarios. After the execution is over, it also provides all the logs and components' performance data, etc. for analyses. The obtained results can be incorporated in the SUT.

7.2.1 Need for Simulation Environment

Simulation environments have been in popular use over the decades majorly for education, network research, and for problem solving in critical infrastructures.

- In education sector, simulation environments are ideal for teaching purposes as they help student in visualizing complex relations and for enhancing problem solving skills (Kincaid *et al.* 2003). Technical subjects like science and mathematics can be taught in collective and applied approach. It also helps in training the students in cybersecurity aspects implemented widely in today's industries.

- For research, simulation environments are useful as they are event-based. They are capable of modeling distinct events like packets' arrival and exit. It can also be used for conducting evaluations of anomaly detectors (Ringberg *et al.* 2008).

- Simulation testbeds are also used for experimenting security mechanisms and ensuring cybersecurity of HANs against cyberattacks and threats (Tong *et al.* 2014).

- It is often used in assessing the vulnerabilities and developing mitigation processes for critical infrastructures like smart grids (Le *et al.* 2019), supply chains (Li *et al.* 2021), and IoT devices (Ahanger 2018).

- It is also required for modeling cyberattacks on military-based autonomous vehicle like UAV, UGS (Bergin 2015).

- It is also used for construction of flexible and scalable virtual laboratories for understanding and studying IA and IO concepts (Murphy *et al.* 2014).

7.2.2 Simulators

This subsection discusses some of the most prominently used simulators: NS_2, NS_3, OMNET++, and QualNet.

7.2.2.1 NS$_2$

It was developed in 1995 as part of VINT project (Siraj *et al.* 2012). It is an event-specific simulator used for studying and analyzing dynamic characteristics of different communication networks and protocols like TCP and UDP. This simulator has been used for analyzing the performance of routing protocols like DSR, AODV, DSDV, and OLSR (Mohapatra *et al.* 2012). Its one major advantage is its lack of visualization. This makes it difficult to modify parameters and assemble the components (Jubair *et al.* 2016).

As shown in Figure 7.9, its architecture is composed of (Issariyakul *et al.* 2009):

- **SEC**: it is responsible for accepting the input argument and name of the Tcl script. It also generates simulation trace files for analyses.
- **Programming languages**: it supports C++ and OTcl. C++ is responsible for defining the backend of simulation object. OTcl is responsible for arrangement and configuration of object and its frontend. OTcl manages user interactions. Both languages are connected via TclCl.

7.2.2.2 NS$_3$

It is an event-specific simulator used majorly for education and research. It is like the NS$_2$ simulator, but it is not its newer version. Both are independently developed simulators. Unlike NS$_2$, it completely supports both python and C++. Its architecture composes of internal interface and application interface (Zarrad *et al.* 2017). It was coded in C++ constituting a scripting interface in python as in Figure 7.10. It also offers virtualization capabilities and supports open-source contribution.

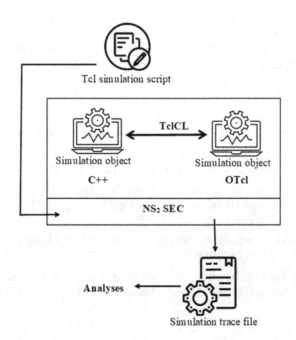

FIGURE 7.9
Architecture layout of NS$_2$.

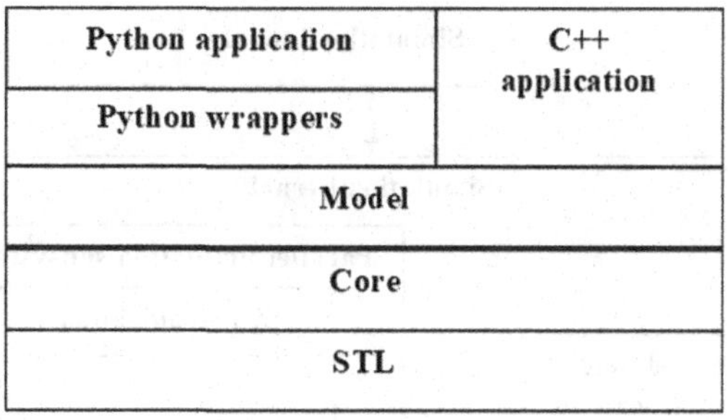

Python application	C++ application
Python wrappers	
Model	
Core	
STL	

FIGURE 7.10
NS$_3$ architecture.

As shown in Figure 7.11, NS$_3$ comprises the following modules (Carneiro 2010):

- **Core**: it is responsible for logging, tracing, and callback operations. It consists of random variables, smart pointers, attributes, etc.
- **Common**: it composes of packets and information like packet tags, headers, and other files.
- **Simulator**: it is responsible for scheduling events.
- **Node**: it is the node class comprising address types, queues, sockets, etc.
- **Mobility**: it comprises mobility models.
- **Helper**: it composes of high-level wrapper(s). It is concerned with scripting.

7.2.2.3 OMNET++

It is a modular, component-based, open-architecture, and event-specific simulator (Siraj *et al.* 2012). It is most commonly used for computer network and queuing simulations. It comprises C++ library used for creating simulation module, channels, etc. It can also support parallel execution of simulations. As shown in Figure 7.12, its architecture comprises a configurable communication library (Varga *et al.* 2008). The modules communicate via message passing. The active modules are coded in C++. Active modules can also

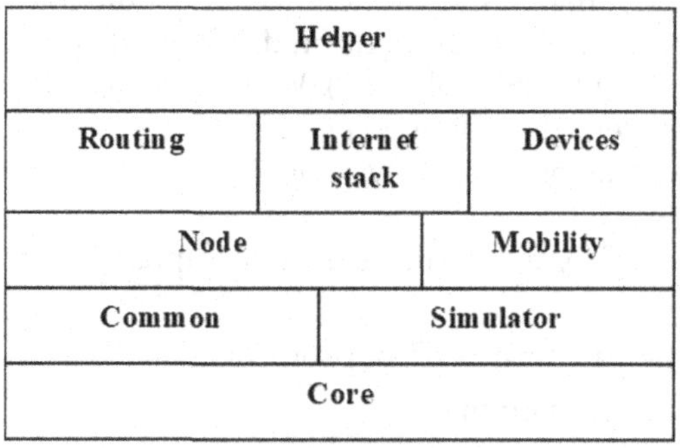

Helper		
Routing	Internet stack	Devices
Node		Mobility
Common		Simulator
Core		

FIGURE 7.11
NS$_3$ modules.

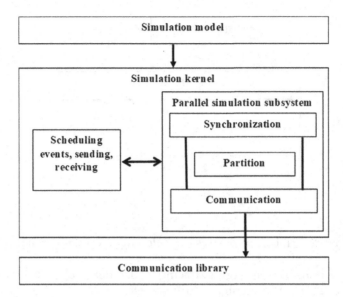

FIGURE 7.12
OMNET++ logical architecture.

be grouped together forming compound modules. The most common tasks executed by active modules include sending and receiving messages.

Its class library covers many common tasks providing the ability for random number generations from independent streams. The library comprises queues and container classes. The simulator also supports the simulation's routing traffic conditions (Varga *et al.* 2008). The simulator uses NED as its GUI, thus enabling parametric topologies (Varga *et al.* 2008). This is an advantage of the simulator over NS₂. As topologies in NS_2 are coded in Tcl. Thus, OMNET++ is favorable for executing extensive simulations.

7.2.2.4 QualNet

It provides network simulations of high fidelity for predicting device performance in wired and wireless networks (Varga *et al.* 2008). It is ideal for conducting extensive and heterogeneous network simulations. It uses C++ for implementation of latest protocols. It uses PARSEC for executing simple operations on distributed systems. It is used in evaluating the performance of WiMAX (Shuaib 2009). With QualNet 5.0 comes GUI program for development of network scenarios (Dinesh *et al.* 2014).

The simulator provides the following advantages:

- As shown in Figure 7.13, its architecture is composed of layered and modular stacks.
- Provides rapid prototype formation of protocols.
- Each layer has a fixed measurement.
- It has APIs for protocol arrangement across various layers.
- It is scalable and flexible and supports parallel execution of simulations.
- Protocol and system modeling are possible via GUI.

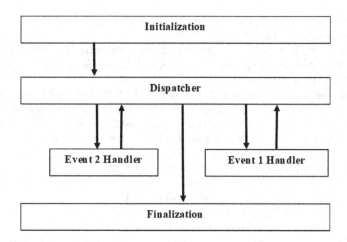

FIGURE 7.13
QualNet architecture.

References

Ahanger, T. A., 2018. Defense scheme to protect IoT from cyber attacks using AI principles. *International Journal of Computers Communications & Control*, 13(6), 915–926.

Ahmad, N., Wahab, A., Schormans, J., 2020. Importance of cross-correlation of QoS metrics in network emulators to evaluate QoE of video streaming applications. *In: 2020 11th International Conference on Network of the Future (NoF)*, 12–14 October 2020 Bordeaux. New York: IEEE, 43–47.

Bergin, D. L., 2015. Cyber-attack and defense simulation framework. *The Journal of Defense Modeling and Simulation*, 12(4), 383–392.

Carbone, M., Rizzo, L., 2010. Dummynet revisited. *ACM SIGCOMM Computer Communication Review*, 40(2), 12–20.

Carneiro, G., 2010. NS-3: Network simulator 3. *UTM Lab Meeting April*, 20(1), 4–5.

Carson, M., Santay, D., 2003. NIST Net: A Linux-based network emulation tool. *ACM SIGCOMM Computer Communication Review*, 33(3), 111–126.

Dinesh, S., Sonal, G., 2014. Qualnet simulator. *International Journal of Information & Computation Technology*, 4(13), 1349–1354.

Fanney, H., Healy, W. M., 2014. Design challenges of the NIST net zero energy residential test facility. *NIST Technical Note*, 1(1), 1–73.

Garcia, J., Conchon, E., Pérennou, T., Brunstrom, A., 2007. KauNet: Improving reproducibility for wireless and mobile research. *In: Proceedings of the 1st International Workshop on System Evaluation for Mobile Platforms*, 11 June 2007 San Juan Puerto Rico. New York: Association for Computing Machinery, 21–26.

Göktürk, E., 2007. A stance on emulation and testbeds, and a survey of network emulators and testbeds. *Proceedings of ECMS*, 1(1), 13–18.

Guruprasad, S., Ricci, R., Lepreau, J., 2005. Integrated network experimentation using simulation and emulation. *In: First International Conference on Testbeds and Research Infrastructures for the DEvelopment of NeTworks and COMmunities*, 23–25 February 2005 Trento. New York: IEEE, 204–212.

Hemminger, S., 2005. Network emulation with NetEm. *Linux conf au*, 18–23 April Canberra. Australia: Linux, 5, 1–9.

Herrscher, D., Rothermel, K., 2002. A dynamic network scenario emulation tool. *In: Proceedings of Eleventh International Conference on Computer Communications and Networks*, 16–16 October 2002 Miami. New York: IEEE, 262–267.

Ingalls, R. G., 2011. Introduction to simulation. *In: Proceedings of the 2011 Winter Simulation Conference (WSC)*, 11–14 December 2011 Phoenix. New York: IEEE, 1374–1388.

Issariyakul, T., Hossain, E., 2009. Introduction to network simulator 2 (NS2). *In: Introduction to Network Simulator NS2*. Cham: Springer, 1–18.

Jubair, M., Muniyandi, R., 2016. NS2 simulator to evaluate the effective of nodes number and simulation time on the reactive routing protocols in MANET. *International Journal of Applied Engineering Research*, 11(23), 11394–11399.

Jurgelionis, A., Laulajainen, J. P., Hirvonen, M., Wang, A. I., 2011. An empirical study of NetEm network emulation functionalities. *In: 2011 Proceedings of 20th international conference on computer communications and networks (ICCCN)*, 31 July–4 August 2011 Lahaina. New York: IEEE, 1–6.

Kincaid, J. P., Hamilton, R., Tarr, R. W., Sangani, H., 2003. Simulation in education and training. *In: Applied System Simulation*. Cham: Springer, 437–456.

Le, T. D., Anwar, A., Beuran, R., Loke, S. W., 2019. Smart grid co-simulation tools: Review and cybersecurity case study. *In: 2019 7th International Conference on Smart Grid (icSmartGrid)*, 9–11 December 2019 Newcastle. New York: IEEE, 39–45.

Li, Y., Xu, L., 2021. Cybersecurity investments in a two-echelon supply chain with third-party risk propagation. *International Journal of Production Research*, 59(4), 1216–1238.

Lochin, E., Perennou, T., Dairaine, L., 2012. When should I use network emulation? *Annals of Telecommunications – annales des télécommunications*, 67(5), 247–255.

Mirkovic, J., Benzel, T. V., Faber, T., Braden, R., Wroclawski, J. T., Schwab, S., 2010. The DETER project: Advancing the science of cyber security experimentation and test. *In: 2010 IEEE International Conference on Technologies for Homeland Security (HST)*, 8–10 November 2010 Waltham. New York: IEEE, 1–7.

Mohapatra, S., Kanungo, P., 2012. Performance analysis of AODV, DSR, OLSR and DSDV routing protocols using NS2 Simulator. *Procedia Engineering*, 30(1), 69–76.

Murphy, J., Sihler, E., Ebben, M., Wilson, G., 2014. Building a virtual cybersecurity collaborative learning laboratory (VCCLL). *In: 2014 World Congress in Computer Science, Conference Proceedings: Computer Engineering and Applied Computing*, 21–24 July 2014 Las Vegas. CSREA Press, 1–5.

Ringberg, H., Roughan, M., Rexford, J., 2008. The need for simulation in evaluating anomaly detectors. *ACM SIGCOMM Computer Communication Review*, 38(1), 55–59.

Rizzo, L., 1997. Dummynet: A simple approach to the evaluation of network protocols. *ACM SIGCOMM Computer Communication Review*, 27(1), 31–41.

Shuaib, K. A., 2009. A performance evaluation study of WIMAX using Qualnet. *Proceedings of the World Congress on Engineering*, 1(1), 1–3.

Siraj, S., Gupta, A., Badgujar, R., 2012. Network simulation tools survey. *International Journal of Advanced Research in Computer and Communication Engineering*, 1(4), 199–206.

Tong, J., Sun, W., Wang, L., 2014. A smart home network simulation testbed for cybersecurity experimentation. *In: International Conference on Testbeds and Research Infrastructures*, 5–7 May 2014 Guangzhou. Switzerland: Springer, 136–145.

Van der Hoeven, J., 2012. The need for emulation services. *PIK-Praxis der Informationsverarbeitung und Kommunikation*, 35(4), 235–239.

Van der Hoeven, J., Lohman, B., Verdegem, R., 2007. Emulation for digital preservation in practice: The results. *The International Journal of Digital Curation*, 2(2), 123–132.

Vanhonacker, W. A., 2003. Evaluation of the FreeBSD dummynet network performance simulation tool on a Pentium 4-based Ethernet Bridge. *M CAIA Technical Report 0312*, 1(1), 1–8.

Varga, A., Hornig, R., 2008. An overview of the OMNeT++ simulation environment. *In: Proceedings of the 1st International Conference on Simulation Tools and Techniques for Communications, Networks and Systems & Workshops*, 03–07 March 2008 Marseille. Brussels: ICST (Institute for Computer Sciences, Social-Informatics and Telecommunications Engineering), 1–10.

Weingärtner, E., Schmidt, F., Heer, T., Wehrle, K., 2008. Synchronized network emulation: Matching prototypes with complex simulations. *ACM SIGMETRICS Performance Evaluation Review*, 36(2), 58–63.

Zarrad, A., Alsmadi, I., 2017. Evaluating network test scenarios for network simulators systems. *International Journal of Distributed Sensor Networks*, 13(10), 1–17.

8

Designing a Cyber Range

8.1 Planning Phase

This phase is necessary for brainstorming and discussing:

- **The purpose for constructing a CR**: it is necessary to have well-defined objectives, as they would guide the further design processes, for example, the CR can be constructed for training purposes, education, operations, testing, or research.
- **Architecture**: the size of the CR and types of equipment and resources to be used for its construction need to be properly estimated for providing a consistent and realistic platform.
- **Cost**: constructing a CR is an expensive project. Therefore, it is important to conduct cost analyses for determining a budget and recognize sources for funding.
- **Approach**: developing and deciding the most suitable approach for CR construction, facilitates timely progress.

For successful designing and construction of a CR, it is crucial to compare and decide on these matters. Frank *et al.* (2017) describe seven steps as shown in Figure 8.1 of design life cycle of a CR.

8.1.1 Security Challenges Supported by the CR

Most of the existing CRs are event specific or role specific. Therefore, the tasks of the CR must be predefined in the planning phase. Some of the most common categories of security challenges as shown in Figure 8.2 and appearing in CRs are as follows (Chouliaras *et al.* 2021):

- **Web**: challenges in this category involve finding vulnerabilities in the provided web applications or websites. Finding the vulnerability gains the participants' secret flags. These challenges assist in learning web security-related concepts and procedures.
- **Cryptography**: challenges in this category involve breaking basic cryptographic protocol or rectifying errors in its implementations. Decrypting secret messages gains the participants' points and access to subsequent rounds. These challenges provide an insight into cryptography-related protocols.
- **Forensics**: challenges in this category involve finding-specified information that is hidden in the provided network traffic, memory dumps or log files, etc. These challenges are often used for incident response trainings.

DOI: 10.1201/9781003206071-8

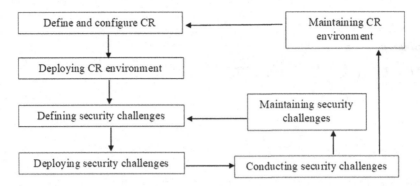

FIGURE 8.1
CR design life cycle steps.

- **Exploitation:** challenges in this category involve locating vulnerabilities in provided applications and exploiting them. These challenges are beneficial for improving offensive and defensive security-related skills.

- **Steganography:** challenges in this category involve finding-hidden encrypted data among the provided files or applications. These challenges are beneficial for understanding the importance of steganography and other related concepts.

- **Reversing:** challenges in this category involve discovering the working of a binary file into revealing a hidden flag. These challenges are beneficial for understanding reverse engineering and related analyst skills.

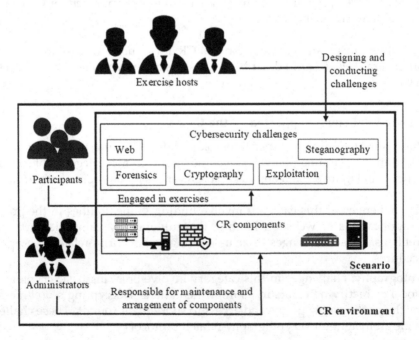

FIGURE 8.2
Security challenge setup.

8.1.2 Components for CR

Modern CRs use different virtualization, like VMWare (Nieh *et al.* 2000), and open source technologies, like OpenStack (Sefraoui *et al.* 2012) and Terraform (Brikman 2019), for implementing scenarios, replicating network settings, etc. The quantity and types of components may vary in different CRs. It depends on the size of the CR and its functionalities. However, some of the core components are common in the architecture of most CRs:

- **Compute power**: the CR's physical servers should adequately support the use of multiple VMs simultaneously. Interoperability between both kinetic and cyber elements of the CR is essential for smooth execution of scenarios. CAAJED comprises both cyber and kinetic interfaces (read more in Section 9.2.2).
- **Storage**: the CR must have permanent raw-data-storing capabilities. Many CRs use containers for collecting, storing, and maintaining datasets. These datasets can be results of the exercise, analyses report, log files, details of potential threats, exiting cyberattacks, etc. Datasets can be used for designing new security procedures, applying ML algorithms (Xin *et al.* 2018), evidence learning (Maennel 2020), or other research purposes.
- **Network**: the CR should be able to support low-latency and high-bandwidth Internet and other important network communication protocols. Specifications of network devices like routers, firewall, switches, VPN, and DNS should also be considered (Priyadarshini 2018).
- **Automation and management system**: the CR components must be regularly audited, updated, and maintained. It is necessary to avoid low utilization of assets, incomplete reporting of processes, lack of integrity, etc. (Reynolds 2019).
- **Backup**: is essential to protect the CR from external attacks, as the configurations and architecture would be unique to the specific organization. For example, the architecture of RINSE has a backup instance (Liljenstam *et al.* 2005).

8.1.3 Defining CR Teams

Teams' definition has already been discussed in Chapter 6. This subsection focuses on defining different considerations for types of teams commonly participating in the majority of modern CRs. Considering and fulfilling necessary technical requirements are beneficial for the teams to efficiently execute their respective tasks. The number of teams and their roles can vary in different CRs. However, the four most common CR teams include Red, Blue, Green, and White Teams. The roles and some basic requirements of each team are discussed as follows:

- **Red Team**

    Role: to locate and exploit system vulnerabilities, disrupt security protocols, launch cyberattacks, and compromise assets.

    Technical requirements: OS (Windows or Linux is generally preferred), Internet and server access, workstations, attack tools, metrics tool for reporting MTTC and MTTP details (Diogenes *et al.* 2018), and source IP.

- **Blue Team**

  Role: locate, validate, and report system vulnerabilities, develop and implement mitigation procedures against Red Team attacks.

  Technical requirements: OS (Windows or Linux is generally preferred), Internet and server access, routing series, HMI, firewall and IPAM services, DNS, web services, file services, VPN, vulnerability scanners, metadata of both network traffic flow and packet flow, and metrics tool for reporting ETTD and ETTR (Diogenes *et al.* 2018).

- **White Team**

  Role: supervising and evaluating activities of Red and Blue Teams, ensuring rules' implementation, assisting active teams with any support issues.

  Technical requirements: Internet and server access, workstations, CLI, web and script interface, evaluation criteria automation, and feedback mechanism.

- **Green Team**

  Role: providing fixes and security patches to the Blue Team.

  Technical requirements: Internet and server access, workstations, IDS, IPS, web services, file services, software license, updates, patches, VPN, and SCCS.

8.2 Architectural Considerations

This step involves deciding implementation strategies, design considerations, developing prototype, etc. Having a well-described diagram of the CR architecture serves as a guide in implementing the components. Some of the basic architecture considerations are as follows:

- **Platform**: it is where all the CR functionalities will get hosted and executed. It will comprise all the basic hardware components like workstations, network devices, and computing resources like memory, storage, and processing power.

- **Programming language**: all the libraries, APIs, and other system functionalities are commonly programmed in C++ or Python. The selection of a suitable programming language assists in developing initial prototype applications.

- **Network design**: some of the essential components of network topology are web and email servers, database, firewalls, routers, NTF generators, etc., all connected via LAN or VPN services.

- **Type of environment**: the CR may have a simulation-based, emulation-based, or a hybrid environment. The planned environment can be created using appropriate simulator or emulator devices (read more in Chapter 7).

- **Interface**: it allows communication between the users and the CR environment. The CR may have a GUI interface or a CLI. Many modern CRs support GUI interface for improving user-friendliness.

- **API**: it is responsible for managing the communications taking place between CR infrastructure, subsystems, applications, and microservices as shown in Figure 8.3. It provides user authentication services, resource reservation services, etc. to the clients as shown in Figure 8.4.

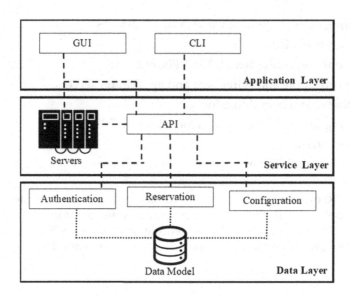

FIGURE 8.3
Working of an API.

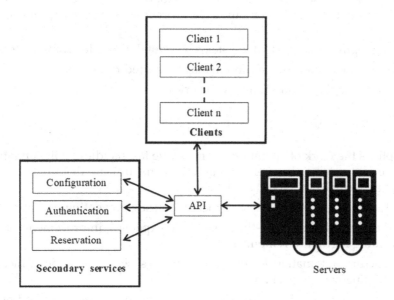

FIGURE 8.4
API services.

8.3 Implementation Phase

Integrating all the components and tools in a proper sequence is critical to accomplish all the initially decided objectives. An ideal sequence for implementation of all the components can be described in the following order:

1. Deploying the platform and related components.
2. Implementing the teams' environment.

3. Implementing network topology and network devices.
4. Arranging core services.
5. Setting up Internet connection, LAN, VPN, etc.
6. Arranging core applications like web and application servers.
7. Coordinating scenario-building tools.
8. Implementing firewalls and network policies.
9. Placing user interface.
10. Tools for metric and evaluations.

For scaling the CR, external physical or virtual components can get integrated with the CR's network topology. It is easier to integrate components having in-built capabilities, which are fit for CR's infrastructure. Implementing an extensive CR is challenging; therefore, the implementation is preferably done using automation and IaC.

8.3.1 IaC

It is defined as an automation approach used for deploying extensive architecture. This approach uses reliable and repeatable procedures for executing or changing specified systems and their respective configurations. Several organizations use IaC for (Morris 2016):

- Applying regular changes to the systems without the need for human interference.
- Allows user to define, execute, and manage required resources.
- Quick and straightforward failure recoveries.

IaC is largely used because:

- It simplifies the work of operations team. While IaC handles all the updating and fixing of components, the operators can utilize that time for deigning of scenarios, mitigation techniques, security patches, etc.
- It timely detects and resolves system inconsistencies, preventing system downtime.
- Instead of implementing one-time, risky, and expensive improvements, it focuses on executing regular developments.
- Infrastructure automation lowers the employees' workloads and difficulties in implementing necessary changes.
- In CRs, IaC can be used for effectively scaling the environment depending on the number of participants.
- IaC promotes the management of subsystems and other resources as a single entity available to all instead of being reserved for only system administrators.

Morris (2016) defines the following principles of IaC:

- Rebuilding any component of the infrastructure should be easily and steadily achievable. This does not require any serious decision-making process. All the necessary details like version update and server installation are included in scripts and tools that will deliver it.

- Resources creation, replacement, resizing, and termination are easier using IaC. Therefore, this dynamic nature of the infrastructure should be considered during the designing phase. This is essential in extensive cloud-based environments where hardware reliability is unguaranteed.

- Consistency in systems and components assists in configuration drift.

- Any changes or actions taking place within the infrastructure are repeatable. Using scripts and configuration tools assists in efficiently making changes as compared to manual changes.

- As designing infrastructure is already a challenging task, extensive changes should be limited after its construction to meet the decided requirements. It is essential to manage and deliver changes in a prompt and secure manner, without drastically affecting the working of the infrastructure. Changes are necessary for developing efficient processes. But too many drastic changes make it difficult to predict the actual working of the infrastructure.

References

Brikman, Y., 2019. *Terraform: Up & Running: Writing Infrastructure as Code*. California: O'Reilly Media.

Chouliaras, N., Kittes, G., Kantzavelou, I., Maglaras, L., Pantziou, G., Ferrag, M. A., 2021. Cyber ranges and testbeds for education, training, and research. *Applied Sciences*, 11(4), 1–23.

Diogenes, Y., Ozkaya, E., 2018. Security posture. *In: Cybersecurity??? Attack and Defense Strategies: Infrastructure Security with Red Team and Blue Team Tactics*. Birmingham: Packt Publishing Ltd, 6–24.

Frank, M., Leitner, M., Pahi, T., 2017. Design considerations for cyber security testbeds: A case study on a cyber security testbed for education. *In: 2017 IEEE 15th Intl Conf on Dependable, Autonomic and Secure Computing*, 6–10 November 2017 Orlando. New York, NY: IEEE, 38–46.

Liljenstam, M., Liu, J., Nicol, D., Yuan, Y., Yan, G., Grier, C., 2005. Rinse: The real-time immersive network simulation environment for network security exercises. *In: Workshop on Principles of Advanced and Distributed Simulation (PADS'05)*, 1–3 June 2005 Monterey. New York, NY: IEEE, 119–128.

Maennel, K., 2020. Learning analytics perspective: Evidencing learning from digital datasets in cybersecurity exercises. *In: 2020 IEEE European Symposium on Security and Privacy Workshops (EuroS&PW)*, 7-11 September 2020 Genoa. New York, NY: IEEE, 27–36.

Morris, K., 2016. Challenges and principles. *In: Infrastructure as Code: Managing Servers in the Cloud*. California: O'Reilly Media, Inc., 3–19.

Nieh, J., Leonard, O. C., 2000. Examining vmware. *Dr. Dobb's Journal*, 25(8), 70–78.

Priyadarshini, I., 2018. *Features and Architecture of the Modern Cyber Range: A Qualitative Analysis and Survey*. Newark, NJ: University of Delaware.

Reynolds, C. T., 2019. Cyber Range as a Service® CRaaS [online]. Available from: https://rdp21.org/wp-content/uploads/2020/11/Cyber-Range-as-a-Service-CRaaS-2019.pdf [Accessed 25 May 2021].

Sefraoui, O., Aissaoui, M., Eleuldj, M., 2012. OpenStack: Toward an open-source solution for cloud computing. *International Journal of Computer Applications*, 55(3), 38–42.

Xin, Y., Kong, L., Liu, Z., Chen, Y., Li, Y., Zhu, H., Gao, M., Hou, H., Wang, C., 2018. Machine learning and deep learning methods for cybersecurity. *IEEE Access*, 6(1), 35365–35381.

9

Military Cyber Ranges

9.1 Need of MCRs

First, it is important to understand the term "cyberwarfare". Cyberwarfare can be defined as the integration of fundamental know-hows of CNOs used for disrupting other network infrastructure while also defending their own. It also supports or gets supported by other capabilities such as psychological operations, military deception, EW, and operations securities. CNO comprises CNA, CND, and CNE. CNA includes events responsible for disrupting, degrading, denying, and destroying information of any computer network. CND includes events dealing with monitoring, analyzing, detecting, responding, and providing protection against any CNAs or any other unauthorized activities. CNE is responsible for enabling intelligence operation capabilities for gathering data from targeted CN infrastructure. Military communities have focused on developing CRs which can provide a holistic view of a cyberwarfare scenario, thus also including the CNO. These MCRs would provide simulations of the CN infrastructure. This would assist in locating system vulnerabilities, developing new security procedures, and improving the overall security of the infrastructure.

With the ever-changing and advancing cyberwarfare scenarios, the USAF required rigorous and professional attitude-oriented cyber warriors. As development of cyberwarfare capabilities, would also extend USAF's reach, power, and vigilance on a global scale. To fulfill all these requirements, a platform for educating and training military personnel in the IT aspects, attack and defense tactics, and developing new capabilities would be developed. Thus, many MCRs also provide the simulations for training and research facilities to educate military personnel. These trainings are useful for providing operational experience, enhancing problem-solving and communication skills, and learning about new tools.

MCRs are also required for conducting various government-funded research programs. These programs are useful for further developing the MCRs and its tools capabilities. Newly developed security patches, software, and tools can be tested in the simulation environment of an MCR. It also facilitates in gaining more insights about previous cyberattacks. Based on this Intel, new security policies and measures can be developed. Simulations and emulations can also be useful in analyzing and assessing the infrastructure's security procedures against potential cyber threats.

The majority of MCRs focus on fulfilling these requirements or to enhance any particular cybersecurity aspect. Over the decades, the USAF along with other military communities have funded various MCRs projects for preparing military personnel

DOI: 10.1201/9781003206071-9

against the new and ever-changing cyberwarfare scenarios. An ideal MCR should be able to provide:

- High fidelity, secure simulation environment with instantaneous feedback.
- Platform that allows teams engagement for supporting the CR's experiments.
- Setups supporting research and experimentations.
- Operation-based evaluation data and metrics.

9.2 Simulation-Based MCRs

This section discusses and presents a comparison between the simulation-based MCRs. The MCRs discussed under this section are SIMTEX, CAAJED, SAST, and StealthNet.

9.2.1 SIMTEX

9.2.1.1 Introduction

The SIMTEX uses the three-tier network design of USAF (Leblanc *et al.* 2011). The simulator mimics the three-tier network architecture of the USAF. It can also be set up to link multiple simulators together for forming an "intra-network" (McBride 2007). Over the years, it has extended to accommodate a wider network connectivity facility via JCOR VPN for the purpose of common and interservice exercise and trainings (Harwell *et al.* 2013). Using the JCOR VPN, SIMTEX is able to connect with other services and COCOM CRs. This CR includes a replicated Internet along with domain name resolution and websites like google.com and cnn.com are mimicked. SIMTEX infrastructure is also used for Bulwark Defender, a training exercise conducted once every year jointly by the military and government agencies (Hernandez 2010).

9.2.1.2 Origin

SIMTEX was designed to overcome the shortcomings of a network security exercise – Black Demon. This was conducted by the USAF in 2002, for developing strategies to respond to CNAs on massive military operational infrastructures and simultaneously train its first ten cyber warriors in cybersecurity. However, there were various shortcomings noted like:

- Simulator resetting was time-consuming.
- It had nominal network traffic for masking the actions of the red team.
- There was no fixed configuration of the components.
- Interconnectivity of this exercise was limited to a 56K-VPN connection.

Following the Black Demon exercise, the AAR recommended designing and developing some permanent simulation environment, with the following requirements:

- A secured environment for training of network operations teams.
- Teams should practice exercises given in cyber ranges and enhance their skills and establish modern defense strategies against cyberattacks.

Following these requirements by AAR, SIMTEX was developed in the year 2003. Initially, it was used for conducting training exercises, once in every three months. These exercises aimed at delivering operational trainings on newly developed defense software and network operations used in the USAF.

9.2.1.3 Architecture

SIMTEX was initially modeled like its network core. Over the years, its architecture underwent many changes and innovations. Currently, SIMTEX uses SLAM-R for providing virtual training environments or simulators (Harwell *et al.* 2013). Collaboratively, they provide a dependable environment for scalable classroom exercises, conducting teams' competitions, development of tools, and rehearsals for any missions.

SIMTEX uses Myrmidon module as its attack engine as shown in Figure 9.1. It is responsible for executing realistic cyberattack simulations. This module creates different attack occurrences against the infrastructure's components, and together these occurrences form a group of scenarios. These attack occurrences can vary from component failures to exploiting system vulnerabilities affecting the operations of USAF.

SIMTEX GUI offers an interface for management of different attack scenarios from their creation to execution. The events are written into an XML file, after which the attack engine runs configuration for automatic generation of distinctive attributes in each attack occurrence. The attack duration, its source, and its target are some of the examples of attributes of an attack occurrence. The configuration of the GUI's execution module is for monitoring all the steps involved in creation and broadcast of the attack occurrence and its attributes in the simulation. All the information gets conveyed to the exercise instructor via a bot in the console window.

SIMTEX's network traffic generator module also known as Legion module is responsible for creating replica patterns of network traffic of the USAF network environment.

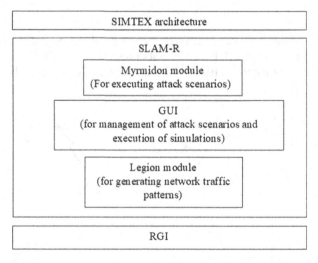

FIGURE 9.1
Main components of SIMTEX.

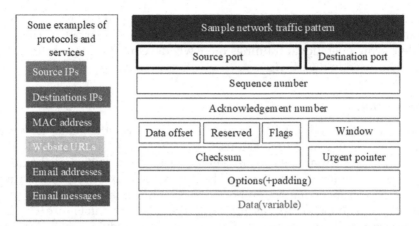

FIGURE 9.2
NTAs and patterns of network traffic.

These replications are useful in the simulation for masking the red teams' activities. The network traffic gets generated among the various devices within the simulation such as routers, servers, and workstations. The legion module is also tasked with creating NTAs and NTSs. NTAs are a group of either one or more than one pattern of the network traffic, as shown in Figure 9.2. NTS are the groups consisting of created NTA and VMs, as shown in Figure 9.3.

For simulation of Internet, SIMTEX simulator uses are accompanied by an RGI. It provides a simulation of the actual Internet. It is ideal for conducting secured and controlled training scenarios independent of the public arena. It is entirely virtualized, and it uses open-source utilities wherever required, and real IP addresses found in the actual web.

9.2.1.4 Evolution

SIMTEX achieved a wider network connectivity via JCOR VPN. It allowed the CR to connect with other simulators as well. Ever since its inception, SIMTEX has underwent major technological advancements for achieving its current architecture. These advancements

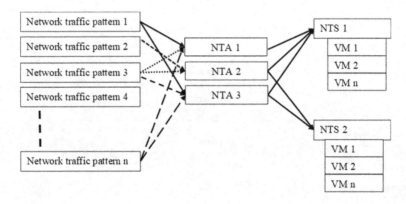

FIGURE 9.3
NTS and its components.

have been possible due to the various shortcomings highlighted during the exercises, a few of them are as follows:

- Lack of practical network traffic.
- Executing the CNAs required the entire CR to be interconnected, this would be very expensive.
- Reconstruction of scenarios needed to be developed rapidly and on demand.
- Training realism was limited

Overcoming its shortcoming, SIMTEX has developed into an interoperable complex network environment. Its architecture remains open system comprising physical and virtual replicated network components. The shortcomings of SIMTEX and other lessons learned are also useful and implemented in the designing of new MCRs.

9.2.2 CAAJED

9.2.2.1 Introduction

CAAJED is an USAF-funded project, designed with the objective to concentrate on advanced cyberwarfare. CAAJED enables simulations for sophisticated attacks. This is achieved by arbitrarily mapping of all the network services to all the available assets in simulations. Overcoming the limitations of other CRs that only focus on information systems, CAAJED conceptualizes the integration of both cyber and air-related assets while creating the exercise environment. CAAJED is successfully able to integrate cyber operations to the simulation of an air battle using a process leaning, cyber inference model (Mudge *et al.* 2008). It acts as a platform for conducting further research and educating new officers about the interoperability of both kinetic and cyber domains. It offers a common arena where interaction of both the domains and their effects on each other can take place.

9.2.2.2 Origin

CAAJED was initially used in 2006 for demonstrating an exercise with showing both kinetic and cyber effects. This project was initiated to fulfill the requirement of providing a sharing learning and research platform for both cyber and kinetic elements. Previous CEs had majorly focused on network systems attacks, thus having a limited scope with no process to reason about (Mudge *et al.* 2008). Since 2007, the program's focus has also incorporated the objective of dealing with advanced cyberwarfare-like situations.

According to the 2007 report of USAF's SAB, three combat levels for cyberwarfare were defined:

The first level, limited to war among system administrators, is also known as the network war. System exploits, malicious logics, and IT vulnerabilities are all classified under this level. The second level considers cyber incidents against kinetic components such as disabling radar site. Attacks under this level are aimed at immobilizing kinetic components with the assistance of cyber incidents or CNAs. The third level is critical in comparison to the previous two levels. Well-planned and coveted CNAs aimed at causing large-scale network disruptions are classified under this level. Such malicious CNAs are orchestrated in a manner where the victims fail to detect cyber-related glitches.

Following SAB's report, CAAJED has incorporated scenarios for dealing with third-level threats and CNAs. After its initial release, its scope has expanded to incorporate

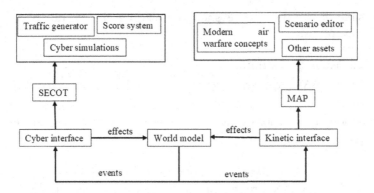

FIGURE 9.4
CAAJED architecture.

cyberwarfare trainings and research. It focuses on enhancing the CND capabilities and trainings for capturing the realities of the ongoing cyberwarfare. Enhancing preparations against level-three attacks can significantly improve the defense tactics and overall team response.

9.2.2.3 Architecture

CAAJED's architecture comprises CKIM along with MAP and SECOT as shown in Figure 9.4. CAAJED's architecture includes both cyber and kinetic war inputs along with a model for interacting effects among these inputs.

CKIM uses the technique to translate the events of one domain into the effects of another domain. It comprises three aspects: kinetic domain, cyber domain, and capabilities. Kinetic domain comprises all the physical assets that are managed through processes. These processes constitute cyber domain. Capabilities are the interactions of physical assets with the processes that manage them. Figure 9.5 elaborates on the collaboration of all the three aspects of CKIM.

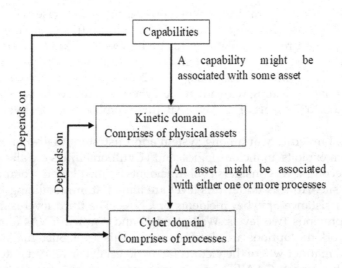

FIGURE 9.5
CKIM model.

Consider the following example. Suppose, the capabilities concern with aircraft refueling. This is enabled by the process that controls it. For this capability, a list of possible processes gets generated on which it will depend on. Refueling the aircraft can be associated with some logistic and planning processes. The processes will again depend on kinetic assets such as destination, personnel, or the terrain.

MAP can be defined an instantaneous, uninterrupted, strategy game comprising unit controls at a flight level. John Tiller Games published this war game. MAP comes under the kinetic interface of architecture of CAAJED. This is because it comprises concepts concerning air warfare, scenario editors along with additional kinetic assets.

Warfare concepts include aircraft refueling, missile control, radar-controlled defenses, and satellites. Scenario editors facilitate the creation of various simulations and their additional customizations.

Communications in MAP are carried out in an .xml file transmitted via network connections. MAP assets comprise command nodes, air bases, radar and missile sites, aircrafts, etc. All the assets have some capabilities associated with them. The control of capabilities is facilitated by the interface. A MAP asset such as an airbase can have capabilities such as radar coverage, launching aircrafts, etc. MAP also provisions three types of interface, between human-human, between human-computer, and between computer-computer.

SECOT is responsible for hosting all the cyber-related components with the help of score system and traffic generator. SECOT is capable of simulating the complete enterprise community. The SECOT framework as shown in Figure 9.6 comprises mobile agents, middleware, and sleep language. The mobile agents are for encapsulating the processes. It follows execute-once property. The state of the agent remains intact even after completing the task and also after migrating to some other location. It can resume its execution without undergoing any changes in its state. The middleware is responsible for employing techniques for protecting the semantic of execute-once.

After the termination of an exercise, the mobile agents migrate and get isolated from the events, which may cause outside band network failures. To prevent such failures, the middleware applies several techniques. Sleep language is responsible for implementation of SECOT. Sleep functions are capable of storing codes, variable, and execution state into different continuation objects. For achieving string mobility, a mechanism of serialization of all the objects is followed.

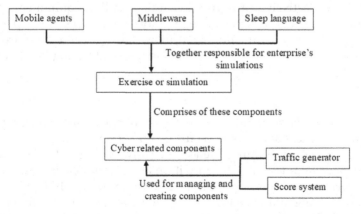

FIGURE 9.6
SECOT framework.

CAAJED's world model, as also illustrated in Figure 9.4, is the software implementation of CKIM. The software receives both MAP events and SECOT events. MAP is connected to the world model using some network socket. MAP provides all the reports via the simulations. Based on these reports, the world model is able to track all the vulnerabilities of each and every physical asset. SECOT provides the states encountered during an event. All the workflow effects are communicated to the world model by SECOT using xml messages.

9.2.2.4 Evolution

After incorporating more sophisticated models for dealing with higher level warfare, CAAJED can easily execute both level-two and level-three cyberattacks in simulation environment. SECOT uses agents for generating points by analyzing process execution outcomes. The exercises promote the teams to focus on achieving persistence, stealth, and smooth flow of communication when dealing with the opponent's network infrastructure. The CAAJED architecture and tools capable of incorporating high-level warfare attacks were put to test in a cyber-defense exercise conducted in 2007.

The students were able to form teams, prepare, and develop an understanding of networks within the ten-week setup time. The SECOT and its agents source code were provided prior to the main event. This enabled the students to focus more on the exercise instead of being concerned about the scoring system. CAAJED had successfully created a proper-scale cyberwarfare simulation that gave the students an opportunity for reasoning w.r.t. targets as well as effects other than network exploits. The concepts covered in CAAJED simulation can also be implemented to other exercises.

9.2.3 SAST

9.2.3.1 Introduction

SAST aims at providing specialized training to the staff of USAF CNO (Wabiszewski *et al.* 2009). It is developed by the PNNL for simulating network setups of most of the DoD organizations. SAST follows the concept of providing a single simulation tool that facilitates the majority aspects of cybersecurity. It is used for carrying out exercises, trainings, tool testing, and evaluations. It also facilitates concepts such as IA and IO. SAST offers an integrated software design for complying with all the applications. Its components may either be individually or collectively put to use depending on the requirements. SAST can be used as a training tool. For inculcating cybersecurity concepts in security personnel, SAST offers operation permissions while training. It allows the user to create, share, and manage virtualized network environment and perform independent testing (Meitzler *et al.* 2009).

9.2.3.2 Origin

SAST project was initially created for simulating national infrastructures in early 2000s. With the rise in awareness about cybersecurity and concerns, the project was reinstated for providing cybersecurity training. Hence, the early objective of SAST was to develop cybersecurity-related simulation platform within a constraining time frame. SAST capabilities were earlier limited to system administrator trainings. With time, it was expanded to accommodate training and exercises of a broader category of personnel, testing environment, IA and IO. Two years following the development of the project, it was distributed to military and academia for feedback.

SAST had later accommodated the objective of fulfilling the lacking cybersecurity experience in freshers. It also started to focus on providing interoperability between the different applications to save cost and minimize complexity. The SAST project was also required to fulfill the need of DoD and other government agencies for protecting their information infrastructure which supported command of weapon systems and other logistics.

To accommodate all these increasing requirements, the SAST project objective was to build an integrated suite comprising all the simulation tools. One of the objectives while developing the SAST platform was to provide simulations in dealing with infrastructure's vulnerable factors like:

- Increasing frequency of sophisticated and stealthy cyberattacks.
- Cyber threats rapidly changing and advancing.
- Scarcity of amply qualified cybersecurity staff.
- Security performance cannot be properly assessed because of insufficient capabilities.
- Significant cost reduction pressure while also maintaining and improving security infrastructure and fixing system glitches.

9.2.3.3 Architecture

Although the SAST platform underwent many changes to accommodate various objectives, all of its components can be categorized into the following (Figure 9.7):

Network infrastructure: all the physical and virtual devices of an infrastructure fall under this category. Components such as routers, workstations, switches, operating systems, routing tables, device interconnectivity, etc. can either exist as physical or

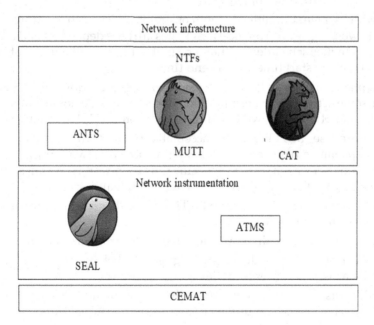

FIGURE 9.7
SAST architecture components.

virtualized components. Not all components may be required for conducting an exercise and are used as per their requirements. The network infrastructure aims to provide maximum flexibility while creating the exercise environment and user autonomy while handling operations. SAST also offers guidance on setting up the environment for carrying out training exercises. SAST operates on the network infrastructure, and so the environment must offer high fidelity and scalability.

NTF: all the components responsible for communication among the components of the network infrastructure and their behavior get placed in this category. These NTFs are either device generated or user generated. Device-generated flows are a result of activities such as logging, automatic backups, updates, system patches, etc. User-generated flows are a result of authorized behavior as well as unauthorized behavior. Authorized behavior can include surfing the web, email and file transfers, etc. Unauthorized behavior includes worms, malware, data exfiltration or unauthorized email, and file transfers. The NTF functionality is provided by SAST via ANTS along with MUTT and CAT capabilities as the plugged-in modules.

ANTS recreates the networks users and devices for carrying out its functions. These representations are referred to as "actors". Some of the features of ANTS include:

- It is capable of providing 16 engines for performing network relation actions.
- It is designed for supporting engine plugins which helps in delivering the latest capabilities when required.
- Simulations of huge network infrastructures with the use of less hardware devices are possible in SAST because ANTS can recreate many actors within one host.

An actor created by the ANTS consists of three attributes, described as follows:

- **Specification dataset**: it includes properties like email account, MAC address, authentication permits, IP address, and other relevant information that explains the properties of any actor.
- **Activities schedule**: limiting to time constraint, an actor can have three states – at lunch, working, and on break. These states are time dependent and are defined using activities schedule. In other words, it defines the likelihood of any task's occurrence, its start time, and its end time.
- **Task plan**: it details all the actions and their rate occurring during or before or after some activity. Some examples of task plan include download and upload of files, email transfers, web surfing, or some other ANTS activity.

During any exercise, MUTT delivers acceptable network traffic activities. MUTT delivers capabilities required for modeling an actual network infrastructure, its behavior, and users. Even scenario-specific time frames and schedules can be simulated using MUTT. MUTT offers following functionalities:

- Automatic generation of saturated NTFs from either one or more than one system in the network range.
- Allows performing realistic activities like web surfing and email transfers.
- It is also responsible for demonstrating realistic behaviors like the task schedules, databases, and user activities.
- MUTT hosts are capable of individually simulating up to 200 users, each with some specific profile and unique IP address and MAC address.

During an exercise, CAT delivers malicious or failed network traffic activities. CAT delivers capabilities required for direct attachment of malicious exploits within a network's infrastructure. These malicious exploits can include equipment failures or user permission errors. CAT offers the following functionalities:

- It automates the majority of its processes and allows the operator to intervene as per their needs.
- Simulates realistic attack vectors responsible for malicious attacks on network traffic and on the infrastructure.
- Performs realistic network attacks like causing failure of systems, reconnaissance, using cover fire, and smokescreen techniques, etc.
- It is capable of performing such attacks both internally or externally.
- Provides live, augmented red teams for exercise.

Network instrumentation: this comprises two components: one is responsible for providing a management system and the other for providing a monitoring system for the CR exercises. The CR's management functionality is fulfilled by SEAL and the monitoring functionality is addressed by ATMS.

SEAL functions are listed as follows:

- It can compartmentalize the CR's access for delivering multiple isolated environments for either research, training, or war games.
- It offers to dynamically reassign control of the CR's resources to some other authorized user or users.
- The CR can be remotely accessed using SEAL.
- It provides users with a multidimensional view of any network attack.
- It allows the user to view, access, and control the resources of the CR and encompass live actors as per requirement in any simulation.

ATMS is responsible for providing an operator with means to uninterruptedly determine the status of any simulation(s) and for collecting metrics to perform analysis.

ATMS functions are listed as follows:

- It provides the user with tools required for introducing, detecting, and recording of the network tracer packets. These packets are responsible for various data types to deliver instantaneous network traffic flows analysis via some control points defined in advance.
- It analyses both authorized NTF and unauthorized NTFs for determining security conditions and effectiveness.
- It provides all the reports and analysis of NTF to CEMAT.

CEMAT offers capabilities for tracking and measuring security performances. SAST components exchange monitored NTF reports with CEMAT using an interface. Based on the reports provides, CEMAT helps in highlighting all the security shortcomings.

9.2.3.4 Evolution

From catering to only system administrator and national infrastructures, SAST has evolved into an independent testing platform with isolated environments for different activities. Over the decade, by 2010, it has incorporated many objectives and expanded its own capabilities. By 2010, SAST version 3.2.1 was released and distributed via a direct download or CDs.

9.2.4 StealthNet

9.2.4.1 Introduction

It is an LVC framework funded by TRMC via US Army program. It aims to provide instantaneous simulations for evaluation and testing of cyber operations and conducting trainings. It has been initially used for the representation of the impacts of DoS and jamming in a cyberwar-like situation. It provided simulations of network architecture comprising tactical radios with network software and network hardware. It provides interface concerning simulated network and physical network devices like router firewalls. The CR also consists of LVC elements like Snort (Roesch 1999). It makes use of LVC technology for creating network system simulations for conducting instantaneous cyber threat analysis. Its framework also facilitates transition of testing and evaluations environments to other similar programs.

9.2.4.2 Origin

This program was initiated in 2010 with a duration of three years (Varshney *et al.* 2011). The focus of the program was to accurately characterize the impacts of any potential cyber threat and IO on the network infrastructure. As most of the simulations were oriented around CNAs, the analysis of cyber threats would only be limited to threats to only physical devices. Consideration cyberattacks centered around passive threats like coordinated threats or eavesdropping were also overlooked by most of the simulations. Therefore, one of the major objectives of StealthNet was to use LVC for delivering detailed analysis of the effects of existing as well as potential cyber threats.

Limited consideration of cyber threats also limited the scalability and intricacy of the CRs to simulate such possible CNAs. This would happen in cases where those threats would actually realize to cyberattacks. Many simulations would be missing the paradigms for modeling scenarios concerning possible cyber threats. Tools used for modeling of large-scale physical attacks like wormhole attack, jamming, etc. would be very expensive. Lack of which would restrict the testing of resilience and intricacy of the simulated infrastructure. StealthNet also incorporated these limitations, thus expanding its objectives.

The use of end-to-end communication technological devices like smartphones in the military also exhibited various cyber threats. Cyberattacks would target any vulnerabilities found in strategical operations, wired as well as wireless devices and networks. Wireless networks were prone to eavesdropping, DDoS, intrusion, etc. Wired networks were prone to service disruption, restriction of resources, and often they were used as source of information gathering. Therefore, it was also required of the CR to consider cyberattacks and threats against the latest technologies by personnel for communications.

9.2.4.3 Architecture

StealthNet is an LVC (as shown in Figure 9.8) environment that allows analyzing the effects of cyber threats and attacks on an actual network system.

LVC also provides tools for evaluation of the success rate of any threat in disrupting BFN communication. BFN can be affected by disrupting bandwidth or meddling with the service metrics. BFN simulation can be carried out with the help of applications, devices, and simulation models. LVC is capable of simulating network systems for conducting tests or assessing viability of new security tools. It is a combination of user behavior model along

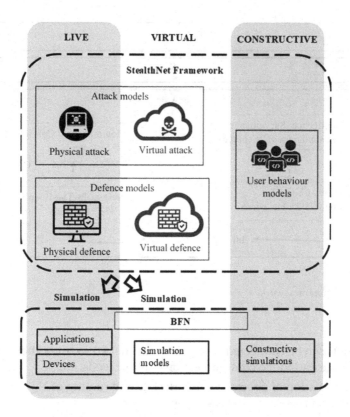

FIGURE 9.8
LVC framework.

with both physical and virtual attacks and defenses. It is capable of launching cyberattacks against the network infrastructure within the simulations. It provides a safe and cheap environment for creating network infrastructure simulations and monitoring its performance when under cyber threats and attacks.

StealthNet framework comprises three main components as shown in Figure 9.9. All these components together are responsible for handling different aspects of a simulations and its smooth execution.

SNA comprises different kinds of interfaces, LVC elements like C2 systems and network hardware. There are three different interfaces – HITL, SITL, and interoperability interface. Network hardware comprises ISR feed, firewalls, routers, etc. LVC elements also include Snort, C2 systems, systems for IDs and IPSs, etc. Cyberattacks are launched against the network within SNA. These attacks are aimed at finding vulnerabilities and exploiting them. Analysis generated from the impacts of such attacks helps in enhancing the security of the overall network infrastructure.

SVN is the core of StealthNet framework. It is responsible for simulating the communication infrastructure with maximum fidelity. It allows the deployment of network applications like NTF, voice communications, video streaming, web conferencing, etc. SVN offers the following listed benefits:

- It provides computation-efficient, greater fidelity, scalable environment for conducting various cyber-related operations.

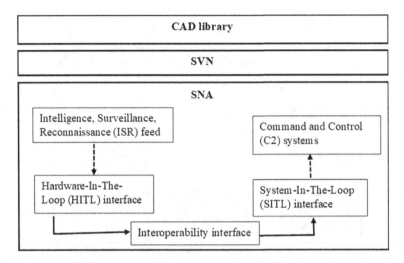

FIGURE 9.9
Components of StealthNet framework.

- Physical tools can be connected with the virtual networks and other NTF applications like voice and video communications, sensor feeds, etc.
- Real-time simulation of effects of network state and routing of NTF to a particular destination with losses and delays is made possible.
- Use of third-party analysis and management network tools for studying completely simulated networks.
- Integration of physical applications with cyberwarfare communications that assist in evaluating the impacts of CNAs on the active systems.

StealthNet framework also comprises CAD library capable of simulating LVC network systems. This is possible as it operates in LVC modes. It comprises models for accurately simulating cyber threats for all network layers. These threats can be either active, coordinated or adaptive, or passive. Some of the models provided by CAD library are DoS, channel scanning, radio jamming, firewalls, etc.

DoS model supports basic attacks, TCP attack, IP fragmentation attacks. Channel scanning model supports framework and APIs for development of information gathering algorithms. Radio jamming model supports wideband, sweep, and custom jamming. Firewall is a stateless software process for inspecting all network packets and determining to allow a packet or deny it access.

9.2.4.4 Evolution

StealthNet development was divided into three phases. By the completion of first phase in 2011, it offered tactical network interface to both wired and wireless devices. Third phase focused on providing interface for handling live tactical radios. With the progress in the development phases, the scalability of the CR also increases. After completion of its first phase, the CR was being designed to scale up to a thousand network nodes. These would aid in delivering the instantaneous NTF. Later on, it was being designed to accommodate

TABLE 9.1

Advantages of Simulation-Based MCRs

SIMTEX	CAAJED	SAST	StealthNet
It delivers practical experience in managing network defenses and responding to real-world cyber threats and cyber C2 processes trainings. It can accommodate a large number of participants. Automated cyberattack setups for training can restart within 10 minutes. It has an intra-network of simulators. It has its own functional Internet with DNS resolution and simulated version of websites like Google and CNN.	It allows the interaction between the cyber and kinetic domains to be investigated. Synergy between the two domains. Kinetic domain comprises physical assets and cyber domain comprises processes controlling these assets. It enhances training and develops TTPs. The simulation replicates the real-world scenario with features like high fidelity, instructors support, programmed performance measurements and replay functionality.	It is comparatively easier to install and operate. It can accommodate a large number of participants. It incorporates concepts like IA and IOs. It offers multiplatform interoperability. It provides a thorough analysis of security performances of the infrastructure.	It provides an assessment of the impacts of any cyber threats on net-centric systems and tactical networks performed during testing. It also focuses on representing the impacts of DDoS and jamming. Real equipment can be connected to the virtual network and real sensor feeds can be sent through it. It also aims to interface with the Army's other LVC simulations.

live and simulated attack tools in the simulations. StealthNet has evolved to accommodate its initial objectives. It supports training environments for determining the robustness of network infrastructures.

9.2.5 Comparison of Simulation-Based MCRs

This section focuses on summarizing all the advantages (in Table 9.1) and features (in Table 9.2) of the above-discussed MCRs.

TABLE 9.2

Features of Simulation-Based MCRs

SIMTEX	CAAJED	SAST	StealthNet
Supports multilocation training arenas (connected to SIMTEX network). Provides remote training network for real hosts and cyberattacks. Uses JCOR VPN for connecting with other simulations. Its architecture remains open system comprising physical as well as virtual replicated network components.	Hosts exercises for training against high-level cyber/air warfare. Covers concepts such as interoperability between both kinetic domain and cyber domain. Gives personnel an opportunity for reasoning w.r.t. targets as well as effects in addition to network exploits. Its architecture includes both cyber and kinetic war inputs along with a model for interacting effects among these inputs.	Offers complete user independence for using different tools. It is a scalable, multiuser platform. The CR can be accessed from any location when required. It provides isolated environments for every activity like software testing, war games or exercises. Offers flexible management and monitoring systems. Provides live, augmented red teams for exercise.	Offers a framework for modeling and assessing impacts existing and potential cyber threats. Offers CAD library, that are capable of simulating LVC based network systems. It uses SVN technology for simulation of high-fidelity communication setup. Ideal framework for performing network defense testing and assessments.

9.3 Emulation-Based MCRs

This section discusses and presents a comparison between the emulation-based MCRs. The MCRs discussed under this section are NCR, JIOR, and DoD CSR.

9.3.1 NCR

9.3.1.1 Introduction

The NCR aims to emulate the complexities of commercial and defense networks and assist in developing defensive strategies. It is ideal for cybersecurity testing as it provides an exclusive environment during the life cycle of program development with methods for assessing resiliency (Ferguson *et al.* 2014). NCR is capable of operating in stand-alone mode or connect with JIOR. It also facilitates instant network designing, reconfiguration, network scaling, and sanitization. End-to-end toolkit assists in automating the extensive process of developing high-fidelity test beds. The CR is also used for creating test environments, research, and experimentation in cybersecurity domain. It is ideal and efficient for conducting major experiments having numerous links and nodes, factor and treatment variables (Haglich *et al.* 2011). It is capable of supporting research and evaluation of initial prototypes and conducting designs verifications and testing (Pridmore *et al.* 2010).

In NCR, creation and execution of any test environment follows a test life cycle (Urias *et al.* 2018) consisting of various steps, as shown in Figure 9.10.

The initial step is defining of test objectives and features using the tools for Test specification. Next, the required resources are selected for designing the test environment from the given resource pool. Hardware assets are wired to the correct configurations using the CR's provisioning tools. The software required are automatically configured using the CR's configuration tools. After the configurations, the test environment is executed using tools for test execution. These tools are used for collecting the data for later analysis. After the execution process, the sanitization tool is used for virtually returning the hardware and software resource back to the resource pool. This allows the resources to be reused for other events. This life cycle process is appropriate for capturing high-level generalized approach for seeing through an event (Urias *et al.* 2018).

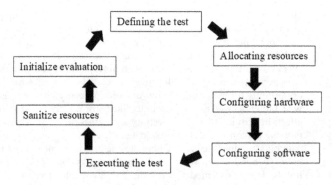

FIGURE 9.10
Test environment life cycle.

9.3.1.2 Origin

NCR was initially developed by DARPA in 2009. Since its inception, the initial vision of NCR was to be acknowledged as the MCR for cyberspace testing, also providing goal-oriented, secured environments for conducting independent testing and assessments of innovative cyberwarfare capabilities. The phase I of NCR development focused on:

- Refining initial designs of the concept.
- Developing model of operation
- Producing a comprehensive systems demonstration and engineering plans.

The other subsequent phases would be responsible for supporting a prototype CR fulfilling the following requirements:

- Providing both classified and unclassified research environments for testing various security hypothesis and products against potential threats, with accuracy and also addressing new capabilities.
- Providing a library of existing and newly developed emulation capabilities.
- Providing sophisticated and detailed emulations of the infrastructure that can be operated from home base.
- Incorporating LVC assets.
- Conducting multiple operations simultaneously at different levels of security.
- Providing an extensive repository of resources.

Development of NCR has also revolutionized the approach toward wide-ranging cyber testing.

9.3.1.3 Architecture

The core independent components of NCR architecture are as follows (Figure 9.11):

- **Secure facility**: it is a reliable base for setting up the CR, its operator rooms, support centers, operation centers and data centers. The facility comprises reconfigurable test suites along with conference and test rooms. Data centers contain the consortium of resources. Security office is responsible for file storage and conducting security operations. The facility caters the following functions:
  - A wireless testing setup.
  - Supporting more than one independent simultaneously occurring events on the site.
  - Remote access via JIOR.
  - Supporting mobile computing.
- **Operational procedures and network architecture**: the CR's infrastructures have a consortium of resources. The CR utilizes tools as per test specifications for defining its end-to-end features. It is responsible for automatic allocation of resources and configuration of tools. It also involves monitoring and evaluating

Secure facility

Operational procedures
and network architecture

Software Testing
Toolkit

Cyber Test Teams

FIGURE 9.11
Components of NCR architecture.

the data collected from the test. After completing test execution, the earlier allocated resources are returned back to the consortium for later usage.

- **Software testing toolkit**: this allows the researchers to formulate test specifications for creating specific test beds for participants to practice. These specifications are achieved via analysis of data, sensors, visualization, and NTF generation
  tools. Building and verifying the test bed requires event execution language and
  test management verification control. The different toolsets of the toolkit are also
  presented in Figure 9.12.

- **Cyber test teams**: These teams provide the following services:
  - Complete test supports.
  - Customized data analysis.
  - Development of threat vectors and NTF generation for design and execution
    phases.
  - Test bed designing support.
  - Integration of variety of resources like wireless, wired components, hardware,
    software, and remote blue/red teams support.
  - Training and exercise expertise.

9.3.1.4 Evolution

The NCR project was transitioned to DoD TRMC after 2012. Ever since its inception, NCR
has developed to support innumerable cybersecurity-related events like testing, system
and target emulations, forensic and architectural analyses, mission rehearsals, etc. NCR
teams works with its consumers in defining the test requirements and providing a veri-
fied CR and resource sanitization at the end. Other than planning, the consumers can
concentrate only on executing the created test and analyzing the data collected and event
report generated. By 2014, NCR has been used in conducting various cyberflag exercises
and supporting other CRs.

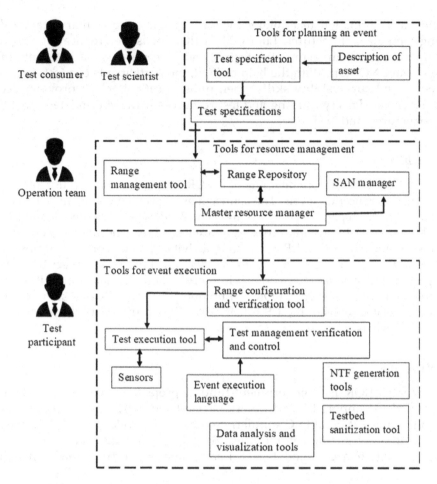

FIGURE 9.12
Software testing toolkit.

9.3.2 JIOR

9.3.2.1 Introduction

The US JIOR can be described as a real-life network setup for practicing techniques, tactics, and procedures for IO. The infrastructure of JIOR can support CNO exercises, testing, and training of cybersecurity concepts. Participants can use multiple sites for the exercise through encrypted links. It is capable of creating numerous realistic setups by the combinations of CNO labs, NTF generators, computing infrastructure, EW, telecommunications equipment, threat systems, communications systems, red teams, SCADA systems along with other simulations (Prinetto *et al.* 2018). It provides a realistic environment allowing the participants to discover vulnerabilities timely, perform software testing for all stages of the development cycle. It is a unique "live fire" CR that supports IO- and cyberwarfare-related goals of the US JTF.

9.3.2.2 Origin

JIOR was developed by the US JFCOM. JFCOM focuses on the experimentation and development in information technology. It also focuses on the interoperability and integration of information technology tools for shaping the military standards and designing common architectures (Luddy 2005). JIOR focuses on replicating realistic set-ups for training cadets in techniques, tactics, and procedures. JIOR is essential for the training of the CNO staff. With the help of JIOR, the participants can test their combat effectiveness and survivability skills when under an IO attack. It provides access to high demand, low-density training and test resources with cyber-related targets, critical infrastructures, and NTF, etc.

9.3.2.3 Architecture

As shown in Figure 9.13, the architecture of the CR can support numerous isolated activities at distinct classification levels. The connections between the systems'and the CR are controlled by the patch panels. The ports and type-3 VPNs have one-one relationship. The CR is a closed-loop network that provides an exclusive, realistic environment with multilevel security for conducting CE along other activities like test group trainings, experimentation, and testing in cyberwarfare and IO domain. It can interconnect 145+ sites. The CR can provide a distributed network having service nodes situated at multiple sites for conducting simultaneous events. JIOR is a unique "live fire" CR that supports IO- and cyberwarfare-related goals of the US JTF. By 2014, JIOR could support up to 90 network nodes and 60+ events.

9.3.2.4 Evolution

Development of JIOR is a government-funded project. By the end of 2016, JIOR had expanded to support IO and other cyber-related activities. It had successfully improved the integration of LVC simulations, operational relevance, and threat representation with other testing communities. By 2017, this integration assisted in JIOR's increased capacity to accommodate 6000+ candidates for certifications and trainings.

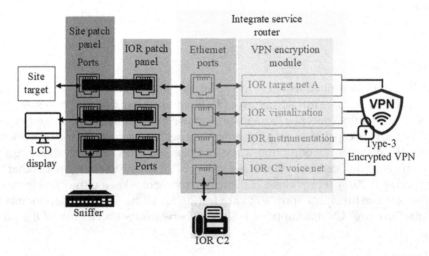

FIGURE 9.13
JIOR activities.

JIOR would also carry out assessments on cyber-related vulnerabilities. By 2018, the CR was capable of evaluating and deploying tools supporting network automation for better management. Over these years, modernization of JIOR resulted in reducing the time taken for configuration of network settings and reusing the CR. The response time for instant, on-demand setting up of the CR also improved. JIOR had sufficient agility and capacity for supporting cybersecurity assessments and development of new resources.

9.3.3 DoD CSR

9.3.3.1 Introduction

DoD CSR has been administered and operated by the US Marine Corps since 2009. The CR is used for DoD personnel trainings in operational networks and defending against network intrusion. The CR replicates the characteristics of Global Information Grid, IA, CND, and other test bed requirements for increasing the security of DoD network. This CR also allows evaluations and testing of the latest resources; immersive training, techniques, procedures, tactics; with advancements and validations; integration testing and interoperability of the system; and certification processes. It provides a persistent environment, maintained by network experts, available to DoD clients for use at minimal pricings. DoD clients requiring the CR can get access by numerous secure transport methods at customer's base stations. This eliminates the need for funding, or designing, or purchasing a CR for only definite purpose. Clients do not have to pay any direct charges unless they have some exclusive requirements currently not built-in the CR. In such cases, the clients can fulfill that specific requirement and give it to the staff for integrating it to the CR's construct. The clients can also give necessary funds for the purchase of that specific hardware or software on their behalf.

9.3.3.2 Origin

DoD CSR was developed with the mission of having a stand-alone combat-oriented MCR supporting tier 1 network infrastructure. The tier 1 infrastructure included the following components:

- A core router as the infrastructure's backbone
- Core services
- Sensing nodes
- Routing
- JRSS
- Access points

The JRSS was a virtual environment for supporting training and management systems. Users could also bring in their own certified devices to train the operational infrastructure container. It could also be used for distant learning and conducting training events or lab activities. The initial version of DoD CSR comprised majority of physical devices, and its configuration was labor intensive. This often led to a conflict in allocating computing resource. The segments of the CR were not aligned with each other. The need for integrated, automated framework led to the development of the DoD CSR version 2.0.

9.3.3.3 Architecture

DoD CSR version 2.0 is considered the next-generation design. It addressed resource and event authoring and event orchestration. The new version of the CR provided the following benefits:

- It provided a constant consortium of resources that stabilized event authoring.
- Automation framework supported validation, configurations, control, and monitoring of capabilities
- Event topology and its validation were automated.
- Event metrics, responses, and control were also automated.

The new version of the CR was a complete hybrid CR architecture along with other components like JRSS, UNCLASS tier 1, and cross-domain services, as also shown in Figure 9.14.

9.3.3.4 Evolution

The CR's prime objective is to support DoD environment. It is a realistic, closed, network setup that allows training and testing operations for removing risks to the networks that are operational. To overcome doing manual configurations in the CR, its version 2.0 was released. This new version CR provides automatic and instant event topology, its validation, and usage metrics of the resources, control, and assessment reports. The version 2.0 virtualizes the majority of physical equipment's and uses browser technology for managing the virtual infrastructure. Its services comprise NTF generation, easily configurable

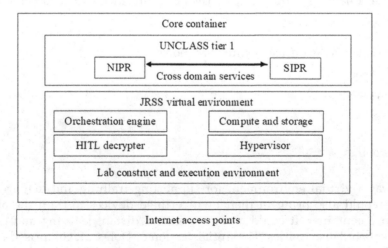

FIGURE 9.14
DoD CSR version 2.0 architecture components.

TABLE 9.3

Advantages of Emulation-Based MCRs

NCR	JIOR	DoD CSR
• It provides realistic and high-fidelity, test beds for conducting advanced cyberwarfare trainings. • The NCR allows incorporating cybersecurity features early for avoiding costly integration at end of development life cycle. • It is institutional-funded and cost effective. • NCR capabilities are independently validated. • Different events can occur either exclusively or simultaneously. • Secure and isolated test beds. • An extensive repository of major resources.	• It provides a seamless, flexible, and persistent setup for training in IO and cyberwarfare concepts. • It is a live-fire CR. • It can run numerous events simultaneously at numerous security levels. • It can provide both tactical event environment and persistent environment. • It provides enterprise services as well. • Accommodates 6000+ candidates for certifications and trainings. • It can interconnect 145+ sites. It can support up to 90 network nodes and 60+ events.	It provides a persistent environment for testing, evaluation, CE support and training. A replica of the GIG environment, with complete network services. It can operate in stand-alone mode or it can be used jointly with other CRs like JIOR using VPN. It also provides tier 2 and tier 3 capabilities. Hosting emulation environment is less costly. Clients do not have to pay any direct charges unless they have some exclusive requirements currently not built-in the CR.

emulation. It allows the emulation and use of malware, botnets, and spyware within the environment for training simulations.

9.3.4 Comparison of Emulation-Based MCRs

This section focuses on summarizing all the advantages and features of the above-discussed CRs in tabular form.

TABLE 9.4

Features of Emulation-Based MCRs

NCR	JIOR	DoD CSR
• Its multilevel independent security architecture support running various simultaneous tests of differing classification levels. • It provides scalable and rapid emulation of sophisticated CN environment. • Automatic software testing toolkit increases the efficacy of the created events by reducing timeline and minimizing human errors. • Restoring all the resources back to the consortium after completion of an event for later use. • Supporting a geographically diverse base of users and communities. Along with a variety of events ranging from testing, to exercises to competitions to research.	• It provides access to network emulations, blue team capabilities, threat environments and NTF generation. • It supports 110+ access points across five countries. • It supports secure connectivity and secure transport facilities for associated partners. • The infrastructure of JIOR can support CNO exercises, testing and training of cybersecurity concepts. • It provides access to high demand, low-density training, and test resources with cyber-related targets, critical infrastructures, and NTF, etc.	It is a hybrid CR. DoD clients requiring the CR can get access by numerous secure transport methods at customer's base stations. Its version 2.0 virtualizes majority of physical equipment's and use browser technology for managing the virtual infrastructure. Its environment supports distant learning and conducting lab activities and training.

9.4 MACRs

This section discusses and presents a comparison among the MACRs. The MACRs discussed under this section are USMA IWAR, Estonian CR, and KYPO Czech.

9.4.1 USMA IWAR

9.4.1.1 Introduction

It is an USMA remote network that is used in training and educating cadets in the information assurance and technical operations (Dodge *et al.* 2005). Initially, the IWAR lab had focused on familiarizing the students in concepts like computer security, information assurance and taking technical measures and responding to network attacks (Lathrop *et al.* 2003). The IWAR CR is an isolated laboratory having no contact with the outside world. The main purpose of the IWAR is to provide an authentic, isolated environment for conducting simultaneous activities, for example, training, research, and analyses. Most of the researches conducted in IWAR are focused on IO and cyberwarfare concepts. It also focuses on developing techniques for both offensive approach and defensive approach. It is imperative to understand the techniques used by the intruders for exploitation of infrastructure's vulnerabilities. These insights assist in developing techniques for protecting, detecting, defending, and fixing these vulnerabilities.

9.4.1.2 Origin

The initial objectives of the CR were focused on creating a reliable, authentic environment fulfilling the following requirements:

- Comprises heterogenous systems.
- Provides multilevel security facilities.
- Sharing of resources is possible across various isolated setups.
- Swift system rebuilds with backups and admin servers.
- Reconfiguration of the lab should be centralized.
- Avoiding external or local disruptions.
- Reuse resources and reduce expenditures.

In its initial years, the lab comprised 40+ systems, 2 firewalls, software for vulnerability detection and scanning, 10 networking components, and 8 different operating systems. The initial budget of the lab facility was approximately $270K (Lathrop *et al.* 2003).

9.4.1.3 Architecture

The CR is divided into four different networks: Gray network, Gold network, Green network, and Black network (Schafer *et al.* 2000); illustrated in Figure 9.15.

9.4.1.3.1 Gray Network

It is the "attack teams" or "attack systems" of the CR. The teams' workstations are located on the Gray subnetwork1. Each team is provided with one main workstation. Each

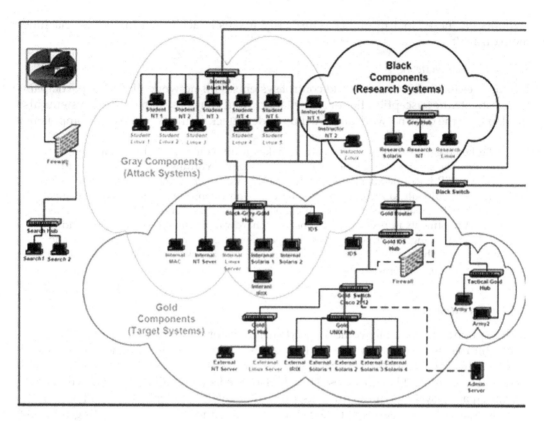

FIGURE 9.15
IWAR schematic.

workstation uses VMWare for running both Windows NT (Hades) and Linux (Inferno) instantaneously on a similar physical machine. All the participants have user accounts on every Gray subnetwork machine. During the exercise, the participants have to download some malicious applet from their Linux-box on a similar physical hardware using their credentials for NT machines. And so, the Gray network is able to launch inside attacks.

9.4.1.3.2 Gold Network

It comprises the "gold components" or the "target systems" of the CR. The target systems are Linux, Unix (SGI and Solaris), Macintosh and Windows NT servers, and workstations. The Gold network assists the participants to understand the competencies and vulnerabilities of the firewalls and routers when under an insider attack.

9.4.1.3.3 Black Network

It comprises the "research systems" of the CR. The Black network is generally used for research purposes. Faculty members operate this network for the information assurance researches (Ragsdale *et al.* 2000). The placement of all the components of this network (as shown in Figure 9.8) allows the researchers to carry out their works on both the offensive and the defensive projects.

Several machines in the topology are Black Gold components. This means that these components are targets, but they are on the Black subnet and so the users don't have any accounts on these Gold machines. This setup makes attacking on these host machines more difficult.

9.4.1.3.4 Green Network

It comprises tactical commands and control systems. This network allows the participants to investigate the susceptibilities of Army tactical and control systems. These systems also overlap with the Gold network and are thus under attack similarly as the gold components.

> The heterogenous and complex nature makes it difficult to scale the components of the lab. The setup of the CR needs to be customized according to the objectives of the CE. The CR is not flexible to be able to accommodate important trade-off functionalities. It is difficult to incorporate new defense and offense techniques and strategies into the CR's environment. The maintenance and implementation of IWAR CR entails hefty investments in resources like software, hardware, human resources for creating and maintaining the physical network topologies of communication components and computers. There may be numerous dangerous cyberattacks that won't be possible to operate on real systems.

9.4.1.4 Evolution

With its popular use, the lab would support various information and cyber-related courses, research projects in fields like operating systems, designing of information systems, artificial intelligence, computer networks, etc. All the lectures would include hands-on and technical training and lab activities. The CR also faced some challenges such as exceeding the lab capacity, system administrations, providing newly developed tools and other functionalities. The heterogenous nature of the lab also led to some issues. Setting up of the lab would be tedious and time-consuming. These shortcomings in the initial lab design needed to be addressed.

9.4.2 Estonian CR

9.4.2.1 Introduction

Estonian CR is one of the government-financed CRs operated under the military's command. The CR not only fulfills the military requirements but also provides supports national and/or international programs. These programs are dedicated to enhancing the cyber defense resources, increasing multinational cooperation and enhancing resilience of cybersecurity. The CR's platform can be operated anywhere in the world, generally for purposes like education, trainings, and conducting CE. Apart from Cyber Coalition and Locked Shields exercises, it has also been used for multiple trainings like for the Tallinn University of Technology and the CCDCoE (Valtenberg *et al.* 2017).

9.4.2.2 Origin

With the objective of supporting the enhancement of Estonia's cyber defense resources, this CR project got initiated in 2011 (Valtenberg *et al.* 2017). This CR supported two NATO exercises: Cyber Coalition and Locked Shields (Čeleda *et al.* 2015). Locked Shields is organized by the NATO CCDCoE as an annual exercise since 2010. This exercise focuses on providing simulations of an entire massive and complex cyber incident for enhancing the participants' decision-making, communication, and legal characteristics.

This exercise provides an exclusive opportunity for encouraging trainings, experimentations, and cooperation among the NATO, CCDCoE, and partner nation members (CCDCOE 2021). The participants include over 12,000 cyber defense professionals from over 30 nations who work together in teams training against highly skilled adversaries' attacks in a secure training environment. Cyber Coalition has been among the major cyber exercises conducted in the world, providing a practical scenario and allowing the participants to train against any cyber incidents (NATO CSC 2020). In 2020, over 1000 people had participated in this exercise from the European Union, the Alliance, and four Partner Nations.

9.4.2.3 Architecture

The infrastructure of the CR comprises the following components (Figure 9.16):.

- **Cisco UCS servers**: the CR consists of three generations of the UCS blade servers having 12 TB of RAM and 1400 CPU cores.
- **XtremIO and EMC VNX platforms**: these platforms are used for data storage purposes and these are connected with the CR's data centers using several 8 Gbit/s links(fiber-channel). VNX provides 140-TB capacity slower spinning drives. These drives are used for the operations having least resource demands. XtremIO provides the storage units (SSD ultrafast) with 30-TB usable capacity.
- **Network connections**: the CR uses the ASOnet connections for daily operations. Another Internet connection is delivered by Telia for CE. Telia gives both one 1 Gbit/s as well as several 10 Gbit/s Internet connections to the CR. Although the network devices are all duplicated and the interconnections among these devices are done using the replicated 10 Gbit/s connectors.
- **Firewalls and VPNs**: the CR uses SourceFire IPs solutions and Cisco firewalls. These firewalls are responsible for providing a safe VPN connection to approximately 500 end users and indefinite site-to-site channels. The VPN concentrators get configured in the active-passive modes for fault tolerances.

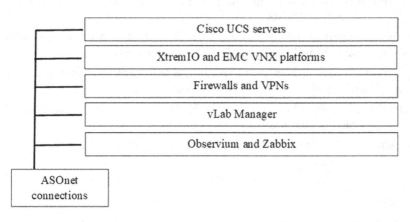

FIGURE 9.16
Estonian CR architecture.

- **vLab Manager**: this is an automation software used for configuring and designing the training environments of the CR. It is also responsible for the CR's resource management and workflow visualizations.
- **Observium and Zabbix**: these tools are used for monitoring the CR's environment.

9.4.2.4 Evolution

The CR and its functionalities are fundamental in the development of NATO CR with Estonian government. It provides dynamic environments comparatively to cloud environments in use. It also supports activities of short durations. Numerous systems get activated or deactivated, they get consistently modified. This is in contrast with cloud environments that support long duration running systems.

9.4.3 KYPO Czech

9.4.3.1 Introduction

This CR was a government-funded project, developed and operated by CSIRT-Masaryk University (Valtenberg and Matulevičius 2017). KYPO is designed as a modular distributed platform with the aim to provide real-world scenarios. The CR's architecture can run on any platforms, for example, OpenStack. KYPO's architecture fulfills the following requirements:

  i. **Flexibility**: the CR supports the development and configurations of arbitrary (or as required) network topologies that may range from single node to several nodes connected networks.
 ii. **Scalability**: the CR's environment and components can be scaled proportionally to the number of users. Resources like numbers of sandboxes and topology nodes, bandwidth network size, and processing power can be scaled according to the number of participants.
iii. **Isolation versus interoperability**: the CR can be remotely accessed anywhere in the world and can be integrated with other external resources and systems.
 iv. **Cost-effectiveness**: the CR's operating and maintenance expenses are quite less in comparison to other MACRs.
  v. **Built-in monitoring**: the CR monitors the flow data, captured packets and provides real-time logs and node metrics for each exercise.
 vi. **Easy access**: as the CR is cloud-based, it is able to provide web-based accesses to its central functionalities to all the participants.
vii. **Service-based access**: the cloud-based CR offers PaaS, thus, making the platform easily accessible via web interfaces for even the amateur users.
viii. **Open source**: KYPO is currently an open-source software distributed under MIT license.

9.4.3.2 Origin

With the rising cyberwarfare scenarios, time-efficiency and cost-effectiveness were prime factors while considering the development of any CR. KYPO was developed for simulating

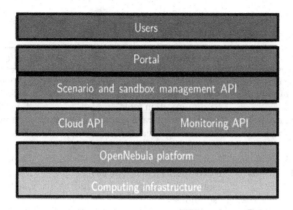

FIGURE 9.17
Components of KYPO.

complex cyber networks and systems. It provides virtualized environment with complete control and monitoring capabilities. It is both time and cost-efficient. This is possible, as the CR uses cloud resources instead of some physical infrastructure.

9.4.3.3 Architecture

The following are the main building blocks of KYPO's architecture (Figure 9.17):

i. **Computing infrastructure**: it comprises computing resources like physical machines, data center resources, network devices, etc. (Valtenberg *et al.* 2017).

ii. **OpenNebula platform**: the purpose of this platform is to manage the computing infrastructure, provide cloud management, and virtualization management (Joint Staff J7, 2015)

iii. **Monitoring API**: it provides monitoring functionalities for network topologies, hosts, and other components of CR. It also monitors the cloud API responsible for translating OpenNebula commands into commonly used API methods (Joint Staff J7, 2015).

iv. **Scenario and sandbox management APIs**: they are for managing various sandboxes (Chaskos 2019).

v. **Portal**: the user is able to interact with sandboxes using the portal as an interface. These sandboxes can be used for research and analysis of malwares and for conducting CE. Using the portal, the user is able to manage and analyze the CE, access sandboxes, create, and test new cyber situational awareness sensitive network topologies and implement new security scenarios.

9.4.3.4 Evolution

The CR conducts various exercises and training sessions supporting hundreds of participants. These activities assist in providing useful feedback for the improvement of the CR. The CR has evolved to incorporate not only simulations of critical infrastructures but also support academic-related activities.

TABLE 9.5

Advantages of MACRs

USMA IWAR	Estonian CR	KYPO Czech CR
It can provide simulations of defenses like encryption, cryptography and access control techniques. It can provide simulations of cyberattacks like Trojans, viruses, DoS, worms, etc. It provides training in military tactics like reconnaissance and concepts like offense and defense.	It provides the participants with ad hoc backup infrastructure, reporting, and communication tools. It provides interactive trainings for the team using "live-fire" exercises, practical high-stress setups and consistent performance assessments. It is cost-effective for the testing of software-enabled products and solutions.	The CR is completely cloud based. It provides a comprehensive training stack, sophisticated customization tools, forensics on malware, network security, and certifications. It has a flexible and scalable architecture.

9.4.4 Comparison of MACRs

This section focuses on summarizing all the advantages of the above-discussed MACRs in tabular form.

References

CCDCOE, 2021. Locked Shields [online]. Available from: https://ccdcoe.org/exercises/locked-shields/ [Accessed 23 April 2021].

Čeleda, P., Čegan, J., Vykopal, J., Tovarňák, D., 2015. Kypo – A platform for cyber defence exercises. *In: M&S Support to Operational Tasks Including War Gaming, Logistics, Cyber Defence*. NATO Science and Technology Organization, Norway.

Chaskos, E. C., 2019. Cyber-security training: A comparative analysis of cyber ranges and emerging trends [online]. Available from: https://pergamos.lib.uoa.gr/uoa/dl/frontend/file/lib/default/data/2864976/theFile [Accessed 23 April 2021].

Dodge, R., Ragsdale, D., 2005. Technology education at the US Military Academy. *IEEE Security & Privacy*, 3(2), 49–53.

Ferguson, B., Tall, A., Olsen, D., 2014. National cyber range overview. *In*: Military Communications Conference, 6–8 October 2014 Baltimore. New York: IEEE, 123–128.

Haglich, P., Grimshaw, R., Wilder, S., Nodine, M., Lyles, B., 2011. Cyber scientific test language. *In*: International Semantic Web Conference, 23–27 October 2011 Berlin. Switzerland: Springer, 97–111.

Harwell, S. D., Gore, C. M., 2013. Synthetic cyber environments for training and exercising cyberspace operations. *M&S Journal*, 8(2), 36–47.

Hernandez, J., 2010. The Human element complicates cybersecurity [online]. Available from: http://www.defensesystems.com/Articles/2010/03/11/IndustryPerspective-1-human-side-of-cybersecurity.aspx?Page=2 [Accessed 20 March 2021].

Joint Staff J7, 2015. *Cyberspace Environment Division/Joint Information Operations Range (JIOR) Overview* [online]. Joint Staff Public Affairs. Available from: http://www.itea.org/images/pdf/conferences/2016%20Cyber/Proceedings/ROMERO_CED_JIOR_101.pdf [Accessed 23 April 2021].

Lathrop, S. D., Conti, G. J., Ragsdale, D. J., 2003. Information warfare in the trenches. *IFIP Advances in Information and Communication Technology*, 125(1), 19–39.

Leblanc, S. P., Partington, A., Chapman, I. M., Bernier, M., 2011. An overview of cyber attack and computer network operations simulation. *In*: A. G. Stricker, ed., *Spring Simulation Multi-conference*, 3–7 April 2011 Boston. New York: SCS/ACM, 92–100.

Luddy, J., 2005. *The Challenge and Promise of Network-Centric Warfare*. Arlington: Lexington Institute.

McBride, A., 2007. Air force cyber warfare training. *The Defense Standardization Program Journal*, 1(2), 9–13.

Meitzler, W., Oudekirk, S., Hughes, C., 2009. *Security Assessment Simulation Toolkit: SAST*. Technical Report, Pacific Northwest National Laboratory.

Mudge, R. S., Lingley, S., 2008. *Cyber and Air Joint Effects Demonstration (CAAJED)*. Air Force Research Lab Rome, NY Information Directorate.

NATO CSC, 2020. NATO exercises cyber defence capabilities at Cyber Coalition [online]. Available from: https://www.ncia.nato.int/about-us/newsroom/nato-exercises-cyber-defence-capabilities-at-cyber-coalition.html [Accessed 23 April 2021].

Pridmore, L., Lardieri, P., Hollister, R., 2010. National Cyber Range (NCR) automated test tools: Implications and application to network-centric support tools. *In*: 2010 IEEE Autotestcon, 13–16 September 2010 Orlando. New York: IEEE, 1–4.

Prinetto, P., Farulla, D. G. A., Marrocco, D., 2018. *Design and Deployment of a Virtual Environment to Emulate a SCADA Network within Cyber Ranges*. Politecnico di Torino. Available from: https://webthesis.biblio.polito.it/9566/ [Accessed 23 April 2021].

Ragsdale, D., Schafer, J., 2000. USMA information warfare analysis and research IWAR laboratory [online]. Available from: https://slidetodoc.com/usma-information-warfare-analysis-and-research-iwar-laboratory/ [Accessed 23 April 2021].

Roesch, M., 1999. Snort: Lightweight intrusion detection for networks. *Lisa*, 99(1), 229–238.

Schafer, J., Ragsdale, D. J., Surdu, J. R., Carver, C. A., 2000. *The IWAR Range: A Laboratory for Undergraduate Information Assurance Education*. Military Academy West Point, NY.

Urias, V. E., Stout, W. M., Van Leeuwen, B., Lin, H., 2018. Cyber range infrastructure limitations and needs of tomorrow: A position paper. *In*: 2018 International Carnahan Conference on Security Technology (ICCST), 22–25 October 2018 Montreal. New York: IEEE, 1–5.

Valtenberg, U., Matulevičius, R., 2017. *Federation of Cyber Ranges*. Thesis (Master's). University of Tartu.

Varshney, M., Pickett, K., Bagrodia, R., 2011. A live-virtual-constructive (LVC) framework for cyber operations test, evaluation and training. *In*: Military Communications Conference, 7–10 November 2011 Baltimore. New York: IEEE, 1387–1392.

Wabiszewski, M. G., Andel, T. R., Mullins, B. E., Thomas, R. W., 2009. Enhancing realistic hands-on network training in a virtual environment. *In*: Spring Simulation Multiconference, 22–27 March 2009 San Diego. San Diego: Society for Computer Simulation International, 1–8.

10

Existing Cyber Ranges in Academic Sector

10.1 Simulation-Based ACRs

This section discusses and presents a comparison between the simulation-based ACRs. The ACRs discussed under this section are SECUSIM, RINSE, netEngine, OPNET CR, and CONCORDIA consortium.

10.1.1 SECUSIM

10.1.1.1 Introduction

SECUSIM is a seminal-paper-based CR developed in 2001 (Cohen 1999). It was a government and research-center-supported project (Cohen 1999). The CR initially focused on fulfilling its three major objectives. These objectives are listed below:

- Specification of attack-oriented CR's mechanisms.
- Verification of defense-oriented CR's mechanisms.
- Drawing evaluations from their corollaries.

To achieve these objectives, the CR used SES/MB framework, an experimental frame, and DEVS formalism (Cohen 1999). All these were sophisticated simulation and modeling concepts. The CR achieves its objectives by adapting to the hierarchical and integrated types of modeling/simulation environment. The working of the CR's simulation can be summarized in the following points:

1. Defining metrics for vulnerable links and nodes of the network infrastructure. This supports in delivering an appropriate mechanism for evaluating the simulated infrastructure.
2. Characterizing behaviors of defense-oriented mechanisms, cyberattacks, and their consequences. This is completed in state transition diagrams of an isolated event model.
3. The complexity of the simulation is of functional-level developed using DEVS formalism.

The simulation methodology could be divided into four different phases:

Phase I: involves specifying the simulation objectives, requirements, taxonomies, and constraints. SES specifies all these network infrastructure-related concepts.

Phase II: involves generation of behavioral and structural models. DEVS formalism assists in building analyzer and attack models. These models get saved into the MB.

Phase III: involves integration of MB's dynamic models and SES network structure. This results in the construction of a simulation for performing cyberattacks.

Phase IV: involves analyzing the results of the simulation. Each network component, its security policies, and characteristics get evaluated in this phase.

10.1.1.2 Terminologies

This subsection explains some of the above-mentioned terminologies w.r.t the CR:

- **SES/MB framework**: SES comprises know-how of all the components' breakdowns, constraints, simulation taxonomies, objectives, etc. SES along with the use of some transformation operations can be used for generating hierarchal and integrated simulations (Chi *et al.* 2001). MB stores all the constructed models like the analyzer and attack models. SES/MB framework supports the object-oriented programming aspects of the CR's environment.

- **DEVS**: it describes the created event models. It is a structure comprising different event types as the input, a sequential state, and event types (external) generated as the output. It also comprises both internal and external transition functions, an output function, and a function for time advanced (Chi *et al.* 2001).

- **Attack model**: responsible for providing an array of attacking commands as the output that corresponds to the attack settings (Chi *et al.* 2001).

- **Analyzer model**: responsible for gathering the stats of the functioning of all the components. It also analyses the performance index of the components of the infrastructure considering their vulnerabilities (Chi *et al.* 2001).

Figure 10.1 depicts the relation between the working of both attack and analyzer models. The attack model is used for implementing its commands in the network and into the

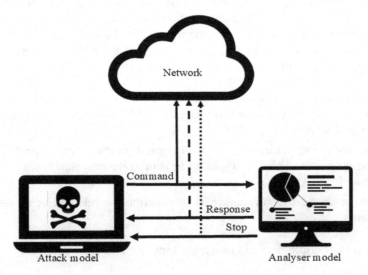

FIGURE 10.1
Working of attack and analyzer models.

analyzer. The network responds to both the attack and analyzer models. Once enough data is collected by the analyzer model, it terminates the simulation by sending the stop command to both the attack model and network. Next, the analyzer model performs analysis on the performance of each component, also considering the results of the attack model.

10.1.1.3 Architecture

With its initial release, SECUSIM CR got implemented on Visual C++ platform. It could support up to 20 attack patterns within a simulation, against approximately 100 network modules (Park *et al.* 2001). Figure 10.2 illustrates the major architectural components of this CR. Their functionalities are discussed as follows:

- **Network configurator**: it delivers editing facilities for graphics, thus aiding in the construction of diverse and as per requirement of network structures.
- **GUI**: it supports tasks like network components, initialization and adjustment attributes. These attributes vary upon the results and conditions of a simulation. Construction of graphic packet-level animations is also supported during a simulation.
- **Simulation engine**: it is responsible for the execution of all attack scenarios and corresponding network models. It also provides the results of the simulations.
- **Component MB**: it comprises physical components like routers, servers, firewalls, and gateways.
- **Attack scenario database**: it comprises authorized cyberattack scenarios that can be incorporated in a simulation using commands.

  Upon its release, SECUSIM allows five different modes based on usage:
  - **Basic mode**: its purpose is to provide information about attack scenarios when retrieved from the database.
  - **Intermediate mode**: it supports the setup of an attack scenario. Users can randomly select target hosts and attacks models from the "component property window".

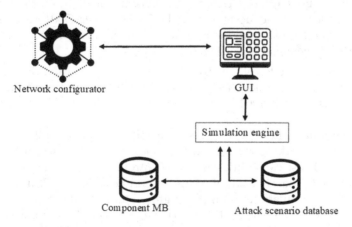

FIGURE 10.2
Components of SECUSIM.

- **Advanced mode**: it supports authorized testing of modulated cyberattacks using the "command input window".

- **Professional mode**: it allows hosting multiple cyberattack simulations. This is helpful in determining and analyzing vulnerabilities in the network infrastructure.

- **Application mode**: it allows creation and editing capabilities to the user for simulating network configurations as per their requirements.

10.1.2 RINSE

10.1.2.1 Introduction

RINSE was developed by the University of Illinois (Liljenstam *et al.* 2005) with the aim of simulating terrorist-level cyberattacks on network infrastructures of national importance. It essentially focused on developing an extensive, real-time simulation system. This simulation system could simultaneously accommodate multiple participants, offer security techniques, and manage any hardware redundancies (Greenspan *et al.* 2004). The CR brings human interaction service together with various simulation features. The CR accommodates institutes of both public and private sectors in cyber wargame exercises. These institutes range from telecom, power, and financial sectors to all the contributing universities and their staff.

In earlier CRs, when the developers required to add more network components to the simulation, a new simulation would be created from scratch. RINSE architecture is developed such that the simulation platform can be scaled instantly, easily, and economically. The CR's APIs are user-friendly (Greenspan *et al.* 2004). The CR achieves scalability by adopting tactics like maintaining a semantic consistency between the different modules, predicting possible variations, and regulating possible decisions. To further enhance its performance, RINSE focuses on the following factors:

- **Resource demand**: the CR uses a parallel processing technique for regulating the occurrences of various events and resources consumed in each event. Well-bounded queue sizes and execution times assist in preventing any overruns.

- **Resource management**: the CR maintains a backup of all the data and simulations in a distantly located backup network. The CR uses over 1500+ processors of high performance and substantial memory for achieving concurrency and increasing its resources (Greenspan *et al.* 2004).

- **Resource arbitration**: for efficiently allocating resources, RINSE uses scheduling strategies like FIFO queues, fixed priority scheduling, and deadline monatomic tactics (Greenspan *et al.* 2004).

RINSE simulation offers the following user capabilities – packet filters installations for attack or defense, networking tools for diagnostics, simulator data, and device controls (Leblanc *et al.* 2011). These capabilities assist in controlling the simulation output for highlighting any vulnerabilities. Instead of a GUI-based interface, the CR uses command line. Majority of the CR's simulations comprise highly intense traffic (network) flow cyberattacks like worms and DDoS. The participants have to defend the simulated network infrastructure against such attacks. They also have to detect the vulnerabilities and diagnose the same. The attack teams' task is to disable the infrastructure's servers by bombarding it with junk traffic (network). The traffic is voluminous and so the server is unable to deliver its services. Defense teams need to ensure that all the servers are properly functioning and diagnose the affected servers. The participants' performances are monitored by the simulation controller. The CR aims to educate and train network security personnel against such extensive cyberattack scenarios.

10.1.2.2 Architectural and Business Influences

The architecture of the CR is contributed by various teams of stakeholders, organizations, and university staff. The basic features of the CR like ensuring high performance, security, and fault tolerance are set by the stakeholders and other organizations involved. The technical team is responsible for setting up a technical environment fulfilling the above requirements. Figure 10.3 demonstrates the relation between the various entities involved in designing the architecture of the CR (Greenspan *et al.* 2004).

10.1.2.3 Architecture

The CR comprises five major components as discussed below and as shown in Figure 10.4.

- **iSSFNet**: it is a network simulator supporting a network of parallel running simulations. Its kernel pattern is responsible for managing all its support functions. This network simulator assists in hosting various extensive, instantaneous, live simulations. Its distinctive synchronization mechanism supports distributed execution.

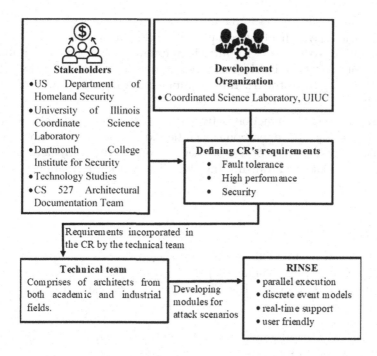

FIGURE 10.3
Architectural and business influences.

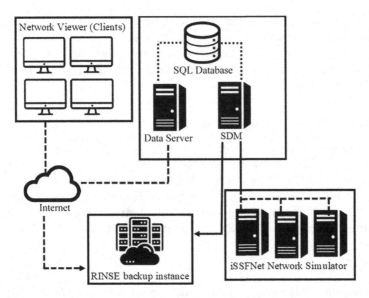

FIGURE 10.4
Components of RINSE architecture.

- **SDM**: it is responsible for the transmission of the data taking place between the iSSFNet and SQL database. SDM is independently connected with all the simulation nodes (Liljenstam *et al.* 2005). It also allocates the database's control signals to simulator.

- **Network viewer**: during a simulation, it assists the users in viewing the simulated network. It is a java client-based application (Liljenstam *et al.* 2005). Simulation admins use network viewer for introducing new scenarios in the simulations. It supports commands of five distinct types: initiating an attack, employing defense tactics, operating the infrastructure's components, diagnosis, and collecting simulation data.

- **Data server**: allows interaction between the simulation and network viewer. It offers monitoring and operational facilities to the admins hosting the simulation. It is also responsible for user authentications, authorizing network viewer to access the database, and transmitting clients' network information.

10.1.3 netEngine

10.1.3.1 Introduction

The aim of constructing this CR was to encourage cybersecurity preparedness among security personnel and policymakers. The CR was capable of creating extensive simulations of national infrastructures. The CR was constructed to incorporate the following objectives (Brown *et al.* 2003):

- Distinguishing the vulnerabilities of the network infrastructure and providing relevant data to the user to make informed decisions.
- Determine the possible consequences of decisions made by the user.

- Conduct relevant cyberattack preparedness exercises by simulating extensive critical infrastructures.
- Provide a communication medium between the diverse, involved communities.

The CR's simulations are generally used for conducting cyberattack preparedness exercises. The simulation assists in streamlining the complex interactions and dependencies of the network infrastructure. The simulation also helps the user in recognizing any overlooked or unforeseen consequences of the attack. Logs of all the participants' activities and teams' communication during the simulations are maintained. Post-exercise analyses are also conducted for ensuring effective decision-making. Participants can communicate in the simulation via emails or instant messages. The CR also provides a realistic experience to the participants by allowing them to view network statuses, topology maps, and response actions of the teams.

The CR platform is C++ based and runs on Linux. It uses Apache as the web server (Brown *et al.* 2003). Thus, with good Internet connection, the simulation is accessible to participants living across different geographical areas. Figure 10.5 illustrates the working of netEngine.

10.1.3.2 Architecture

netEngine is a lightweight CR capable of accommodating thousands of participants whether they are present on the same site or they are geographically distributed. All the participants can access the simulation exercises via browser. Every CPU in the CR can simulate up to a thousand network components like routers, workstations, and firewalls in real time without any graphics involved (Brown *et al.* 2003). Graphics calculation consumes maximum execution time. These graphics calculations include diagrams of network statuses or strip charts of router load.

The strip chart records all the activities affecting the router's performance under specific time periods like:

- The router under a normal network traffic condition.
- The router under cyberattack conditions.

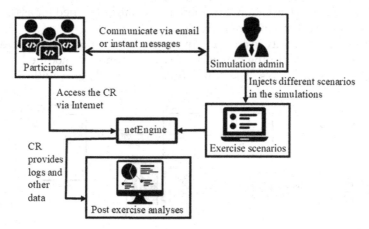

FIGURE 10.5
Working of netEngine.

- Duration of inactivity of router.
- Router reset condition.
- Working of router after reset.

The operational status of all the components is indicated with different colors. The CR interface allows the participants to view any component's load history when clicked upon. It also lets the participants view security policies and routing tables. Communication medium between participants is established using the simulations of email and telephone executed via applet. Participants can exchange dialogue or any other relevant information with each other and with the simulation admins during the exercise. Figure 10.6 illustrates the different physical components used in a simulation.

All the exercise events are pre-configured and stored in the CR's database. The simulation admins decide which event to deploy and the events flow during the exercise. The simulation admins also control the flow of network traffic during the ongoing simulation. They can disable routers or alter routing tables or boot a device. They have the freedom to dynamically revise the network during the simulations (Leblanc *et al.* 2011). Initially, participants deal with events aimed at understanding the CR's network communication and monitoring functions.

All the information communicated, decisions taken, and other activities performed by the participants are maintained in a log. This log is useful in drawing post-exercise analyses. They are also useful in analyzing the individual performance of the participants in maintaining the functionality of the simulated network during any attack.

10.1.4 OPNET CR

10.1.4.1 Introduction

The OPNET CR was developed by the OPNET Technologies incorporation (Pan *et al.* 2008). Till date, it has supported researchers and students from 240+ countries performing multiple projects (OPNET PROJECTS TEAM 2005). These projects have their own teams for guiding students in network research field or development arena. OPNET is an open and free to install and use software. It provides free licenses of the software and discounts on technical support to qualified academic institutes under its university program (Sethi *et al.* 2012). The CR is generally used for studying devices, applications, and protocols in a communication network. The CR environment is specially designed for assisting network-related research task or development activities.

The CR offers great versatility in creating diverse network topology simulations. It already has a definite set of protocols, the behavior of which cannot be modified. Neither does it support creating new protocols. The simulation workflow begins with the creation and

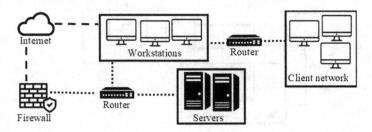

FIGURE 10.6
Simulation components.

configuration of network topology. It is followed by setting up network traffic and statistics. After the completion of the simulation, users can view and publish the outcomes. Users can also duplicate the previously created simulation or develop a new one. The CR makes use of its powerful GUI and integrated platform to enhance user-friendly experience. Simulations can be easily designed using the GUI. The CR also assists in generating charts, animations, and graphs of the outcomes of the simulations for analyses and distribution.

Other than its own modules and libraries, the CR also supports integration of external libraries in the simulation. Simulation events occur according to various scenarios setup by the user. All the networks are organized using hierarchical modeling technique. OPNET is designed to incorporate the following design requirements:

- Object-oriented simulations
- Hierarchical modeling
- Powerful graphical interface capabilities

Hierarchical modeling highlights the various often overlooked attributes of each level of the simulated structure. The user first needs to define the simulation objectives or a problem statement. Then using the in-built libraries and protocols, they built the simulation model. The model gets complied into a form of executable code. Thus, the simulation could be either debugged or directly get executed. Users can modify these models as per the initially set objectives. Lastly, users are provided with all the simulation data, outcomes, and analyses. The CR successfully supports instantaneous simulation generation, scalability, simulation packages, and libraries (Chang 1999).

10.1.4.2 Architecture

All the components and tools of the CR can be sorted according to their use as shown in Figure 10.7. The CR requires these tools for:

- **Building hierarchical model**: consists of four main editors for supporting reuse of newly created or existing models. A model developed at one level (or layer) can

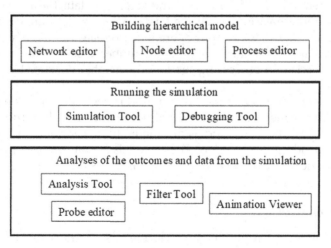

FIGURE 10.7
OPNET architectural components.

be used in another. Network editor specifies communication network's physical topology. This includes defining the locus of network components (like links and nodes) and their interconnection. The editor realizes all capabilities of nodes in the "network model". Each model is used for customizing a node's or a link's behavior. Node editor specifies all the created and interconnected components in network model within the "node model". These models are interconnected and can be categorized into predefined and highly programmable models. Packet generators, radio receivers, etc. fall under the predefined models as they already have a built-in set of parameters. Queues and processors are highly programmable models.

The functionalities of every programmable block within node model get defined using the "process model". Process editor is responsible for creating these models. These models define behavior and logic flows of queues and processors. Proto-C language is used for expressing the process models. This language comprises all the functionalities of C language, state transition diagrams, and kernel procedure libraries. New process can be created for executing sub-tasks.

- **Running the simulation**: all the above-mentioned models assist in executing the exercise in the simulations. Both debugging and simulation tools assist in executing the simulation and gathering the data. Simulation tool is responsible for executing simulations within OPNET with its GUI capabilities. The tool specifies simulation sequences, their execution, storage, and future use.

- **Analyses of the outcomes and data from the simulation**: data generation after a simulation is achieved using tools like probe editor, filter, and analysis tools. Probe editor defines the source of data and the type of data to be collected. Simulation data like statistics and animations get generated by various OPNET models. Probe editor assists the user to streamline huge chunk of data to only provide the relevant information. OPNET comprises different probes for different types of data. For monitoring rate of bit errors and throughput, user can apply statistic probe. For generating animation sequences, users can apply automatic animation and, for customized animations, they can use custom animation probes. Coupled statistics probe is only applied in the case of radio receivers.

  With the generation of different types and volume of data, the analysis tool assists in graphical representation of collected data. All the graphs are displayed within analysis panel. Users have various operations to create and modify the panel. The panel area comprises plotting region with numbered coordinate axes. The analysis tool also assists in processing the latest generated datasets by plotting them into graphs.

  Filter elements are interconnected and used in the representation of filter models. These filter elements are either a reference to filter models or pre-built processing elements. All the filter models are hierarchical and most of them comprise other corresponding filter models. These models operate on one or more than one vector (numeric data entries) and their combinations form the output.

10.1.4.3 Simulation Workflow

With the specification of various hierarchical models, the next procedure involves the execution of the exercise within a simulation. It is also important to collect the output data such as individual performances and statuses of the network components after the termination of a simulation. Therefore, the first step in simulation execution includes the specification of the type of data to be stored. Users need to decide in advance what information would be necessary as per their requirements. Different types of data can include component's behavior and statistics of an application and its visualization.

The step followed by this focuses on the construction of the simulation. After defining the hierarchical models and data probes, developers can create an executable code file for the simulation. This code file can also be stored for future use. It can also be debugged according to the latest requirements. OPNET is flexible in executing the simulation. It supports both internal and external execution processes and attributes. The CR offers a versatile range of options that support the simulation execution. Simulations can independently run on OPNET platform but with the exception of graphical tools.

10.1.5 Concordia Consortium

It is one of the European-Union-funded projects under Horizon 2020 program (The CONCORDIAns 2020). The consortium comprises various European academic institutions and organizations from communication, e-health, e-mobility, finance, and telecom industries. The consortium also supports some CRs under its project. The consortium also hosts various webinars, workshops, conferences, and cybersecurity-related events year-round.

The consortium was formed for fulfilling the listed objectives:

- Delivering the latest know-hows of cybersecurity aspects to the industry's policymakers. The scenario of cybersecurity, cyberwarfare is ever-changing and dynamic. Therefore, it is necessary to be updated and prepared for every kind of possibility affecting the security of critical infrastructures.

- Incorporating goals, perspectives, and priorities of all the diverse involved communities. The consortium must serve as a medium where all the communities are able to share and discuss their research.

- Design a resilient, secure cybersecurity ecosystem, which can make its resource accessible to various communities involved.

- Support the development of a road map for cybersecurity. Diverse communities should be able to come together for developing more sophisticated, reliable solutions for cybersecurity, data security, application and user security, etc.

- The consortium should also be able to provide streamlined virtual courses, certifications, competitions, and other workshops or activities for both students and professionals.

- The existing resources, virtual services, and platforms should be scalable to accommodate a maximum number of participants and activities carried out.

- Support execution of cyber-defense exercises, learning and training of professionals and students. It should also be able to support research facilities and crises management as well.

- Develop a system of governance to ensure community guidelines are executed and followed. This would also assist in building a strong, secure, and respectable community.

- Develop a framework for economic aspects. The consortium must be able to provide a framework to assess the impacts of both direct and indirect economic factors.

The CRs supported by the consortium are listed as follows and will be discussed in the upcoming subsections:

- TELECOM Nancy CR
- RISE CR
- Airbus CR
- CODE CR
- KYPO CR

10.1.5.1 KYPO CR

It was developed and operated by CSIRT – Masaryk University (Valtenberg *et al.* 2017). This platform depends on OpenStack cloud provider and consists of containers, microservices, and infrastructure as code (Feller 2020). This is a user-driven range with the objective of providing practical solutions for student education and cybersecurity professionals training. Since it is a cloud-based CR, it provides the advantage of being scalable and flexible. The CR is already been discussed in the previous chapter. For further details, refer to Chapter 9 (Section 9.4.3).

10.1.5.2 TELECOM Nancy CR

It was initially developed at the University of Lorraine, France for supporting the training of students and professionals in the Grand Est. region (Tncy 2020). The CR facilitates building, deploying, and experimenting realistic and sophisticated IT setups for the simulation and analysis of different cyberattacks and defense settings. It comprises two training rooms that are interconnected with a server room used for hosting the range's servers. This CR also provides graphical interface for the creation and editing of network topologies and importing or exporting external functionalities.

It offers services like learning and training activities, cyber-defense-related exercises, and hardware/software testing and research. It also offers certifications in cyber-related studies. The servers used by the CR are called HNS. DIATEAM company had developed these servers. The servers assist in establishing network connections between the virtual topologies and physical platforms and resources.

10.1.5.3 RISE CR

It is the part of RISE, KISTA, Stockholm, Sweden cybersecurity demo and test arena (RISE 2020). The CR aims to provide realistic cybersecurity awareness and training for the public sector. It also supports response handling and provides a setup for research and development in cybersecurity arena. It also supports forums for participation and organization of international competitions in ethical hacking and CTF.

It also provides the same services as the above-discussed CR. The CR also serves as a testing platform for latest security software, patches, or hardware before their release in the market. All the necessary security analyses can be easily conducted in the CR's environment. It also allows the user to constantly monitor the performance of the simulated infrastructure and its components. The CR uses private cloud for executing simulations. It also uses both virtualized topologies and physical hardware components in the creation of simulated critical infrastructures.

10.1.5.4 Airbus CR

It is a multipurpose CR platform comprising various virtual components and capabilities like virtual machines, topologies, containers, traffic generators, attacks, and scenarios (Airbus 2020). The CR offers the following capabilities:

- **User-friendly platform:** the CR is accessible via web interfaces. No additional software needs to be installed by the users. The interfaces cover the complexities of component management. It assists the users to focus on the simulation aspects of their systems.
- **Ease of operations:** the CR minimizes the work of administration during an operation as it uses suitable virtualization technologies like Docker and VMWare.
- **Open, scalable, and customizable platform:** the CR's platform can concurrently support and run numerous simulation environments. The platform also integrates its attack models and virtual assets to build the simulation as per the user requirement.

The CR also supports crises management exercises. They are multisite exercises comprising up to 50 participants from educational institutes and also industrial professionals. This CR's benefits are as follows:

- Transportable, easy to deploy, and use physical components. It also includes servers and power supply. The platform gets deployed using a transportable box.
- The cloud platform of the CR provides multisite collaborative and flexible experience. The price of hosting platform in cloud is quite competitive.
- The CR team offers services like hosting professional training and crises management exercises, resources for conducting components' testing.
- All the CR's elements are backed up and stored in structural layout called "bundle". These bundles can be used for backups, and resource sharing among geographically distributed communities.
- The CR can run multiple isolated simulation environments using its advanced APIs.

10.1.5.5 CODE CR

It was originally developed by the Research Institute CODE of Universität der Bundeswehr Munich, Germany (CODE 2020). This CR provides the training environment for CNOs. The CR aims to provide isolated virtual setups for cybersecurity and CNO trainings. As the CR is isolated from other networks, it also offers evaluation and testing of new IT prototypes or tools. Its flexibility and modularity allow the creating, editing, and importing of the content using VMWare.

It is a virtual-based CR. This is a useful factor as the CR provides flexibility in the integration of both physical and virtual components. The users can create, import, and edit contents of the simulation using VMWare. However, it still requires implementing export functionality for authorized export of resources and user-created scenarios. It also includes 80 different types of exercises such as the red teaming, SCADA, and blue team exercises. The CR also allows customization of topologies and creating new topologies by the users.

10.1.6 Comparison of Simulation-Based ACRs

This section focuses on summarizing all the advantages (in Table 10.1) and features (in Table 10.2) of the above-discussed CRs.

TABLE 10.1

Advantages of Simulation-Based ACRs

SECUSIM	RINSE	netEngine	OPNET CR
It supports construction of security models. It deploys vulnerability metrics to analyze different components of the infrastructure. It offers five different working modes depending on the usage requirements – basic, intermediate, advanced, professional, and application modes. Provides an ideal integrated environment serving multiple goals like creating attack models and analyzing components' performances. Cyberattacks of diverse scale and complexity can be systematically categorized, understood, and used in simulations.	It is a user-friendly platform. It coordinates extensive exercises and war games, accommodating numerous participants from diverse fields of study. Majority of the CR's simulations comprise highly intense traffic (network) flow cyberattacks like worms and DDoS. The pace of the simulation can be varied according to the requirements of the users. The CR efficiently handles resource demands, resource allocation, and resource backup. The CR maintains a backup of all the data and simulations in a distantly located backup network.	The CR is scalable. It can accommodate up to thousand participants present on-site or geographically distributed. Focuses on the consequences of cyberattacks on critical infrastructures. Offers post-exercise analyses. It maintains a log of all the activities taking place during a simulation. Trains participants in cyberattack preparedness and informed decision-making. Simulation assists in streamlining the complex interactions and dependencies of the network infrastructure. It also helps the user in recognizing any overlooked or unforeseen consequences of the attack.	It is an open, free software. It provides free licenses of the software and discounts on technical support to qualified academic institutes under its university program. Supports a variety of extensive network and communications topologies. Offers advanced graphical interface capabilities. Proto-C supports dynamic creation of simulation protocols and functions. It comprises pre-existing library of models and also allows the user to create new models and modify them. Simulation data can be analyzed and presented in form of a graph within analysis panel.

TABLE 10.2

Features of Simulation-Based ACRs

SECUSIM	RINSE	netEngine	OPNET CR
It uses Visual C++ for its implementation. It comprises SES/MB framework, DEVS formalism, and an object-oriented experimental framework concept. Offers a hierarchical and integrated simulation environment. Generates authorized cyberattack scenarios. Supports analysis of all components' vulnerabilities.	It provides instantaneous interface and simulation support. It allows traffic (network) modeling that is of multi-resolution. It offers professional attack models, licensed routing simulations, and physical resource models (CPU, memory, etc.). It is a flexible and scalable platform for training and conducting exercises. It also implements latency absorption techniques.	Implemented on C++. Accessible to participants via web browser. The CR interface allows the participants to view any component's load history when clicked upon. Communication among participants and with simulation admins is achieved via email and telephone applet. Can run on Linux machine All the exercise events are pre-configured and stored in the CR's database.	Supports creation of scalable, flexible, extensive, and discrete event simulator. Uses hierarchical and object-oriented modeling of simulation models. Supports both external and internal simulation libraries and attributes. Offers an integrated platform for running simulations of complex network and communications infrastructures along with data analysis capabilities. Dynamically allows processes to different in-use models. Supports applying probes to the model to streamline big chunks of data. This is useful when the user wants to focus on analyzing only a specific type of data.

10.2 Emulation-Based ACRs

This section discusses and presents a comparison between the emulation-based ACRs. The ACRs discussed under this section are VCSTC, LARIAT, Emulab, DETER, and Virginia CR.

10.2.1 VCSTC

10.2.1.1 Introduction

It is another DoD-funded academic project for an automated testing capability to assess the security impact of a new device before deployment (Pederson *et al.* 2008). The CR primarily focused on achieving an emulation system capable of integrating both physical resources and virtualization techniques. The CR also uses TDL. This language would facilitate security devices' specifications. The CR offers the following functionalities (Shu *et al.* 2008):

- **Advanced fidelity**: hybrid nature of the emulation system makes it possible to recreate realistic emulations of the original infrastructure. The CR supports automatic configuration of the network nodes as per the users' requirements.
- **Scalable and competitive testbed**: duplicating the network infrastructure as realistic as possible is expensive in concern with resources utilized. The CR uses VMWare servers, which assist in instantaneous scaling of the testbed as required. Advanced virtualization methods preserve the resources and other applications when scaling the testbed.
- **Automatic execution of emulations**: the CR covers all the complicated security sequences and coordination among virtual and physical components, so that the user can only focus on the running of the emulation.
- **Incorporate latest security-related testbed solutions**: the CR supports creation of test cases, emulation of the infrastructure and its execution. Before their execution, the test cases get compiled into an executable form using TDL.

10.2.1.2 Architecture

The essential components of the CR supporting security testing include test cases and models. Both of these components are developed separately but independently operational. The network model must incorporate information required to emulate the original infrastructure. The CR's network models are reusable because they are not assisted by any specific devices. For test cases, it is imperative to specify a set of observations to be recorded and provide the necessary outcomes. Users must also set the required parameters before the execution of the test.

Before execution of the test cases, the network model is compiled with the supporting libraries. If only they are compatible, they get successfully compiled in an executable form. The next step involves the automatic emulation of network models and setting up of all the test cases and their parameters.

The VCSTC architecture comprises a modeling module, test executor, hybrid network, database, test outcome analyzer, and a web frontend. All these major components are illustrated in Figure 10.8 and their working is discussed below.

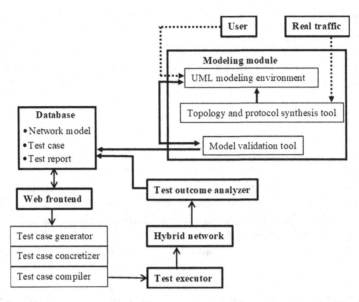

FIGURE 10.8
VCSTC architecture components.

Modeling module provides the user with a UML-based and compatible environment, which facilitates the creation and validation of the network models. After validation, these models get stored in the database for further usage. The web frontend supports the test case generator, concretizer, and compiler. All these three components assist in accepting the user-created test case, setting up test parameters, and then compiling everything in an executable binary file. Using the file, the test executor then forms the emulation of the original infrastructure and then executes the test cases. The emulated network is basically a hybrid network comprising various network interfaces. These are helpful in providing an interface for establishing a connection between the external and internal networks. All the transferred virtual network packets are monitored throughout the execution process. After termination of the emulation, the test outcomes are analyzed and stored in the database. The database stores the test results, test cases, and the network models of the executed emulation.

10.2.2 LARIAT

10.2.2.1 Introduction

It was originally built as an extension to the DARPA 1998 and 1999 intrusion detection data generation testbed (Rossey *et al.* 2002). It was designed as a deployable testbed for information assurance by generating background traffic, real attacks, and verifying success or failure. Initially, the CR aimed at fulfilling these predefined objectives:

- Support instantaneous evaluations.
- Provide a configurable, instantly deployable, and user-friendly testbed.
- Support development and assessments of information assurance systems.

- Generate attack vectors from either single or multiple components.
- Reduce time consumed during execution.
- Can be distributed and operated on numerous sites.
- Includes defense technologies like firewalls.
- Test cases can be reused and reconfigured easily.

The CR is capable of automating all the phases involved in the setup of the emulation. The user only requires to setup the test conditions, select a test scenario profile, and edit and schedule attacks and logs. The CR then distributes all the configurations to all the hosts. The next step involves the execution of the emulation system and keeping track of the performance of the hosts in real time. After the termination of the emulation, the CR examines the collected data like the attack logs, success of attack, outputs, and individual performances. Next, the CR cleans up the platform by either reinitializing the hosts or resetting changes by attack vectors. To run another test, the user requires to again select a test scenario profile.

10.2.2.2 Architecture

The CR's differentiating feature is its ability to generate realistic user traffic through user simulation. Testbed staff are still required to build the test network, install operating systems on hosts, install applications, and deploy defensive host and network tools. CR then deploys virtual hosts and users on top. The virtual users are driven by Markov models, each with a different user role interacting with applications, content, and other users. Some Internet traffic is also simulated. In this way, the CR is a mixture of simulation and real hardware. It is suitable for testing information operations, as well as for security research. It runs applications and services natively, so vulnerabilities and flaws can be found and investigated. To simplify the process of setting up the CR's testbed, a GUI-called Director was created. This improves test specification and control such as software deployment, troubleshooting, control, and monitoring. This CR is one of the few simulation tools used within the USAF for training (Wabiszewski *et al.* 2009). It has also been used for real-time automated testing of systems for intrusion detection. All the details of the emulation system are stored in an .xml file, which is configurable and portable. Using XML is ideal for interpreting the configuration data of hosts by Java-based Director and Perl-based scripts. This also assists in reconfiguring the hosts and scaling the quantity of network traffic.

10.2.3 Emulab

10.2.3.1 Introduction

Originally developed by University of Utah, Emulab is a multiuser, open-source testbed for virtual network emulations. It accommodates different network devices in a common interface within one experimental framework (Eide *et al.* 2006). There are two networks connected via nodes in the physical topology of Emulab – control and experimental networks (Hermenier *et al.* 2012). Control network is used for controlling network file systems and disk-loading tasks in the testbed. Experimental network is an isolated network and it is reconfigurable according to the requirements of the user's virtual topology. One of the significant operating entities of the CR is an "experiment" (Stoller *et al.* 2008).

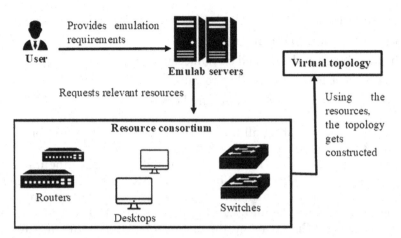

FIGURE 10.9
Emulab network topology creation.

The steps involved in the life cycle of an Emulab experiment, as shown in Figure 10.9, are as follows:

- The first step involves providing a detailed description of the components required for virtual topology of the network. This is done using experiment script because it enumerates comparable components as distinctive instances of the same type of component. It helps in creating predefined templates for various components that are reusable, automatically deployable, and configurable. The other users can recreate similar setups using experiment script for reproducing the previous results.

- The second step is swap-in of components. For running an experiment in Emulab, it is instantiated for automatic reservation and allocation of the required physical resources from pool of accessible components. Returning these components back to the resource pool is called swap-out.

- The third step involves configuring network switches. This is done by using various VLANs to connect experimental nodes for recreating virtual topology. The software uses delay, bandwidth, and packet loss strategies for the emulation of network link.

- The last step involves packet capturing configuration of predefined links. This is performed for the purpose of monitoring before releasing the testbed for experimentation.

10.2.3.2 Architecture

The control infrastructure of Emulab, as illustrated in Figure 10.10, comprises three different types of hosts:

- **Boss node**: it is responsible for hosting the essential components of the infrastructure like webs server, database, boot, imaging, and DNS servers. It is also used to access VLAN-protected components like SNMP interfaces. During swap-in and swap-out processes, boss is responsible for configuring the switches.

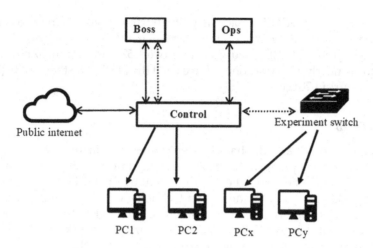

FIGURE 10.10
Control infrastructure (Emulab).

- **Sub-boss nodes**: for extensive installations, sub-boss nodes are required for imaging and boot services. For avoiding intricate state synchronizations between the two types of nodes, the sub-boss nodes deliver read-only services.
- **Ops**: its main functionality is to provide the users with a place for substituting as a fundamental fileserver and get an experiment independent shell. It also acts as bastion host where user logs in before reaching the interfaces of control network of the experiment nodes.

The CR also serves as a reliable disk-loading system because it provides the users with root access to the physical systems; these systems are reusable for different experimentations and they also get reconditioned according to the experiment requirements using boss (Cutler *et al.* 2010).

10.2.4 DETER

10.2.4.1 Introduction

DETER was developed as an open testbed for experimentation in cybersecurity domain by the DHS, NSF, and DoD. It was initially hosted as a testbed facility with the aim of significantly advancing its infrastructures, methodologies, and tools. Since its inception in 2003, the DETER community has been developing advanced tools that are publicly accessible online from its website (DETER project 2012). During its initial phase, when it became operational in 2004, the DETER project focused on the assembly of physical and network resources, integration of software like network testbed operations, employing the existing tools, and defining and developing user interfaces and controls.

Later on, around 2007, the DETERLab facility comprised works on worm propagation and defense, DDoS defense, network intrusion deterrence, BGP routing attacks, and malware analyses. DETERLab technology could now support and enable research works in malware containment, experiment automation, and benchmarking. During its third phase, the DETER project focused on research in cybersecurity infrastructure, experimentation, and tools. Currently, the DETER project is in its fourth phase; it is managed by SPAWAR and focuses on reaching other cyber researchers, expanding the community and helping other sites in using the DETERLab. Furthermore, over 157 classes from 37 educational institutions, including nearly 10,000 students, have used the DETER testbed (DHS [Department of Homeland Security] 2012).

10.2.4.2 DETERlab

The DETERLab is an advanced, shared, scientific testbed facility for the cybersecurity researchers. It provides a platform to the researchers for discovery, development, testing, and experimentation of modern cybersecurity technology. DETERLab is generally used for projects in behavior analysis, defensive technologies comprising worm and botnet attacks, DDoS attacks, pattern detection, and encryption. DETERLab supports allocation of testbeds among various parallelly running experiments, an expanding library of interfaces, tools, and datasets, and building a community of researchers.

DETERLab offers numerous local area and wide area networking at different locations where the lab setup is deployed. It can also provide on-demand integration of third-party networks with the computing facility. DETERLab uses nodes that are configurable with existing operating systems, VMs, network emulation components and simulators, and application software. The testbed users can remotely and locally access the node console.

DETERLab offers the following capabilities supporting more reliable, scalable, complex experimentations – for example, SEER (Schwab et al. 2007) – within the testbed environment:

- **DETER Core** comprises hardware and software resources, interface, software, and staff support. The core resources of the testbed are based on Emulab. The interface consists of a web-based GUI. The GUI offers remote access to the lab, experiment and account management, third-party tools, and MAGI. My DETERLab is an open-source software consisting of dashboard and command line interface. The staff works regularly to improve the size and scale of available resources evolving the testbed.

- **Multi-resolution virtualization** assists in modeling large and sophisticated systems and allocating computation power where required. The experiment might require varying fidelity and scalability resources. It can also model cyber-physical systems with the help of nodes functioning as cluster computers, and emulating the system using DETER capabilities (Mirkovic *et al.* 2010).

- **Predictive modeling of human behavior** is carried out using DASH. As human activities have an effect on the networked system, it must be modeled to provide accurate assessments of the security assets. It is used for modeling end users, attackers, and defenders. It is useful for testing and exploring new software or security policies in a realistic and recurring scenario involving human subject experiments without affecting the working of the original systems.

- **Risky experiment management** allocates gateway nodes in an experiment for enabling certain communication paths inside and outside of testbed regarding sources and addresses with particular traffic type.

- **MAGI** is used for managing the experiment workflow. It can run identical workflows several times for evaluations, parameterizing the workflows and creating alternative workflows via derivations of the original.

10.2.4.3 Architecture

DETERLab subsystems comprise four main components:

- **DETER containers**: these containers as shown in Figure 10.11 are useful for creating wide-ranging DETERLab topologies. The lab's core comprises 400+ computers (DETER documentation 2018). It is useful for managing complexities making the construction of the experiment framework easy (Benzel 2011). If a topology requires more systems, the users can use simulations or virtualization for representing the topology.
  The containers guide this process and allow the users to create extensive experimental environments. It also provides numerous applications of the virtual nodes and also allocates resource according to the specified configuration.
  There are three types of DETER containers with different fidelity and scalability. Physical machine offers complete fidelity with one container per physical machine. Qemu VM offers virtual hardware with tens of containers per machine. Openvz container offers partitioned resources with hundreds of containers per machine.

- **DASH**: it is used for simulating human behavior and decision-making in scenarios like response to a phishing email or making decisions to control a power plant. DASH models the observed behavior with the help a dual-process cognitive architecture (*DASH User Guide*). The system consists of two modules. One module is used for replicating rational behavior. It also contains sub-modules used for projection and reactive planning using mental models (*DASH User Guide*).
  The second module replicates instinctive behavior and other reasoning. Together, these modules can duplicate human biases in reasoning and describe the effects of time pressure and cognitive load on human performance, which are documented in various fields. The platform also provides GUI for controlling DASH agent parameters and viewing the condition of the modules.

- **DETER federation**: it is a mechanism and model used for the creation of experiments that extent to multiple testbeds. It allows the researcher in acquiring the resources on-demand from other testbeds and using them in one experiment. It also uses ABAC for constructing authorized scalable systems.

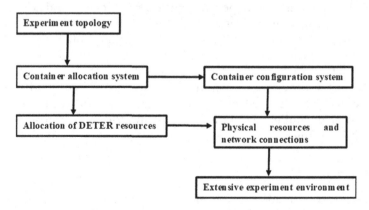

FIGURE 10.11
DETER containers.

- **MAGI**: it is the lab's control and communications system used for recurring experimentation. It provides the user with deterministic control of numerous components in any experiment. It also provides a detailed log for understanding the execution of the experiment. It is also used in GENI, mininet, and Emulab environments (Hussain *et al.* 2020).

10.2.5 Virginia CR

10.2.5.1 Introduction

This CR is the initiative of the Commonwealth of Virginia for improving cybersecurity learning for its students. The range is administrated by the executive committee comprising educational institutes in Virginia designated by the National Security Agency as Centers of Academic Excellence in Cybersecurity Education (Luth 2020). One of its objectives is to have a greater number of completely prepared students enter the cybersecurity workforce in fields such as development, operations, and research (Raymond 2021). The range allows faculty contributions and provides students with modules having series of lessons with associated labs (Kalyanam *et al.* 2020). The CR offers the following functionalities:

- No specific software installation is required; students can access the range's virtual machines via their web browsers.
- The cloud-based range supports faster deployment and scalability.
- The range supports capture the flag and other extensive exercises.
- The Virginia's educational institutes are provided with the range's resources at no costs.
- The range's resource contents can be accessed using a web portal.
- It provides on-demand virtual environments.
- The range allows replicating big target networks for various, real-time uses.

The CR also hosts Cloud CTF, which is provisioned from range's exercise arena for competitions, practice, labs, etc. (Knowledge Base 2019). Cloud CTF features two-user roles, players, and admins. CTF admin comprises institute's instructors who are responsible for team management, permission control, scoring, and administrating the competition. The admins are also responsible for defining the objectives of the competition that help in improving the cybersecurity education proficiency. CTF players are the students who are provided with the task of solving challenges from the categories chosen by the CTF admins. These challenges can be created and customized by the admins themselves or they can be from the library of previous Cloud CTF challenges. CTF players refer to the CTF admin for any queries regarding the challenges. The players can also view challenges, statistics, their individual progress, and other team placement in the rankings.

10.2.5.2 Architecture

Virginia tech worked with AWS for developing the infrastructure of their cloud-based CR (AWS 2019) as shown in Figure 10.12. It is hosted on a public cloud, which contributes

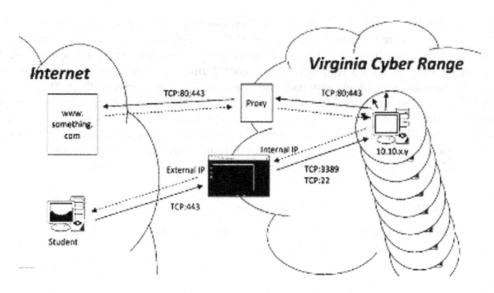

FIGURE 10.12
Virginia CR.

to cost effectiveness and rapid scalability. Registered users can access the range and its resources anywhere and anytime using a web portal. The range also provides various laboratory environments, namely, forensics, cyber basics, and subnets like Ubuntu, Windows, and Kali Linux virtual machines.

The users are provided access to subnet Kali Linux VM (by default) for accessing the exercises resources. The VM accesses the Internet via a proxy to allow HTTP and HTTPs connections. It also allows students to run commands like sudo, install packages, and access webpages as the root user. Descriptions of various VMs used by the range are given below:

- **Kali Linux VM**: it is a desktop instance of Debian Kali which uses Xfce desktop environment. Kali also comprises numerous cybersecurity research and testing tools.
- **Windows VM**: it operates as a Windows 10 system with Windows server 2016. It is a standalone Windows VM in its own virtual subnet.
- **Ubuntu Linux VM**: it is a desktop instance of Ubuntu 16.04 which uses Xfce desktop environment.
- **Vulnerable web server**: it is a LAMP-based web server that operates DVWA for teaching introductory-level web applications security and penetration testing.
- **Samba server**: it is a VM operating software, a vulnerable and outdated version of Samba 4.6.0 version. The services of this server are exploited by the Red Team during a cybersecurity exercise or training.
- **File server**: this VM operates the vsftpd service. During a cybersecurity exercise, the file server is used for directory traversals by anonymous users, anonymous logins, etc. by the Red Team.

The CR also provides a massive Courseware Repository (Virginia Tech 2019) for the educators and a cloud-hosted training arena (VCR 2019) for applied cybersecurity exercises and labs. The range also offers a catalogue of exercises from beginner to complex topics such as cryptography, password examining, forensics, buffer-overflow attack, server hardening, reconnaissance, incident response, and scanning (VCR Knowledge Base 2019). Cyber Basics lab includes introductory exercises on web applications security, cryptography, password auditing, network scanning, and reconnaissance. Forensics lab environment uses the SANS SIFT Workstation consisting of open-source forensic and incident response tools for performing comprehensive digital forensics analyses. It comprises memory, browser, Windows registry, Windows log, and network forensics analysis.

10.2.6 Comparison of Emulation-Based ACRs

This section focuses on summarizing all the advantages (in Table 10.3) and features (in Table 10.4) of the above-discussed CRs.

TABLE 10.3

Advantages of Emulation-Based ACRs

VCSTC	LARIAT	Emulab	DETER	Virginia CR
It is a hybrid emulation system. It successfully integrates both the physical components and advanced virtualization methods. It offers high-fidelity testbed capabilities. It can support up to 1000+ emulated nodes. Test cases can be compiled with the supporting libraries in an executable binary file. All the test cases, network models, are emulation results that get stored within a database.	It is user-friendly. It supports automatic emulation execution. It provides a configurable, instantly deployable, and user-friendly testbed. It can be distributed and operated on numerous sites. It allows the users to examine the collected data like the attack logs, success of attack, outputs, and individual performances.	It provides a combination of realistic hardware emulation and software. This allows scalability and validating the experimental simulation. It keeps the log of most substantial user interactions and provides all the previous data of failures and root causes. Limitations of Emulab served as insightful reference in effective designing of other testbeds like DETER and GENI. The software uses delay, bandwidth, and packet loss strategies for the emulation of network link. It accommodates different network devices in a common interface within one experimental framework.	It provides maintenance with faster turnaround times. It provides realistic emulation environment for evaluating practices, policies, and procedures. It provides extensive physical testbed having sophisticated emulation and simulation abilities. This assists in researchers to build technical experiment, network attack setups on-demand and rapidly. DETERLab offers numerous local area and wide area networking at different locations where the lab setup is deployed. The DETERLab facility comprises works on worm propagation and defense, DDoS defense, network intrusion deterrence, BGP routing attacks, and malware analyses.	It supports the hosting of Cloud CTF competitions. It also helps in expanding NSA/DHS CAE certifications among Virginia educational institutions. Instructors can customize the virtual environment according to the objectives of the cybersecurity exercises. The Virginia's educational institutes are provided with the CR's resources at no costs. No specific software installation is required; students can access the CR's virtual machines via their web browsers.

TABLE 10.4

Features of Emulation-Based ACRs

VCSTC	LARIAT	Emulab	DETER	Virginia CR
It offers lightweight, flexible, and scalable testbed facilities. The CR supports automatic configuration of the network nodes as per the users' requirements. It incorporates the latest security-related testbed solutions. The CR's network models are reusable because they are not assisted by any specific devices. The emulated network is basically a hybrid network comprising various network interfaces.	Its GUI improves test specification and control such as software deployment, troubleshooting, control, and monitoring. All the details of the emulation system are stored in an XML file, which is configurable and portable. It is able to generate realistic user traffic through user simulation. The virtual users are driven by Markov models, each with a different user role interacting with applications, content, and other users.	Supports networks connected via nodes in the physical topology of Emulab – control and experimental networks. Assists in creating predefined templates for various components that are reusable, automatically deployable, and configurable. It is instantiated for automatic reservation and allocation of the required physical resources from pool of accessible components. The CR also serves as a reliable disk-loading system.	DETERLab interface consists of a web-based GUI, which offers remote access to the lab, experiment and account management, third-party tools, and MAGI. DETERLab CR is an open-source software consisting of dashboard and command line interface. DETERLab CR can model cyber-physical systems with the help of nodes functioning as cluster computers, and emulating the system using DETER capabilities. MAGI can run identical workflows several times for evaluations, parameterizing the workflows and creating alternative workflows via derivations of the original. There are three types of DETER containers with different fidelity and scalability.	Virginia tech worked with AWS for developing the infrastructure of their cloud-based CR. The CR also provides various laboratory environments, namely, forensics and cyber basics. It supports subnets like Ubuntu, Windows, and Kali Linux virtual machines. The VM accesses Internet via a proxy to allow HTTP and HTTPs connections. Students can run commands like sudo, install packages, and access webpages as the root user. The CR also provides a massive Courseware Repository. Cyber Basics lab includes introductory exercises on web applications security, cryptography, password auditing, network scanning, and reconnaissance.

References

Airbus [online], 2020. Available from: https://www.concordia-h2020.eu/airbus-cyber-range/ [Accessed 07 May 2021].

AWS, Public Sector Blog Team, 2019. Virginia tech launches U.S. Cyber Range to support cyber-security education nationwide [online]. Available from: https://aws.amazon.com/blogs/publicsector/virginia-tech-launches-u-s-cyber-range-to-support-cybersecurity-education-nationwide/ [Accessed 25 April 2021].

Benzel, T., 2011. The science of cyber security experimentation: the DETER project. *In: Proceedings of the 27th Annual Computer Security Applications Conference*, 5–9 December 2011 Orlando. New York: ACM, 137–148.

Brown, B., Cutts, A., McGrath, D., Nicol, D. M., Smith, T. P., Tofel, B., 2003. Simulation of cyber attacks with applications in homeland defense training. *Sensors, and Command, Control, Communications, and Intelligence (C3I) Technologies for Homeland Defense and Law Enforcement II*, 5071(1), 63–71.

Chang, X., 1999, December. Network simulations with OPNET. *In: WSC'99. 1999 Winter Simulation Conference Proceedings,* 5–8 December 1999 Phoenix. New York: IEEE, 307–314.

Chi, S. D., Park, J. S., Jung, K. C., Lee, J. S., 2001. Network security modeling and cyber attack simulation methodology. *In: Australasian Conference on Information Security and Privacy,* 11–13 July 2001 Sydney. Switzerland: Springer, 320–333.

CODE [online], 2020. Available from: https://www.concordia-h2020.eu/code-cyber-range/ [Accessed 07 May 2021].

Cohen, F., 1999. Simulating cyber attacks, defences, and consequences. *Computers & Security,* 18(1), 479–518.

Cutler, C., Hibler, M., Eide, E., Ricci, R., 2010. Trusted disk loading in the Emulab Network Testbed. *In: USENIX CSET'10,* 11-13 August 2010 Washington. California: USENIX, 1–8.

DASH User Guide [online]. Available from: https://deter-project.org/sites/deter-test.isi.edu/files/files/dash_users_guide.pdf [Accessed 24 April 2021].

DETER documentation, 2018. Containers Quickstart [online]. Available from: https://docs.deterlab.net/containers/containers-quickstart/ [Accessed 24 April 2021].

DETER project [online], 2012. Available from: https://deter-project.org/[Accessed 24 April 2021].

DHS (Department of Homeland Security), 2012. DETER [online]. Available from: https://www.dhs.gov/science-and-technology/deter [Accessed 24 April 2021].

Eide, E., Stoller, L., Stack, T., Freire, J., Lepreau, J., 2006. Integrated scientific workflow management for the Emulab Network Testbed. *In: USENIX Annual Technical Conference, General Track,* 1-3 June 2006 Boston. California: USENIX, 363–368.

Feller, A. 2020. CONCORDIA releases an open-source Cyber Range platform! [online]. Available from: https://cybercompetencenetwork.eu/1563-2/ [Accessed 06 May 2021].

Greenspan, R., Laracy, J. R., Zaman, A., 2004. Real-time Immersive Network Simulation Environment (RINSE). *Software Architecture, UIUC, Urbana,* 1(1), 1–39.

Hermenier, F., Ricci, R., 2012. How to build a better testbed: Lessons from a decade of network experiments on Emulab. *In: International Conference on Testbeds and Research Infrastructures,* 11–13 June 2012 Thessaloniki. Switzerland: Springer, 287–304.

Hussain, A., Jaipuria, P., Lawler, G., Schwab, S., Benzel, T., 2020. Toward Orchestration of Complex Networking Experiments. *In: 13th {USENIX} Workshop on Cyber Security Experimentation and Test ({CSET} 20),* 10 August 2020 [online]. California: USENIX, 1–10.

Kalyanam, R., Yang, B., Willis, C., Lambert, M., Kirkpatrick, C., 2020. CHEESE: Cyber Human Ecosystem of Engaged Security Education. *In: 2020 IEEE Frontiers in Education Conference (FIE),* 21-24 October 2020 Uppsala. New York: IEEE, 1–7.

Knowledge Base, 2019. Cloud CTF Overview [online]. Available from: https://kb.virginiacyberrange.org/cloud-ctf-player/cloud-ctf-overview.html [Accessed 25 April 2021].

Leblanc, S. P., Partington, A., Chapman, I. M., Bernier, M., 2011. An overview of cyber attack and computer network operations simulation. *SpringSim (MMS),* 1(1), 92–100.

Liljenstam, M., Liu, J., Nicol, D., Yuan, Y., Yan, G., Grier, C., 2005. Rinse: The real-time immersive network simulation environment for network security exercises. *In: Workshop on Principles of Advanced and Distributed Simulation (PADS'05),* 3-1 June 2005 Monterey. New York: IEEE, 119–128.

Luth, N., 2020. VIRGINIA CYBER RANGE [online]. Available from: https://www.vtcrc.com/tenant-stories/vcr_may2020/ [Accessed 25 April 2021].

Mirkovic, J., Benzel, T. V., Faber, T., Braden, R., Wroclawski, J. T., Schwab, S., 2010. The DETER project: Advancing the science of cyber security experimentation and test. *In: 2010 IEEE International Conference on Technologies for Homeland Security (HST),* 8-10 November 2010 Waltham. New York: IEEE, 1–7.

OPNET PROJECTS TEAM, 2005. OPNET projects [online]. Available from: https://opnetprojects.com/ [Accessed 24 April 2021].

Pan, J., Jain, R., 2008. A survey of network simulation tools: Current status and future developments. *JSTOR,* 2(4), 45.

Park, J. S., Lee, J. S., Kim, H. K., Jeong, J. R., Yeom, D. B., Chi, S. D., 2001. Secusim: A tool for the cyber-attack simulation. *In*: *International Conference on Information and Communications Security*, 13-16 November 2001 Xi'an. Switzerland: Springer, 471–475.

Pederson, P., Lee, D., Shu, G., Chen, D., Liu, Z., Li, N., Sang, L., 2008. Virtual cyber-security testing capability for large scale distributed information infrastructure protection. *In*: *2008 IEEE Conference on Technologies for Homeland Security*, 12–13 May 2008 Waltham. New York: IEEE, 372–377.

Raymond, D., 2021. Virginia Cyber Range [online]. Available from: https://it.vt.edu/administration/units/virginiacyberrange.html [Accessed 25 April 2021].

RISE [online], 2020. Available from: https://www.concordia-h2020.eu/rise-cyber-range/ [Accessed 07 May 2021].

Rossey, L. M., Cunningham, R. K., Fried, D. J., Rabek, J. C., Lippmann, R. P., Haines, J. W., Zissman, M. A., 2002. LARIAT: Lincoln adaptable real-time information assurance testbed. *In*: *Proceedings, IEEE aerospace conference*, 9–-6 March 2002 Big Sky. New York: IEEE, 6–15.

Schwab, S., Wilson, B., Ko, C., & Hussain, A. 2007. Seer: A security experimentation environment for deter. *In*: *Proceedings of the DETER Community Workshop on Cyber Security Experimentation and Test on DETER Community Workshop on Cyber Security Experimentation and Test 2007*, 6–7 August 2007 Boston. New York: ACM, 1–2.

Sethi, A. S., Hnatyshin, V. Y., 2012. *The practical OPNET user guide for computer network simulation*. Florida: CRC Press.

Shu, G., Chen, D., Liu, Z., Li, N., Sang, L., Lee, D., 2008. VCSTC: Virtual cyber security testing capability—An application oriented paradigm for network infrastructure protection. *In*: *Testing of Software and Communicating Systems*, 10–13 June 2008 Tokyo. Switzerland: Springer, 119–134.

Stoller, M. H. R. R. L., Duerig, J., Guruprasad, S., Stack, T., Webb, K., Lepreau, J., 2008. Large-scale virtualization in the Emulab Network Testbed. *In*: *USENIX Annual Technical Conference*, 25–27 June 2008 Boston. California: USENIX, 255–270.

The CONCORDIAns [online], 2020. Available from: https://www.concordia-h2020.eu/consortium/ [Accessed 06 May 2021].

Tncy [online], 2020. TELECOM Nancy CYBER RANGE [online]. Available from: https://www.concordia-h2020.eu/tncy-cyber-range/ [Accessed 07 May 2021].

Valtenberg, U., Matulevičius, R., 2017. *Federation of Cyber Ranges*. Thesis (Master's). University of TARTU.

VCR Knowledge Base, 2019. Exercise Environment Catalog [online]. Available from: https://vacr.supportbee.io/450-virginia-cyber-range-knowledge-base/1081-resources/2418-exercise-environment-catalog [Accessed 25 April 2021].

VCR [online] 2019. Available from: https://www.virginiacyberrange.org/ [Accessed 25 April 2021].

Virginia Tech, 2019. Courseware [online]. Available from: https://www.virginiacyberrange.org/courseware [Accessed 25 April 2021].

Wabiszewski, M.G., Andel, T. R., Mullins, B. E., Thomas, R. W., 2009. Enhancing realistic hands-on network training in a virtual environment. *In*: *Proceedings of the 2009 Spring Simulation Multiconference*, 22–27 March 2009 San Diego. New York: ACM, 1–8.

Index

Note: Locators in *italics* represent figures and **bold** indicate tables in the text